INTRODUCING MACROECONOMIC MODELLING

INTRODUCING MACROECONOMIC MODELLING

AN ECONOMETRIC STUDY OF THE UNITED KINGDOM

P. ARESTIS and G. HADJIMATHEOU

First published 1982 by
THE MACMILLAN PRESS LTD

London and Basingstoke
Companies and representatives
throughout the world

ISBN 0 333 30014 9 (hard cover)
ISBN 0 333 30015 7 (paper cover)

Printed in Hong Kong

To our children

Chloe, Katerina, Natalia

Contents

Introduction

The analysis and forecasting of national economies on the basis of formal macroeconometric models on the scale pursued presently has been a relatively recent phenomenon. The enhanced economic role of governments, especially in the form of discretionary stabilisation and control policies, following the adoption of Keynesian policy prescriptions, has led to a marked reassessment of the need for both more accurate forecasting and a better understanding of the structure and working of the economy. The concomitant proliferation of economic research on macroeconomic and policy-related issues in conjunction with the development of appropriate statistical techniques and the subsequent availability of powerful computing machines provided the prerequisites for the pursuit of progressively more sophisticated econometric models. Despite their shortcomings present-day econometric models are, for lack of a better alternative, widely used both within and outside the government sector, first as the main instrument for more systematic and less subjective forecasting than before and, second, as the means for the study of the consequences to the economy of alternative economic policies and substantial exogenous shocks to the system.

In this context an economic model is perceived as a system of interrelated relationships, the specification of which is based on economic theory. The quantification of such relationships on the basis of historical data has become the subject-matter of econometrics. Sophisticated statistical techniques have been developed that account for the interdependence of the relationships, and which lead to unbiased and efficient estimates of the model's parameters. A choice between alternative specifications of the same relationship is possible on the basis of a host of statistical tests - including tests for parameter stability over time and the validity of parameter restrictions suggested by economic analysis. Furthermore, considering any model as a whole, historical simulation and *ex post* forecasting (see Chapter 9) can be used to assess how closely each endogenous variable tracks its corresponding historical data series.

The estimated model can then be used for the following different but related purposes:

(a) To make conditional forecasts of the future - the conditions being the alternative assumptions on future values of exogenous variables or policy strategies.
(b) To simulate the consequences of alternative economic policies.
(c) To search for an optimal way - in terms of welfare loss - of controlling certain targets through manipulation of certain instruments.
(d) To experiment with, by evaluating the explanatory power and testing the internal consistency of alternative theoretical perceptions of how the economy or particular sectors of it work, for example by examining the problem of choosing between rational and adaptive expectations hypotheses.

The value of adopting an econometric model-building approach to economics arises, and is indeed necessitated, because of the fact that both governments and industry are involved in some kind of planning and target-setting. Furthermore, there is no serious alternative to economy-wide model-building in carrying out such functions. Even in academic research a large model is sometimes the only vehicle by which the implications and dynamic effects of a theoretical argument can be evaluated. Thus despite the persistence of doubts concerning the theoretical foundations of stochastic economic models (Hicks, 1979) and their performance (McNees, 1979), work on improving them is flourishing. In the meantime, and in the hope of real progress, the models currently available should be used critically, carefully and cautiously.

At present there are four main, non-government, academic teams engaged in economic modelling on a national basis: the London Business School (LBS), the National Institute of Economic and Social Research (NIESR), the Cambridge Growth Project (CGP) and the Cambridge Economic Policy Group (CEPG). Each of these teams is usually identified with a particular strand of economic thought. The specification of the LBS model has increasingly been influenced by monetarist views, whereas the NIESR is assumed to be closer to the traditional Keynesian approach than any of the other models. The CEPG seems to follow a more radical approach to economic modelling and policy within a post-Keynesian framework - emphasising the importance of institutional factors and traditional decision-rules and rejecting the equilibrium or optimisation approach of orthodox economics. The CGP does not seem to conform to a single school of thought, but a different type of model is produced - a markedly more disaggregated one - than the other three. Parallel to these, similar exercises are carried out in the public sector - one in the Treasury and the other in the Bank of England.

Although there is a great deal of duplication in the work accomplished by all these concerns, it can be argued that the discipline of economics is such that there are necessarily differences between economists based on valid disagreements about the theoretical specification of a model, its estimation, its size and the set of questions it purports to answer. Given these differences it is not surprising that the teams compete with one another.

The Treasury and the Bank of England teams are subject to constraints to which academics do not have to conform. They rarely publish forecasts and/or recommendations which may be in contrast to a particular government's policy or its economic philosophy. They are also disinclined to allow themselves to appear to be closely or explicitly identified with a particular school of economic thought and its underlying political undertones. Their work is mainly for internal purposes, i.e. servicing the government, and so it is not usually produced to compete in the arena of economic persuasion.

In addition to the above establishments, there are certain private units which provide a substantially narrower and more specific service. They are not, usually, engaged in economic modelling as such, but they use existing models, mainly the Treasury one, to arrive at forecasts which they subsequently make available to their clients. The most notable ones are the Henley Centre for Forecasting, Phillips & Drew, SCI CON and the St James Club (*The Economist* newspaper group). Two of the academic teams, the LBS and the CGP, have also developed a commercial side to their activities.

Building and continuously updating an economy-wide model is a costly and demanding pursuit that draws heavily on economic theory and econometric techniques. Developing the model is therefore a multi-faceted educational process, because:

(a) It uses a large amount of historical data, covering many aspects of economic activity which is examined and used to highlight and, it is hoped, to explain the working of an economic system.
(b) The initial specification and subsequent improvements in the structure of an economic model require continuous study of economic theory and reflect an increasing experience from the past performance of the model.
(c) An increasing efficiency in estimation of the model depends on the extent to which developments in econometric methods are adopted.
(d) In modelling practice, measurement problems, lag responses, dynamic steady-state paths and stability are recurrent issues which have to be faced and to be fully specified.

Despite the fact that in the recent past considerable progress has been made, there is still a great deal of scepticism as to whether big models in their present form can be relied upon to guide policy-makers. Objections arise on the basis of persisting problems. The mere size of the models frequently leads to the use of *ad hoc* relationships and the adoption of specifications which are not firmly based on economic analysis; the data sets available for estimation and stability testing are still relatively small, especially so when asymptotic tests are involved, which very often results in short-term relationships which lack historical background;

the universal forecasting failure of models in the mid-1970s has raised important questions concerning their parameter stability; and parameter instability, in turn, may be the result of all sorts of mis-specification of the underlying structure. A potentially more damaging criticism is the view that the structural relationships employed are not invariant to policy, and are therefore unlikely to be sufficiently reliable for both forecasting and policy evaluation (Lucas, 1976) - the introduction of the concept of *rational expectations* can be considered as an attempt to allow for this kind of structural change.

The acceptance of these problems and their consequences have led to a more realistic assessment of the models' contribution to economics and policy-making and to a recognition of the need for more research. However, modelling activity and econometric forecasting are going to stay with us.

In 1973 Ash and Smyth argued that the UK macroeconomic models had not been a waste of time. Their argument, however, had been developed before the oil crisis of the 1970s, before the failure to predict the stagflation and stagnation of the decade, and before the concurrence of high and rising inflation and high and rising unemployment. All these events imposed some severe problems to model-builders and model-handlers. Nevertheless, they seem to have managed rather well: 'Recent studies based on the 1970s experience and more current versions of macroeconometric models indicate that structural models out-perform time-series models for most (though not all) variables and that the margin of superiority increases over longer horizons' (McNees, 1979, p.259). Furthermore, with improvements in their performance, models will be more widely used and studied both within and outside the economics profession.

The existing models are too big and too complicated to constitute the object of study in the context of a textbook in economic modelling. The present study is an attempt to carry out a small-size modelling exercise, based on an annual aggregate model of the UK economy, mainly for teaching purposes. Chapter 1 explains the main issues encountered in econometric modelling practice and provides the necessary technical background for the understanding of the specification and estimation of the model. It presupposes a level of econometric knowledge usually attained in a standard introductory course in econometric methods. We feel that econometric textbooks are usually more boring than necessary, in that they are too rich on technical details concerning estimation methods, but rather poor on specification (Rao and Miller, 1971, is an exception), something which is now increasingly recognised by econometric practitioners. In discussing econometric practice, therefore, we have decided to concentrate mainly on specification problems, on testing procedures and on the correct interpretation of the reported statistics. As Hendry (1980, p.399) observes: 'The rapid development of computer speeds and storage capacity should by now have relegated most of estimation theory to footnotes about numerical approximations and refocussed attention on all of the issues surrounding methodology, inference, model formulation and equations selection.'

In Chapters 2-7 the following pattern is followed: after a brief discussion of the main developments in a particular sector of the economy - consumers' expenditure, fixed and inventory investment, public expenditure and revenue, demand for and supply of money, unemployment and inflation, exports and imports - behavioural equations are formulated and estimated. In the process of specifying these relationships and, subsequently, while discussing the estimation results, extensive references are made to the relevant theoretical and empirical literature in the particular area. Key studies recommended for further reading are indicated by asterisks in the Bibliography at the end of the book (pp. 226-41). The methods of ordinary least squares and instrumental variables are used for estimation. The instrumental-variables estimates form the basis of the discussion of both the individual relationships in the various chapters and the model as a whole as summarised in Chapter 8. The ordinary least squares estimates are given in an appendix at the end of the book (pp. 211-17). A comparison of the two sets of estimates gives some idea of the consequences on ordinary least squares estimators of the presence of endogenous variables among the regressors. The use of annual rather than quarterly data was dictated by a number of considerations, including our intention to discuss developments in the UK economy over a relatively long period of time, which inevitably generates problems of reliable data when quarterly data are required. Given the purpose of the book we also wish to avoid making relationships too complicated, especially in the search for appropriate distributed lags and the correct resolution of the seasonality problem. Within the limits set by these considerations, and given that our sample period, allowing for lags, consists of only twenty-two observations (1955-78), the selection of the estimated forms finally included in our model was based on a series of diagnostic tests which have only recently been made available in modelling practice.

Following the sectoral analysis, the estimated behavioural relationships are brought and linked together with the help of well-known identities - including the government's budget constraint - so as to provide an integrated model. The outcome is a standard expenditure-based aggregate model. Its special features include an explicit endogenous treatment of government expenditure and revenue, culminating in the full incorporation of the budget constraint. A summary of the model, together with a discussion of its main features and a flow chart, appear in Chapter 8.

Finally, in Chapter 9, after an explanation and illustration of the simulation process using a simple three-equation model, the performance of the main model is assessed on the basis of simulated results. Subsequently the model is used for policy evaluation. The latter is carried out, first, by changes in policy instruments and repeated simulations, and, second, by introducing a simple welfare-loss function and the application of optimal control techniques.

Throughout this study we have tried to be explicit about the shortcomings of our model in particular and the whole exercise in general.

Some of these shortcomings are confined to this study and some are the result of the state of econometrics and economics as well as the nature of the object of study, i.e. economic behaviour. In all existing models a large part of the latter is left unexplained, so only a limited number of questions can be answered on the basis of present-day modelling. Furthermore, these answers are dependent upon the specific structure of the model and the underlying economic 'philosophy' adopted. Given that complete validation of a model is far from feasible and that parameter stability is probably a very rare occurrence in estimated relationships, any 'illumination' offered must be viewed with considerable caution. Unless (a) assumptions used in the course of a study are made explicit, (b) appropriate statistical tests, whether carried out or omitted, are reported or referred to, and (c) measurement problems and relevant institutional changes are discussed, econometric results are likely to be misleading and thus regressive in the effort to understand the working of the economy. They can of course continue to be used for short-term forecasting.

We hope that we offer a fair picture of economic modelling - a step-by-step explanation of the procedure and work involved in developing and using an economy-wide model of the United Kingdom. We believe that the book will be useful to advanced undergraduates and postgraduates in macroeconomic courses - especially for empirical economics, applied econometrics and economic dynamics and control. It will also be useful for economists interested in economic modelling.

August 1981 *P. Arestis and G. Hadjimatheou*

Acknowledgements

It would seem true to say that no author is without debts. In the course of this work we have incurred debts which are not easily repayable. We have benefited a great deal from suggestions and comments, both specific and general, from friends and colleagues. We wish to thank Robin Becker and Elias Karakitsos, whose help on the computing as well as theoretical aspects of optimal control has been substantial, Edward Clark, Sanjay Dabysing, Sami Daniel, Vince Daly, Cieran Driver, Gregor Koolman, Ron McQuaid and Berc Rustem. In the same context special thanks are due to Gerard Dummett, Keith Povey and John Winckler of the Macmillan Press for encouragement and constructive suggestions at various stages of this project. We also wish to thank Pat Vass, Pat Knight, Norma Phayer, Shirley Angel and the ladies of the secretariat at Penrhyn Road, Kingston Polytechnic, for typing earlier drafts and the final manuscript.

To our wives who have for long endured our tendency to drift into interminable discussions about model-building, even at clearly inappropriate occasions, the end of this work should be a great relief.

P. A. and G. H.

1

Economic Modelling

Economic modelling encompasses a multitude of related activities; it includes the specification, estimation and validation of single- and multiple-equation models for policy analysis and forecasting. A model in this context is broadly defined as a system of interdependent quantitative relations. Various types of relationships are considered: *behavioural*, which constitute attempts to describe certain aspects of economic agents' behaviour; *technical*, an example of which is a production function; and *identities*. The following simple, stochastic and dynamic, macroeconomic model can be used to illustrate this and to introduce some standard terminology:

$$Y = C + \bar{G} + X - M \tag{1.1}$$

$$Y = AK^{a}\bar{L}^{1-a}u_{1} \tag{1.2}$$

$$C = m_{0} + m_{1}Y^{d}_{-1} + u_{2} \tag{1.3}$$

$$I = b_{0} + b_{1}\Delta Y + b_{2}\bar{r} + u_{3} \tag{1.4}$$

$$Y^{d} = Y - \bar{T} \tag{1.5}$$

$$M = c_{0} + c_{1}Y_{-1} + u_{4} \tag{1.6}$$

$$K = K_{-1} + I \tag{1.7}$$

where Y = income or output, C = consumption, I = investment, G = government expenditure, X = exports, M = imports, K = fixed productive capital, L = labour, Y^d = disposable income, T = tax revenue, $\Delta Y = Y - Y_{-1}$, r = interest rate, and u_i = disturbance term. The seven equations determine the values of seven variables, i.e. Y, C, I, M, Y^d, K and X, which are therefore endogenous to the system. The variables $\bar{G}$, $\bar{L}$, $\bar{r}$ and $\bar{T}$ are exogenous (determined outside the system). Equations 1.3, 1.4 and 1.6 are behavioural (based on economic analysis), equation 1.2 is technical and equations 1.1, 1.5 and 1.7 are definitional (or identities). Numerical values of the parameters a, m_0, m_1, b_0, b_1, b_2, c_0 and c_1 can be estimated using statistical data on the variables and an appropriate estimation technique. After estimation the model can be solved for its reduced form so that every endogenous variable is expressed in terms of exogenous and predetermined variables (all lagged variables). The reduced form can then be used to study the impact effects on endogenous variables. For the long-term or dynamic effects the final form is needed. A final-form equation is an equation by which an endogenous variable is expressed in terms of exogenous variables and predetermined values of itself. The final form is used to simulate the economy, to study alternative policy scenaria and to forecast. One of the main aims of this book is to explain and illustrate the procedure for carrying out these functions on the basis of a fully developed model of the UK economy.

The size and degree of sophistication of a model are determined by the purpose that it is supposed to serve. Single-equation, and small multiple-equation, models are used mainly for testing hypotheses and for the explanation of key variables or sectors of the economy, e.g. a consumption function or a model explaining the behaviour of building societies. Such models, as well as small highly aggregate economy-wide models, have certain advantages in comparison with large, all-embracing, disaggregate ones: they are easier to handle and understand, less expensive to run and their properties are easily derivable and directly studied. The small analytically soluble model has been for some time now the main vehicle for carrying out rigorous academic research on macroeconomic issues. Most of our insights in this area and our understanding of the behaviour of macroeconomic systems come from such models. This does not mean that they are for all purposes superior to large-scale macroeconomic models. The latter are richer in detail, more realistic in terms of the complex interdependence of the various sectors of the economy, better equipped - because of their sheer coverage - to provide an effective simulation of the economy and to lead to comprehensive and broadly useful forecasting and policy evaluation (Pearce, 1976). They are relatively freer from aggregation bias (Barker, 1970), but because of the plethora of the variables they include and the relationships they explain, they suffer more from measurement problems and *ad hoc* assumptions and specifications.

Economic reasoning, statistical inference and mathematical techniques are inputs to the modelling process. The non-experimental nature of economic research, in conjunction with the high degree of complexity and the relative lack of stability of economic relationships, has led to the development of appropriate and sophisticated techniques. However, despite the considerable progress that has been made on the technical aspects, the effectiveness of econometric research in model selection and forecasting has still to be established. Some of the major and outstanding issues in economic modelling emanate from (i) the fact that many variables are not easily measurable or directly observable, with the consequence that a researcher has to use proxy and dummy variables, (ii) the presence of errors of observation or measurement, (iii) the lack of knowledge of dynamic responses and lag structures, (iv) the use of inadequate tests of causality, (v) the occurrences of structural changes and parameter instability, (vi) the problem of correctly distinguishing the effects of individual factors in the presence of multi-collinearity, and (vii) the endemic problem of mis-specification. A consequence of this state of the discipline, which makes testing of hypotheses rather ineffective, is the coexistence of competing economic theories. Mayer (1980) ends a review of econometric practice and problems with the suggestion that 'given all the weaknesses of econometric techniques, we should be open-minded enough to accept that truth does not always wear the garb of equations, and is not always born inside a computer. Other ways of testing, such as appeals to qualitative economic history, should not be treated as archaic' (p. 176). A candid assessment of the present state of econometrics is provided by Hendry (1980).

Our aim in this chapter is to attempt to highlight the main issues encountered in economic modelling. It is hoped that the arguments advanced here will provide the background against which the modelling exercise carried out in this book can be comprehended, assessed and evaluated. In the following sections we deal in turn with the problems of specification, measurement, estimation and model selection.

SPECIFICATION

We start at a very elementary level by assuming that economic reasoning suggests the following relationship:

$$Y = f(X_1, X_2, X_3, \ldots, X_n) \tag{1.8}$$

This is a very general statement, that Y (the regressand) depends on X_1 to X_n (the regressors), and is usually supplemented by a specification of the signs of the partial derivatives of Y with respect to each X_i. In estimating this relationship, however, it is necessary to specify the nature of dependence in the form of an explicit equation. If formulation 1.8 is as far as economic theory can go, then the mathematical form of the equation to be estimated will have to be decided on empirical grounds. Linear and non-linear forms can be tried, with the ultimate choice depending on the performance of the estimated regressions in terms of R^2, the standard errors of estimate, t-statistics, signs of individual parameters, etc. In certain cases, however, economic analysis provides further guidance on the specification of a relationship. For example, according to the permanent income hypothesis,

$$C_t = K(i, w, u)Y_t^p \tag{1.9}$$

where C = consumption, Y^p = permanent income, i = the rate of interest, w = the ratio of non-human wealth to total wealth and u = a portmanteau variable for other influences. In this case consumption is proportional to permanent income irrespective of the level of Y^p. In other words, for given i, w and u the marginal propensity to consume (MPC) is equal to the average propensity to consume (APC). The assumption of proportionality does not, however, apply in the case of the absolute income hypothesis, usually expressed as

$$C_t = a + bY_t + u_t \tag{1.10}$$

where Y = measured income. In both cases the form of the relationship is given *a priori*. (Chapter 2 provides further discussion of these and other consumption functions.) In other cases, a particular mathematical form is chosen on the basis of a preference for its implications in interpreting the parameters of a relationship. Consider, for example, the following expression of the Engel curve, estimated from cross-section data:

$$\ell n\ E_j = b_0 + b_1\ \ell n\ Y_j + b_2\ \ell n\ N_j + u_j \tag{1.11}$$

$$(b_1 < 1,\ j = 1, 2, \ldots, n)$$

where E_j, Y_j, and N_j are, respectively, the expenditure on food, the income and the size of the jth household; we presume that the income elasticity of expenditure on food (b_1) is constant, thus the choice of logarithmic form, and less than one - an assumption which has been confirmed by a plethora of studies over time and over different countries. In this case there is no *a priori* theoretical reason for choosing this particular algebraic form of the Engel curve, but past evidence on its comparative performance strongly suggests it (Prais and Houthakker, 1971, ch. 7). A further, and probably more familiar, case where prior empirical observation guides the choice of the algebraic specification of a relationship is the aggregate production function. Whereas the Cobb-Douglas production function was based on the observation that the wage rate was a constant proportion of output per head, the constant elasticity of substitution production function was based upon the more recent observation that output per head is a changing proportion of the wage rate (Heathfield, 1971, ch. 3).

The exponential form and its log-linear equivalent, as in (1.11), has been a popular specification in economic research mainly because it implies constant elasticities. Very often, however, the economic implications of different forms of mathematical dependence are not clearly spelled out. For an illustration consider the following specification of a linear demand for money function:

$$\left(\frac{M}{p}\right)^d = a_0 + a_1\ Y_t + a_2\ r_t + u_t \tag{1.12}$$

The strong assumption incorporated in this equation is that the impact of a given change in the rate of interest (r) on the demand for real money balances (M/p) is the same for the whole of the sample period irrespective of the level of the variables. But given the upward trend over time in M/p, not usually accompanied by a commensurate rise in r, equation 1.12 implies that the interest elasticity of the demand for money, $a_2(M/p)/r$, declines over time. Since on theoretical grounds this is rather unlikely, an exponential equation is preferable. Similar implications, arising from the form of the specification one adopts, abound in econometric practice but are not always thoroughly assessed. Associations in terms of slopes and elasticities must be clearly distinguished and their plausibility in terms of economic reasoning should be examined. For example, a linear Phillips curve relationship, as in a study by Lipsey and Parkin (1972), implies a constant trade-off between *absolute* changes in the rate of change of wages and the level of umemployment, while a non-linear Phillips curve relationship, as in a study by Archibald (1969), implies a constant trade-off between *percentage* changes in the same variables. The difference is important. Another example is the frequent use of shift seasonal dummy variables which imply that the seasonal effect is constant in absolute terms and invariant to the level of the regressand - an assumption which is hardly justified when the variables are non-stationary. In all these examples it should be clear that the choice of a particular specification entails constraints for some or all of the parameters in a relationship. It is not therefore surprising that in recent empirical work there has been an increasing tendency to pay more attention to parameter constraints which, thus, become part of the specification and are subsequently tested. Sometimes such constraints are imposed on the basis of economic-theoretic considerations. Frequently the use of constraints helps tremendously in discriminating between alternative hypotheses. Assume, for example, the following demand for nominal money balances:

$$M = b_0 Y^{b_1} r^{b_2} p^{b_3} u \tag{1.13}$$

and $b_3 = 1$. The constraint $b_3 = 1$ leads to a demand for real money balances

$$M/p = b_0 Y^{b_1} r^{b_2} u \tag{1.14}$$

frequently forming the basis of estimated demand for money functions. Choosing to start with an estimation of 1.13, however, has the advantage that a test, for the restriction $b_3 = 1$, can be carried out, thus providing evidence on the validity of 1.14. Also it is perhaps familiar that a Cobb-Douglas production function

$$Q = A\, L^a K^b u \tag{1.15}$$

with $b = 1 - a$ can be expressed as

$$Q/L = A\, (K/L)^b u \tag{1.16}$$

which, for estimation purposes, is preferable to 1.15 in that it avoids the problem of multicollinearity which is encountered when, in 1.15, L and K are highly correlated. Very frequently such constraints are imposed before estimation, without any attempt to test their validity. The same thing happens occasionally when parameter constraints are the consequence of various transformations of a relationship. For example, consider the following relationship:

$$Y_t = b_0 + b_1 X_t + b_2 Y_{t-1} + u_t \quad (1.17)$$

where

$$u_t = \rho u_{t-1} + \varepsilon_t \text{ and } E(\varepsilon_t \varepsilon_{t+s}) \begin{cases} \sigma_\varepsilon^2 \text{ for } j = 0 \\ 0 \text{ for } j \neq 0 \end{cases} \quad (1.18)$$

The usual procedure in dealing with the first-order autoregressive scheme, 1.18, is to subtract from 1.17 its multiple, lagged by one period, that is

$$\rho Y_{t-1} = \rho b_0 + \rho b_1 X_{t-1} + \rho b_2 Y_{t-2} + \rho u_{t-1}$$

so as to obtain the transformed equation

$$Y_t = c_0 + c_1 X_t + c_2 X_{t-1} + c_3 Y_{t-1} + c_4 Y_{t-2} + \varepsilon_t \quad (1.19)$$

where $c_0 = b_0 (1 - \rho)$, $c_1 = b_1$, $c_2 = -b_1\rho$, $c_3 = b_2 + \rho$ and $c_4 = b_2\rho$. Five parameters are eventually estimated (c_0, c_1, c_2, c_3, c_4) but there are only four original parameters to be determined, that is, b_0, b_1, b_2 and ρ. This gives rise to an over-identification of b_2, in that for given $\hat{\rho}$, $\hat{c}_3$ and $\hat{c}_4$ (estimates) two different values for $\hat{b}_2$ can be obtained from $\hat{c}_3 = \hat{b}_2 + \hat{\rho}$ and $\hat{c}_4 = -\hat{\rho}\,\hat{b}_2$. However, the parameters of 1.19 are not independent of each other, and by imposing the non-linear restriction

$$c_3 = (c_4/c_2)\, c_1 - (c_2/c_1) \quad (1.20)$$

a restricted estimate of 1.19 can be obtained, thus resolving the problem. A statistic, to be discussed later, tests for the validity of the restriction 1.20. The estimation procedure used in this study and described later on in this chapter provides restricted and unrestricted estimates of transformations similar to 1.19. As will be discussed in a subsequent section, a rejection of 1.20 casts doubt on the validity of the original specification 1.17.

In econometric practice the most frequent constraint imposed in estimating a relationship is the exclusion of variables from the chosen specification. This is tantamount to assigning a value of zero to the coefficients of the excluded variables. It is, of course, obvious that a selection of a limited set of variables which are considered relevant for the particular problem is inevitable. In many cases economic theory is specific in suggesting which variables are relevant. But in the presence of competing theories and an imperfect knowledge of economic behaviour a clear distinction between relevant and irrelevant variables is not always possible on an *a priori* basis. The consequence of this is that in practice estimated relationships may include irrelevant variables or exclude relevant variables or both. In such cases we say that our relationships are mis-specified. In both cases of mis-specification there are important consequences. If, for example, for various reasons instead of the true model

$$y_t = \beta_1 x_{1t} + \beta_2 x_{2t} + u_t \tag{1.21}$$

where variables are deviations from their means, the estimated model omits x_2, so that

$$\hat{y}_t = \hat{\beta}_1 x_{1t} \tag{1.22}$$

the consequence is that $\hat{\beta}_1$ is a biased estimate[1] with the bias

$$E(\hat{\beta}_1) - \beta_1 = \beta_2 \frac{\Sigma x_1 x_2}{\Sigma x_1^2} \tag{1.23}$$

depending on the size of β_2 and on the ratio $\Sigma x_1 x_2 / \Sigma x_1^2$, which is the estimated slope coefficient in the following simple regression:

$$\hat{x}_2 = b_{21} x_1 \tag{1.24}$$

The sign of the bias will depend on the signs of β_2 and b_{21}. When both pairs of variables, i.e. y and x_2 and x_1 and x_2, are positively or negatively related, then we have a positive bias, otherwise we have a negative bias; in each case part of the influence of the omitted variable on the dependent variable is captured by the included variable. On the other hand, the variance of the estimate of β_1 from the mis-specified model 1.22

$$\text{Var}(\hat{\beta}_1) = \sigma_u^2 / \Sigma x_1^2 \tag{1.25}$$

is smaller than the variance of the estimate of β_1 from the true model

$$\tilde{y}_t = \tilde{\beta}_1 x_{1t} + \tilde{\beta}_2 x_{2t} \tag{1.26}$$

that is

$$\text{Var}(\tilde{\beta}_1) = \sigma_u^2 / [\Sigma x_1^2 (1 - r_{x_1 x_2}^2)] \tag{1.27}$$

where $r_{x_1 x_2}$ is the correlation coefficient between x_1 and x_2. Therefore, in case of doubt as to whether x_2 should be included or not, a researcher must consider the trade-off between bias and inefficiency: by wrongly choosing to leave out variable x_2 he obtains a biased but more efficient estimate (an estimate with a smaller variance).[2] On the other hand, if x_2 is an irrelevant variable and 1.21 is estimated the outcome is an unbiased estimate of both β_1 and β_2 ($\beta_2 = 0$) but a less efficient estimate of β_1. The trade-off can be formulated in terms of the size of the mean square error (MSE) of the two alternative estimates of β_1. For the first estimate of β_1, $\hat{\beta}_1$

$$\begin{aligned} \text{MSE }(\hat{\beta}_1) &= E\ (\hat{\beta}_1 - \beta_1)^2 \\ &= E[\hat{\beta}_1 - E(\hat{\beta}_1) + E(\hat{\beta}_1) - \beta_1]^2 \\ &= E[\hat{\beta}_1 - E(\hat{\beta}_1)]^2 + [E(\hat{\beta}_1) - \beta_1]^2 \\ &= \text{Variance }(\hat{\beta}_1) + [\text{Bias }(\hat{\beta}_1)]^2 \\ &= \sigma_u^2/\Sigma x_1^2 + \beta_2^2 b_{21}^2 \end{aligned} \tag{1.28}$$

The MSE of the second estimate of β_1, $\tilde{\beta}_1$, is

$$\text{MSE }(\tilde{\beta}_1) = \sigma_u^2/[\Sigma x_1^2\ (1 - r^2_{x_1 x_2}) + 0] \tag{1.29}$$

Rao and Miller (1971), comparing the two mean square errors, show that for

$$(\beta_2/\sigma_{\tilde{\beta}_2}) < 1,$$

where

$$\sigma_{\tilde{\beta}_2} = \frac{\sigma_u^2}{\Sigma x_2^2\ (1 - r^2_{x_1 x_2})} \tag{1.30}$$

MSE $(\hat{\beta}_1)$ < MSE $(\tilde{\beta}_1)$. For $\beta_2 = 0$ this would always be so since $\hat{\beta}_1$ is unbiased, and inclusion of β_2 makes things worse in terms of loss of efficiency; but even if $\beta_2 \neq 0$ it is conceivable, according to 1.30, to have a MSE of the estimate of β_1 from the mis-specified equation which is smaller from its counterpart corresponding to the true relationship. But this is less likely to be the case for large samples since x_2^2 is an increasing, and therefore $\sigma_{\tilde{\beta}_2}$ a decreasing, function of the sample size, thus reducing the likelihood of 1.30 being satisfied. It should be noted, however, that condition 1.30 is not very helpful in practice since both β_2 and $\sigma_{\tilde{\beta}_2}$ are not observable. These results can be generalised for the case of a relationship with more than two regressors. If, for example, the true relationship is

$$y_t = \beta_1\ x_{1t} + \beta_2\ x_{2t} + \beta_3\ x_{3t} + \beta_4\ x_{4t} + \beta_5\ x_{5t} + u_t \tag{1.31}$$

while the estimated equation, resulting from a mis-specification, is

$$y_t = \hat{\beta}_1\ x_{1t} + \hat{\beta}_2\ x_{2t} \tag{1.32}$$

the estimates $\hat{\beta}_1$ and $\hat{\beta}_2$ will be biased, with the bias in each case being

$$E(\hat{\beta}_1) - \beta_1 = \beta_3\ b_{31.2} + \beta_4\ b_{41.2} + \beta_5\ b_{51.2} \tag{1.33}$$

$$E(\hat{\beta}_2) - \beta_2 = \beta_3\ b_{32.1} + \beta_4\ b_{42.1} + \beta_5\ b_{52.1} \tag{1.34}$$

where $b_{ij.k}$ = the coefficient on x_j in the regression of x_i on x_j and x_k.

Perhaps a more fundamental issue in relation to the specification problem arises from the fact that most of the relationships derived in economic theory are steady-state or equilibrium paths. Given, however, that economic processes unfold over real time, and that deviations from equilibrium paths are the norm rather than the exception, equilibrium forms are clearly unsuitable for explaining dynamic adjustments and systems in disequilibrium; model specifications should therefore incorporate adjustment mechanisms and movements of variables between equilibrium positions. In order to illustrate this problem, consider the following example from investment theory:

$$K_t^* = cY_t \tag{1.35}$$

or

$$I_t^* = \Delta K_t^* = c\ \Delta Y_t \tag{1.36}$$

where K^* = desired capital stock, Y = output and I^* = desired investment. These equations express the steady-state or 'desired' path of capital and investment according to the simple accelerator hypothesis. It is apparent, however, that observations on these variables are not expected to be consistent with these relationships. Even if changes in output were the dominant determinant of investment in the long run, it would be unlikely that equation 1.36 would constitute a fair expression of the data-generation process over time. The main reason is that the adjustment of actual stock towards a new optimum, after an initial shock, is not instantaneous. Assume that in addition to equations 1.35 and 1.36 we have the following cost function:

$$C = c_1(K_t^* - K_t)^2 + c_2(K_t - K_{t-1})^2 \tag{1.37}$$

where $c_1(K_t^* - K_t)^2$ measures the cost of being out of equilibrium and $c_2(K_t - K_{t-1})^2$ the cost of adjustment. The minimisation of C with respect to K_t gives

$$\frac{dC}{dK_t} = -2c_1(K_t^* - K_t) + 2c_2(K_t - K_{t-1}) = 0$$

or

$$K_t = \frac{c_2}{c_1 + c_2} K_{t-1} + \frac{c_1}{c_1 + c_2} K_t^*$$

and

$$K_t = K_{t-1} + \frac{c_1}{c_1 + c_2} (K_t^* - K_{t-1}) \tag{1.38}$$

Denoting $c_1/(c_1 + c_2)$ by λ we have

$$K_t = K_{t-1} + \lambda(K_t^* - K_{t-1}) \tag{1.39}$$

where $0 < \lambda < 1$.

Equation 1.39 is known as the partial adjustment hypothesis and can be expressed in the following alternative ways:

$$K_t = \lambda c Y_t + (1 - \lambda)K_{t-1} \tag{1.40}$$

$$I_t = \lambda c \Delta Y_t + (1 - \lambda)\Delta K_{t-1} \tag{1.41}$$

making use of $K_t^* = cY_t$.

It is interesting to note that the dynamic relationships 1.40 and 1.41 can be obtained from an alternative specification of the steady-state equation 1.35 as follows:

$$K_t = cY_t^e \tag{1.42}$$

where Y_t^e = anticipated income; and

$$Y_t^e = Y_{t-1}^e + \delta(Y_t - Y_{t-1}^e)$$

or

$$Y_t^e = (1 - \delta)Y_{t-1}^e + \delta Y_t \quad (0 < \delta < 1) \tag{1.43}$$

which is known as the *adaptive expectations hypothesis*. It implies that economic agents adapt their current expectations on the basis of past forecasting errors, with the adaptive expectations coefficient, δ, indicating the degree of adaptiveness. After repeated substitutions for Y_{t-i}^e in 1.43 we have

$$Y_t^e = \delta Y_t + \delta(1-\delta)Y_{t-1} + \delta(1-\delta)^2 Y_{t-2} + \delta(1-\delta)^3 \; Y_{t-3} + \ldots$$

$$+ \; \delta(1-\delta)^n Y_{t-n}$$

or

$$Y_t^e = \delta \sum_{j=0}^{n} (1-\delta)^j Y_{t-j} \tag{1.44}$$

Substitution of 1.44 into 1.42 gives

$$K_t = c\delta \sum_{j=0}^{n} (1 - \delta)^j Y_{t-j} \tag{1.45}$$

This relationship is not suitable for estimation because of the indefinite number of lagged values of Y which appear as regressors. An estimable equation is obtained by applying the Koyck transformation, a procedure by which a subtraction from 1.45 of the following constant multiple of itself, lagged once, i.e.

$$(1 - \delta)K_t = c\delta \sum_{j=0}^{n} (1 - \delta)^{j+1} \; Y_{t-j-1}$$

leads to the dynamic relationship

$$K_t = c\delta Y_t + (1 - \delta)K_{t-1} \tag{1.46}$$

which is indistinguishable from 1.40. Finally, a more complicated lag structure of the same relationship results when the steady-state hypothesis

$$K_t^* = cY_t^e \tag{1.47}$$

is accompanied by both a partial adjustment and an adaptive expectations hypothesis (Feige, 1967; Laidler and Parkin, 1972).

With the advent of 'rational expectations' (discussed in Chapter 7) the appeal of these rather *ad hoc* formulations has declined considerably. It must be noted that their adoption in the first place was mainly dictated by the need to reduce formulations like 1.47 to estimable relationships not including unobservable variables. For an alternative derivation of 1.41 which highlights the specific nature of 1.39 assume that

$$K_t^* = cY_t \text{ but } K_t = cY_t + Z_1$$

$$K_{t-1}^* = cY_{t-1} \text{ but } K_{t-1} = cY_{t-1} + Z_2$$

where Z is the divergence of actual from desired capital, so that

$$I_t = K_t - K_{t-1} = c\Delta Y_t + Z_1 - Z_2$$

Since $Z_1 = K_t - K_t^*$ and $Z_2 = K_{t-1} - K_{t-1}^*$ the above becomes

$$I_t = c\Delta Y_t + (K_t - K_t^*) + (K_{t-1}^* - K_{t-1})$$

Using 1.35 and 1.39 to substitute for K and K^* we have the special case

$$I_t = \lambda c\Delta Y_t + (1 - \lambda)\Delta K_{t-1}$$

which is equation 1.41.

Another illustration is offered in terms of our estimated demand for money function. The following equation is hypothesised as our steady-state:

$$(M/p)^* = b_0 Y_t^{b_1} r_{1t}^{b_2} (r_{2t}/r_{2t-1})^{b_3} u_t \tag{1.48}$$

where $(M/p)^*$ = desired real money balances, Y = real GDP, r_1 = rate of interest on other assets, r_2 = rate of interest on money (what is called 'own' rate of interest). Assuming a partial adjustment hypothesis

$$(M/p)_t/(M/p)_{t-1} = [(M/p)_t^*/(M/p)_{t-1}]^{\lambda} \tag{1.49}$$

and obtaining a logarithmic transformation of 1.49 after substitution of $(M/p)^*$ from 1.48 we have

$$\ell n(M/p) = \lambda[\ell n\ b_0 + b_1\ \ell n\ Y_t + b_2\ \ell n\ r_{1t} + b_3\ \ell n\ \frac{r_{2t}}{r_{2t-1}} + \ell n\ u_t] + (1 - \lambda)\ \ell n\ (M/p)_{t-1} \tag{1.50}$$

This equation has been estimated (Chapter 5), thus providing estimates of the speed of adjustment (λ) and the steady-state parameters (b_0, b_1, b_2, b_3).

While steady-state paths are usually derived in economic theory, equations incorporating adjustment processes are very often based on *ad hoc* rationalisations. It should be clear, for example, that equation 1.41 is constructed on the basis of two distinct hypotheses, i.e. expressions 1.35 and 1.39; thus a poor performance can be attributed to failure of either or both of them. Furthermore, unlike steady-state relationships, estimated specifications like 1.41 are not independent of the length of the time unit of observations. This is especially so when (i) lag structures are not *a priori* determined but are decided on empirical grounds on the basis of independent lagged values being added to the set of regressors, and (ii) speeds of adjustment are not proportional to time. In the case of the partial adjustment hypothesis, c_1 is expected to be an increasing function of time, while c_2 is expected to be a decreasing function of time, thus making the value of λ a positive function of the length of the time unit used.

The importance of the observation period is frequently manifested in specification problems. In the contemporary theory of the consumption function the steady-state specification

$$C_t = bY_t + u_t \tag{1.51}$$

is expected to perform better for longer units of time, since over a longer time period measured income (Y_t) tends to be closer to permanent income. On the other hand, for a relatively short unit of time it is unlikely that steady-state formulations or equilibrium assumptions are valid. A further illustration can be provided from supply and demand analysis. In estimating the demand-supply model for money

$$M^d = f_1 (x_1, x_2, \ldots, x_n) \tag{1.52}$$

$$M^s = f_2 (y_1, y_2, \ldots, y_n) \tag{1.53}$$

the unobservable variables M^d and M^s are assumed to be equal to the actual value of M on the basis of the equilibrium condition

$$M^d = M^s = M \tag{1.54}$$

which is likely to be less valid for short time units than longer ones.

Finally, in monetarist models it is frequently assumed that in the long run

$$\ell n (P_t/P_{t-1}) = \ell n (M_t/M_{t-1}) \tag{1.55}$$

i.e. that the rate of growth of the price level is fully explained by the rate of growth of the stock of money. But in explaining inflation over time allowance should be made for a lagged response of prices to changes in money supply as well as for other short-run effects such as changes in indirect taxation and petrol prices. The particular lag structure in the causality debate from money to income is an empirical question. At this level experimentation can take place so as to determine the optimum lag pattern which preserves the long-run property of the relationship. Given the inadequacy of the guidance provided by economic theory for choosing the specification of a relationship, the question arises as to whether one should start with simple equations with a small number of variables or a general model which on the basis of specified constraints could give rise to a series of special cases. The latter methodology - i.e. from the general to the specific - is recommended by Hendry (1979) and Hendry and Mizon (1978). The following example - drawn from the latter study - illustrates the problem. Assume the following stable short-run dynamic relationship:

$$c_t = \beta_1 c_{t-1} + \gamma_0 y_t + \gamma_1 y_{t-1} + u_t \qquad (1.56)$$

Next, using the lag operator L, such that $L^n c_t = c_{t-n}$, this equation can be written as

$$c_t = \beta_1 Lc_t + \gamma_0 y_t + \gamma_1 Ly_t + u_t$$

or

$$(1 - \beta_1 L) c_t - (\gamma_0 + \gamma_1 L) y_t + u_t \qquad (1.57)$$

If $\gamma_1 = -\beta_1 \gamma_0$, then equation 1.57 becomes

$$(1 - \beta_1 L) c_t = \gamma_0 (1 - \beta_1 L) y_t + u_t \qquad (1.58)$$

which after dividing through by $(1 - \beta_1 L)$ yields the long-run static relationship

$$c_t = \gamma_0 y_t + \frac{u_t}{1 - \beta_1 L} = \gamma_0 y_t + v_t \qquad (1.59)$$

where $v_t = u_t/(1 - \beta_1 L)$, or $v_t = \beta_1 v_{t-1} + u_t$. In estimating the static model 1.59 instead of 1.56 - taking account of the first-order autoregressive scheme for v_t - we implicitly impose the restriction $\gamma_1 = -\beta_1\gamma_0$. Whether or not such a restriction is valid can be tested by comparing the goodness of fit of model 1.56 with that of model 1.59. Furthermore, on the assumption that 1.58 is valid the use of the Durbin-Watson statistic for autocorrelation in equation 1.59 tests the hypothesis that $\beta_1 = 0$. The presence of residual autocorrelation does not of course by itself imply the validity of either 1.56 or 1.59.

In modelling practice first differences of the variables are often used instead of absolute values to avoid 'spurious' (or nonsense) regression and correlation results, especially when macro variables, which are known to be subject to common trends, are used (Granger and Newbold, 1977). The equation

$$\Delta c_t = \gamma_0 \Delta y_t + u_t \tag{1.60}$$

where $\Delta = 1 - L$, follows from 1.58, if $\beta_1 = 1$. But for $\beta_1 \neq 1$ equation 1.59 is expected to perform better than 1.60. Furthermore, if the true model is

$$c_t = \gamma_0 y_t + u_t \tag{1.61}$$

where u_t is 'white noise' (a normal random variable with mean 0, variance σ_u^2, and covariance cov $(u_t \; u_{t+s}) = 0$ for $s \neq 0$) the differencing procedure gives

$$\Delta c_t = \gamma_0 \Delta y_t + \Delta u_t = \gamma_0 \Delta y_t + w_t$$

so that w_t is a first-order moving average with a coefficient of $-1(w_t = u_t - \theta u_{t-1}$ where $\theta = 1$; Pindyck and Rubinfeld, 1976, pp. 452-8), and violates the classic regression assumption regarding errors. Thus differencing should be used with care, so that implicit restrictions are recognised and any residual autocorrelation accounted for.

The implication of the above illustration is that it is preferable that one should start with a 'dynamic process' of the form 1.56 and test the necessary restrictions which, if valid, may lead to 1.59 rather than the other way round. If the restriction is valid, estimates obtained from the latter are statistically more efficient than those obtained from 1.56 - however, if the restriction is invalid, estimates of 1.59 will be inconsistent.[3]

Hendry (1979) suggests that despite difficulties associated with more complicated and lengthy specifications it is wiser that one should start 'from the most general model which it seems reasonable to maintain' and work through sequential testing procedures to simpler models. Due to the lack of evidence on lag responses it is preferable to move from the 'general' to the 'specific', estimating an unrestricted 'rational lag' equation according to the method of 'intended overparameterisation with data based simplification', i.e. a model with many variables which can be simplified on the basis of statistical data, rather than commencing with a parsimonious model (that is, a model with a small number of parameters). This can be illustrated by reference to the above discussion by suggesting that one should commence from 1.56 and proceed to test the validity of special cases, such as specification 1.59, rather than start from 1.61 and test for mis-specification, a procedure which may suggest the adoption of a more general model, such as 1.56. The latter procedure constitutes a relatively less effective search for the true model.

We can recapitulate by repeating that very frequently in empirical work alternative specifications of the same function are put forward. These specifications could be independent or they could be thought of as belonging to a whole nest of models obtained as special cases of a more general model. Having no *a priori* knowledge of the correct specification it seems inevitable that one should proceed to estimate more than one specification and use the information produced by estimation to choose the specification that performs best. Procedures and methods employed to discriminate between different specifications are described in the final section of this chapter.

MEASUREMENT PROBLEMS

Quite often economic hypotheses are expressed in terms of variables which are not easily observable. This arises from the fact that the development of concepts in economic theory is not conditional upon these concepts being measurable. Consider, for example, the following:

$$C = c_0 + c_1 Y_t^p + c_2 r_t + c_3 H_t + c_4 \dot{p}_t^e + u_t \qquad (1.62)$$

where C = consumption, Y^p = permanent income, r = rate of interest, H = the ratio of human to total wealth and $\dot{p}^e$ = expected inflation. Measurement of each one of these variables presents problems. In practice C is usually measured by consumers' expenditure on non-durables, which differs from actual consumption in that it does not allow for the flow of services from durable goods; Y^p is not directly observable and is usually approximated by a weighted average of present and past values of measured income with geometrically declining weights - an *ad hoc* approximation which is far from being a satisfactory device. The choice of the appropriate rate of interest (nominal or real, short term or long term) for an aggregate function is in the last instance an empirical matter. The numerator of the ratio H, i.e. human wealth, is unobservable. Furthermore, data on total wealth, if available at all, are not reliable (for more on this see Chapter 2).[4] As a result H is measured by proxy variables (such as the ratio of earned income to total income) which do not do justice to the theoretical concept. The final regressor, $\dot{p}^e$, is also non-observable; notwithstanding the problems of measuring the actual rate of inflation (see Chapter 7) the expectation-generating functions employed in practice, including adaptive and extrapolative expectations, are mostly *ad hoc* devices which leave the issue open. Furthermore, the reliability of national accounting measurements of personal disposable income has recently been seriously questioned (Hendry and Ungern-Sternberg, 1980). In periods of high inflation interest earnings tend to rise more rapidly than other types of incomes in a way that may compensate for the loss in the real value of fixed-interest financial assets. The inflation-induced interest earnings should therefore be treated as compensation for wealth losses rather than income. In practice, however, such earnings are treated as income, with the consequence that the level of income of the personal sector, which is assumed to be a net lender, is overestimated. This insight is subsequently used to explain the observed rise in the saving ratio in the United Kingdom (Hendry and Ungern-Sternberg, 1980; Taylor and Threadgold, 1979).

Problems of measurement and unobservable variables are widespread in economics. Wherever they occur their presence and importance should be admitted and their implications for any conclusions in empirical work spelled out. One of the main implications is that in the process of testing a particular hypothesis, such as 1.62, subsidiary hypotheses intrude, rendering any pronouncements on the empirical validity of the hypothesis conditional upon the adopted specific measurements of the relevant variables. It is another reason - in addition to specification, estimation and causality considerations - for questioning the generality and definitiveness of specific tests of economic hypotheses. This is so whether we use dummy variables, proxy variables, or expectation-generating functions.

A data problem which comes under this heading is seasonal variation. Until very recently the practice has been either to use seasonal dummy variables as additional regressors or to run regressions using seasonally adjusted data. We now know, however, that these approaches have serious shortcomings. The use of dummy variables is tantamount to imposing an *a priori* and *ad hoc* seasonal pattern which is extraneous to the rest of the relationship. The alternative of using seasonally adjusted data has been shown to lead to a distortion of the true relationship by introducing additional 'noise', i.e. an extra variation of the variables caused by the seasonal adjustment procedure that distorts some aspects of the original series unrelated to seasonality (Wallis, 1974; Prothero and Wallis, 1976). The most recent suggestion is to use changes in the variables which are free from seasonal variation. In the case of quarterly data, for example, the simple model

$$\Delta_4 c_t = \delta \Delta_4 y_t + u_t \qquad (1.63)$$

where $\Delta_4 c_t = c_t - c_{t-4}$, c = the log of consumers' expenditure (C) and y = the log of disposable income (Y), illustrates the essence of this approach. Both $\Delta_4 c_t$ and $\Delta_4 y_t$ are free from seasonal variation since both components of the corresponding ratios, i.e. log (C_t/C_{t-4}) and log (Y_t/Y_{t-4}), refer to the same quarter. The implicit assumption in 1.63 is that any changes in the seasonal pattern of C is the result of changes in the seasonal pattern of Y.

Errors of measurement and their consequences have been neglected in economic research probably because it is usually assumed that their size is not large enough to affect significantly the estimation results. We feel that quite often such a degree of optimism is not warranted. It is, for example, indicative of the seriousness of the problem that in studies of the personal saving ratio, in both the USA and the United Kingdom, the results change significantly with the use of time series on personal savings obtained from different sources (Taubman, 1968; Odling-Smee, 1973). Leontief (1971, p.3), commenting on the problem, observes that

> In all too many instances sophisticated statistical analysis is performed on a set of data whose exact meaning and validity are unknown to the author or rather so well known to him that

at the very end he warns the reader not to take the material conclusions of the entire 'exercise' seriously.

The main statistical consequence of measurement errors in the regressors is that the estimators are no longer consistent. Furthermore, errors in both the regressors and the regressand are very likely to affect the precision of the estimates of all parameters. In the presence of such errors consistent estimators can be obtained by using instrumental-variables estimation but this technique cannot guarantee efficient estimators.

This general discussion of measurement problems is illustrated in subsequent chapters of the book in which we define the variables we use in our model and discuss the quality of the adopted time series. We make it clear that in common with economic modelling practice measurement of quite a number of variables used in our model is far from being beyond dispute: this applies to, among others, trade-union militancy, anticipated inflation, capital consumption, the real rate of interest, money stock and capacity utilisation.

ESTIMATION

The whole system of a multi-equation model may be written in matrix form as

$$By_t + \Gamma x_t = u_t \tag{1.64}$$

where y_t is a vector of contemporaneous endogenous variables and x_t is a vector of contemporaneous exogenous variables and predetermined variables, so that

$$y_t = \begin{bmatrix} y_{1t} \\ y_{2t} \\ \cdot \\ \cdot \\ \cdot \\ y_{Gt} \end{bmatrix} \qquad x_t = \begin{bmatrix} x_{1t} \\ x_{2t} \\ \cdot \\ \cdot \\ \cdot \\ x_{Kt} \end{bmatrix} \qquad u_t = \begin{bmatrix} u_{1t} \\ u_{2t} \\ \cdot \\ \cdot \\ \cdot \\ u_{Gt} \end{bmatrix}$$

$$B = \begin{bmatrix} \beta_{11} & \beta_{12} & \cdots & \beta_{1G} \\ \beta_{21} & \beta_{22} & \cdots & \beta_{2G} \\ \cdot & \cdot & & \cdot \\ \cdot & \cdot & & \cdot \\ \cdot & \cdot & & \cdot \\ \beta_{G1} & \beta_{G2} & & \beta_{GG} \end{bmatrix} \qquad \Gamma = \begin{bmatrix} \gamma_{11} & \gamma_{12} & \cdots & \gamma_{1K} \\ \gamma_{21} & \gamma_{22} & \cdots & \gamma_{2K} \\ \cdot & \cdot & & \cdot \\ \cdot & \cdot & & \cdot \\ \cdot & \cdot & & \cdot \\ \gamma_{G1} & \gamma_{G2} & & \gamma_{GK} \end{bmatrix}$$

$t = 1, 2, 3, \ldots, n$

By making various assumptions about these matrices and vectors we can highlight the need for alternative estimation techniques:

1. For G = K = 1 and

$$E(u_1u_1') = \sigma^2_{u_1} I_n \tag{1.65}$$

where $u_1' = [u_{11}, u_{12}, \ldots, u_{1n}]$, we have the simple regression

$$y_{1t} = c_{11}x_{1t} + v_{1t} \tag{1.66}$$

where $c_{11} = -\gamma_{11}/\beta_{11}$ and $v_{1t} = u_{1t}/\beta_{11}$.

Ordinary least squares (OLS) gives best linear unbiased (BLU) estimates of c_{11} for x_1 as a contemporaneous or lagged exogenous variable, but only consistent estimates when x_1 is a lagged endogenous variable. This is also so in the more general case where there is more than one exogenous variable.

2. For G = 1, K = 2 and

$$E(u_1u_1') = \sigma^2_u\Omega \tag{1.67}$$

$$y_{1t} = c_{11}x_{1t} + c_{12}x_{2t} + v_{1t} \tag{1.68}$$

Equation 1.67 implies serially correlated and/or heteroscedastic disturbances. In this case, for exogenous regressors only, OLS estimates are unbiased but no longer efficient, that is, they no longer have a minimum variance. The appropriate estimation technique is generalised least squares (GLS), which provides BLU estimates. For the case where lagged endogenous variables appear among regressors GLS provides consistent estimators. For $\Omega = I$ OLS is the appropriate technique.

3. For G = 2, K = 2 and

$$E[uu'] = E\begin{bmatrix} u_1u_1' & u_1u_2' \\ u_2u_1' & u_2u_2' \end{bmatrix} = \begin{bmatrix} \sigma^2_{u_1} I_n & 0 \\ 0 & \sigma^2_{u_2} I_n \end{bmatrix} \tag{1.69}$$

we have

$$y_{1t} = b_{12}y_{2t} + c_{11}x_{1t} + c_{12}x_{2t} + v_{1t} \tag{1.70}$$

$$y_{2t} = b_{21}y_{1t} + c_{21}x_{1t} + c_{22}x_{2t} + v_{2t} \tag{1.71}$$

and for $c_{12} = c_{21} = 0$ both equations are exactly identified. If $b_{21} = 0$, the two equations constitute a *recursive*[5] system, and given that v_{1t} and v_{2t} are independent (assumption 1.67) OLS gives BLU estimates as long as x_1 and x_2 are exogenous. For $b_{21} \neq 0$ we have a simultaneous-equations system with its reduced form being (assuming $c_{12} = c_{21} = 0$)

$$y_{1t} = \frac{b_{12}c_{22}}{1-b_{21}b_{12}}x_{2t} + \frac{c_{11}}{1-b_{21}b_{12}}x_{1t} + \frac{v_{1t} + b_{12}v_{2t}}{1-b_{21}b_{12}}$$

$$y_{2t} = \frac{b_{21}c_{11}}{1-b_{21}b_{12}}x_{1t} + \frac{c_{22}}{1-b_{21}b_{12}}x_{2t} + \frac{v_{2t} + b_{21}v_{1t}}{1-b_{21}b_{12}}$$

Since, from the above, the covariances $E(y_{1t}v_{2t})$ and $E(y_{2t}v_{1t})$ are different from zero, OLS estimates of the structural parameters from 1.70 and 1.71 are not unbiased.

In this case the appropriate estimation method is two-stage least squares (TSLS), which in this case, because the two equations are exactly identified, gives the same estimates as the indirect least squares method (ILS) and the instrumental-variables method (IV) (Stewart, 1976, pp. 202-13). In many cases we are interested in estimating a single-equation model, e.g. 1.70, rather than the whole model. In such a case, in specifying the relationship one may be obliged to include endogenous variables among its regressors. The standard estimation technique for such a relationship is IV, with a selected list of instruments usually including the lagged values of the endogenous variables themselves. It should be added that when the disturbance term is serially correlated, an appropriate transformation has to be made according to an autoregressive scheme so as to ensure efficient estimators, irrespective of whether OLS, TSLS or IV is used.

4. For G = 3, K = 3 and the alternative variance-covariance matrices

$$E[uu'] = E\begin{bmatrix} u_1u_1' & u_1u_2' & u_1u_3' \\ u_2u_1' & u_2u_2' & u_2u_3' \\ u_3u_1' & u_3u_2' & u_3u_3' \end{bmatrix} \begin{bmatrix} \sigma^2_{u_1}I_n & 0 & 0 \\ 0 & \sigma^2_{u_2}I_n & 0 \\ 0 & 0 & \sigma^2_{u_3}I_n \end{bmatrix} \quad (a)$$

or

$$\begin{bmatrix} \sigma^2_{u_1}\Omega_1 & 0 & 0 \\ 0 & \sigma^2_{u_2}\Omega_2 & 0 \\ 0 & 0 & \sigma^2_{u_3}\Omega_3 \end{bmatrix} \quad (b)$$

or

$$\begin{bmatrix} \sigma^2_{u_1}I_n & \sigma_{u_1u_2}I_n & \sigma_{u_1u_3}I_n \\ \sigma_{u_2u_1}I_n & \sigma^2_{u_2}I_n & \sigma_{u_2u_3}I_n \\ \sigma_{u_3u_1}I_n & \sigma_{u_3u_2}I_n & \sigma^2_{u_3}I_n \end{bmatrix} \quad (c)$$

or

$$\begin{bmatrix} \sigma^2_{u_1}\Omega_1 & \sigma_{u_1u_2}I_n & \sigma_{u_1u_3}I_n \\ \sigma_{u_2u_1}I_n & \sigma^2_{u_2}\Omega_2 & \sigma_{u_2u_3}I_n \\ \sigma_{u_3u_1}I_n & \sigma_{u_3u_2}I_n & \sigma^2_{u_3}\Omega_3 \end{bmatrix} \qquad \text{(d)}$$

the three equations are

$$y_{1t} = b_{12}y_{2t} + b_{13}y_{3t} + c_{11}x_{1t} + c_{12}x_{2t} + c_{13}x_{3t} + v_{1t} \qquad (1.72)$$

$$y_{2t} = b_{21}y_{1t} + b_{23}y_{3t} + c_{21}x_{1t} + c_{22}x_{2t} + c_{23}x_{3t} + v_{2t} \qquad (1.73)$$

$$y_{3t} = b_{31}y_{1t} + b_{32}y_{2t} + c_{31}x_{1t} + c_{32}x_{2t} + c_{33}x_{3t} + v_{3t} \qquad (1.74)$$

For $b_{13} = c_{11} = c_{12} = b_{21} = c_{22} = c_{23} = b_{31} = c_{32} = c_{33} = 0$, all three equations are over-identified, and since there is an endogenous regressor in each equation TSLS should be used for estimation. For serially correlated disturbances and/or heteroscedasticity (assumption b) GLS estimators should be used in combination with TSLS.

All estimation methods considered so far are single-equation methods, i.e. each equation is estimated individually and independently of the rest of the equations in the model. These methods provide consistent but, in general, not asymptotically efficient estimates. The lack of efficiency arises from the fact that no provision is made for the correlation of disturbances across equations; it could also arise if restrictions on other equations in the model are disregarded. A method that makes use of all the available information is the complete system method known as three stage least squares. An alternative complete system method is the full-information maximum likelihood method. For asymptotically efficient estimates one of these two methods will have to be used for the model 1.72-1.74 with (c) or (d). However, both these methods are generally more sensitive than the others to specification errors and also to errors in variables. Given that misspecification is a likely occurrence in 'large' models, and that both techniques involve extremely complicated computations, single-equation estimation methods, such as IV and TSLS, are nearly always preferred.

For $b_{12} = b_{13} = b_{23} = 0$, the system is recursive, and assuming that there is no correlation of disturbances across equations OLS estimates are BLU. Finally, even if there are no endogenous regressors, as long as disturbances across equations are significantly related, efficient estimates can only be obtained by using a generalised least squares estimation method with a simultaneous estimation of all equations so that the complete system of information is utilised. Systems of this form are known as 'seemingly unrelated equations'.

The model used in this book was initially estimated on the basis of OLS with full provision being made for serial correlation. Subsequently IV estimates were obtained for all relationships with endogenous regressors. Given that annual observations are used, a first-order autoregressive scheme is always assumed and tested. A general instrumental-variable estimation (GIVE) of linear equations with lagged dependent variables and first-order autoregressive errors - a widely used programme in the United Kingdom in the 1970s - was the basis of all estimation in this study. A description and illustration of the estimation procedure using the relationship which explains the average propensity to consume (APC) should be instructive. The final specification chosen mainly on theoretical grounds and partly on estimation experimentation is

$$APC = b_0 + b_1 [(RL)_t - (RPD)_t] + b_2 \left(\frac{LA}{YD}\right)_t + b_3 \left(\frac{TYDR}{YDR}\right)_t + b_4 (RPD)_t + b_5 (RPD)_{t-2} \quad (1.75)$$

where RL = long-term rate of interest, RPD = rate of change of the GDP price deflator, LA = liquid assets, YD = nominal personal disposable income, YDR = real personal disposable income, $(TYDR)_t = \sum_{j=0}^{4} (YDR)_{t-j}/5$ and APC = total consumers' expenditure over total personal disposable income. OLS estimation of 1.75 gives the following results:

$$\underset{}{APC_t} = \underset{(4.17)}{0.577} - \underset{(4.49)}{0.0077} [(RL)_t - (RPD)_t] + \underset{(2.86)}{0.246} \left(\frac{LA}{YD}\right)_t + \underset{(2.01)}{0.205} \left(\frac{TYDR}{YDR}\right)_t - \underset{(5.55)}{0.0069} (RPD)_t + \underset{(0.35)}{0.00023} (RPD)_{t-2} \quad (1.76)$$

$R^2 = 0.932$, D-W = 0.946, S = 0.0098, S/ME = 0.011, $F_1(5,15) = 41.3$

R^2 is the square of the coefficient of multiple correlation; it measures the percentage of variation in the dependent variable explained by the variation in the independent variables on the basis of the estimated relationship. It is calculated according to the expression

$$R^2 = 1 - \frac{\Sigma e_t^2}{\Sigma y_t^2} \quad (1.77)$$

where the ratio of the sum of the squares of the residuals (Σe_t^2) to the total variation of $y_t(\Sigma y_t^2)$ measures the unexplained variation. R^2 increases with every additional regressor. Often in empirical work, instead of R^2 the adjusted coefficient, denoted by $\bar{R}^2$, is preferred. The two are related as follows:

$$\bar{R}^2 = 1 - \frac{n-1}{n-k} (1 - R^2) \quad (1.78)$$

which implies that $\bar{R}^2$ can decrease as additional regressors - the number of which is denoted by k - are added to the regression. Numbers in parentheses are t-statistics, defined as

$$t_i = \frac{\hat{b}_i}{\sqrt{S^2_{\hat{b}_i}}} \tag{1.79}$$

where $S^2_{\hat{b}_i}$ is an unbiased estimate of the variance of $\hat{b}_i$; S = standard error of estimate, defined as follows:

$$S = \sqrt{\frac{\Sigma e_t^2}{n - k}} \tag{1.80}$$

When S is divided by the arithmetic value of the dependent variable (ME) we have the ratio (S/ME), which provides a rough measure of the relative size of the residuals; F_1 is a test for the null hypothesis that none of the explanatory variables has an influence upon the dependent variable and is defined as

$$F_1\ (k - 1,\ n - k) = \frac{R^2/(k - 1)}{(1 - R^2)/(n - k)} \tag{1.81}$$

Alternatively this is a test of the significance of R^2 and is never reported in our results as it is always ensured that for each chosen specification the null hypothesis is rejected. D-W is the Durbin-Watson statistic, calculated according to the formula:

$$\text{D-W} = \frac{\sum_{t=2}^{n}(e_t - e_{t-1})^2}{\sum_{t=1}^{n} e_t^2} \tag{1.82}$$

For twenty-one observations, five regressors and 95 per cent probability level the critical value of the Durbin-Watson statistic is between 0.83 and 1.96 which includes the estimated value. The test is inconclusive as to the presence or not of serial correlation, and equation 1.75 is transformed on the basis of a first-order autoregressive scheme

$$u_t = \rho u_{t-1} + \varepsilon_t \tag{1.83}$$

to give the following:

$$\text{APC} = d_0 + b_1[(\text{RL})_t - (\text{RPD})_t] + b_2\left(\frac{\text{LA}}{\text{YD}}\right)_t + b_3\left(\frac{\text{TYDR}}{\text{YDR}}\right)_t + b_4(\text{RPD})_t$$
$$+ b_5(\text{RPD})_{t-2} + b_6[(\text{RL})_{t-1} - (\text{RPD})_{t-1}] + b_7\left(\frac{\text{LA}}{\text{YD}}\right)_{t-1}$$

$$+ b_8\left(\frac{TYDR}{YDR}\right)_{t-1} + b_9(RPD)_{t-1} + b_{10}(RPD)_{t-3} + b_{11}(APC)_{t-1} \tag{1.84}$$

where

$$d_0 = (1 - \rho)b_0,\ b_6 = -\rho b_1,\ b_7 = -\rho b_2,\ b_8 = -\rho b_3,\ b_9 = -\rho b_4,$$

$$b_{10} = -\rho b_5,\ b_{11} = \rho \tag{1.85}$$

Equation 1.84 provides twelve estimates from which estimates of the following seven parameters must be determined: ρ, b_0, b_1, b_2, b_3, b_4, b_5. For unique estimates the five restrictions indicated by b_6-b_{10} in 1.85 must be imposed in estimating 1.84. Before such restricted estimates are obtained, equation 1.84 can be considered as an autonomous relationship and estimated without any reference to 1.75 and 1.85. Thus 1.84 by itself is called the *unrestricted form estimation*, which gives the following results:

$$\begin{aligned}
APC = &- \underset{(1.1)}{0.208} - \underset{(1.78)}{0.0043}\,[(RL)_t - (RPD)_t] + \underset{(2.09)}{0.343}\left(\frac{LA}{YD}\right)_t \\
&+ \underset{(4.17)}{0.434}\left(\frac{TYDR}{YDR}\right)_t - \underset{(1.51)}{0.0046}\,(RPD)_t - \underset{(1.46)}{0.00095}\,(RPD)_{t-2} \\
&+ \underset{(0.79)}{0.0041}\,[(RL)_{t-1} - (RPD)_{t-1}] - \underset{(0.69)}{0.169}\left(\frac{LA}{YD}\right)_{t-1} \\
&- \underset{(1.64)}{0.265}\left(\frac{TYDR}{YDR}\right)_t + \underset{(1.01)}{0.0052}\,(RPD)_{t-1} + \underset{(1.49)}{0.0013}\,(RPD)_{t-3} \\
&+ \underset{(3.47)}{0.897}\,(APC)_{t-1}
\end{aligned} \tag{1.86}$$

$R^2 = 0.987$, D-W $= 1.70$, S $= 0.006$, S/ME $= 0.0007$, $F_1(11,9) = 52.3$, $F_2(6,9) = 5.09$

where F_2 is a test of the significance of the additional parameters calculated according to the formula

$$F_2(Q - k,\ n - Q) = \frac{(R_Q^2 - R_k^2)/(Q - k)}{(1 - R_Q^2)/(n - Q)} \tag{1.87}$$

where k and R_k are, respectively, the number of parameters and correlation coefficient for 1.76, and Q and R_Q the number of parameters and correlation coefficient for 1.86. The tabulated value of F_2 (6,9) at the 1 per cent significance level is 5.80 implying that the null hypothesis

$$H_0: b_6 = b_7 = b_8 = b_9 = b_{10} = b_{11} = 0$$

should be accepted. (For a 95 per cent probability level the null hypothesis is rejected.) Finally, the restricted estimates for 1.75 are as follows:

$$\underset{}{APC} = \underset{(3.81)}{0.447} - \underset{(3.18)}{0.0041} [(RL)_t - (RPD)_t] + \underset{(3.11)}{0.223} \left(\frac{LA}{YD}\right)_t$$

$$+ \underset{(3.86)}{0.344} \left(\frac{TYDR}{YDR}\right)_t - \underset{(3.73)}{0.0047} (RPD)_t - \underset{(2.26)}{0.00084} (RPD)_{t-2} \quad (1.88)$$

$$\underset{(6.05)}{\rho = 0.819}, \quad S = 0.006, \quad S/ME = 0.007, \quad \chi_1^2 (5) = 8.88, \quad \chi_\rho^2 (1) = 22.21,$$

$$\chi_3^2 (1) = 1.55, \quad F(1,13) = 0.53$$

where ρ = the estimate of the serial correlation coefficient in 1.83. This equation is obtained as follows: a restricted estimation of 1.84 is obtained by imposing the five restrictions, indicated by b_6-b_{10} in 1.85, during the estimation process; at the same time an iteration procedure is applied to obtain the optimum value of ρ, that is, that value that minimises the sum of the squares of the residuals. Values of ρ from -0.92 to 0.98 in steps of 0.1 are tried to check for multiple minima and help ensure that the iteration commences close to the global minimum. The value of ρ chosen is that one for which the restricted estimate of the sum of the squares of the residuals converges. The imposition of the restrictions provides the unique estimates of the parameters depicted in 1.88. χ_1^2 is a test of the validity of autoregressive restrictions, calculated as

$$\chi_1^2(m) = n\ell n \frac{SSR_3}{SSR_2} \quad (1.89)$$

where m is the number of restrictions (in this case the five restrictions referred to above), n = number of observations, SSR_2 = the sum of the squares of the residuals from the unrestricted form, and SSR_3 = sum of the squares of the residuals from the restricted form. SSR_3 is expected to be greater than SSR_2 since the former, unlike the latter, is obtained from a constrained minimisation. However, if the restrictions are correct, the two SSR should not differ significantly - thus the χ_1^2 test, which is a likelihood-ratio-based asymptotic test (Harvey, 1981, pp. 159-65). If the actual value of χ_1^2 is greater than its critical value at a certain probability level, then the restrictions imposed are invalid. This casts doubt upon the validity of the initial specification, which may have to change by incorporating higher-order lags in the light of the estimates of the unrestricted form; also the order of the autoregressive scheme assumed initially may have to change. A stage of specification experiments may therefore ensue with each lag structure being assessed on purely statistical grounds. $\chi_\rho^2(1)$ is an asymptotic test for the significance of $\hat{\rho}$ calculated as follows:

$$\chi^2_\rho(1) = n\ell n \frac{SSR_1}{SSR_3} \tag{1.90}$$

where SSR_1 = the sum of the squares of the residuals of the structural form 1.75, and SSR_3 the sum of the squares of the residuals from the restricted form. An alternative to this is the asymptotic t-test given in parentheses below the value of ρ. In the rest of this book when reporting results only the t-test will be given. The post-sample parameter stability test (χ^2_3) and the Chow test (F) are fully explained in the next section.

The estimation of all structural equations in our model was based on the procedure described above. All three forms (structural equation 1.75, transformed unrestricted 1.84, transformed restricted 1.84 and 1.85) are estimated with the choice made on the basis of the various tests provided. For equations with endogenous regressors IV is used instead of OLS, so that parameter estimators are consistent. For the APC function the preferred equation is the restricted form given below:

$$\underset{(3.94)}{APC = 0.473} - \underset{(3.13)}{0.00413}\,[(RL)_t - (RPD)_t] + \underset{(2.95)}{0.2143}\left(\frac{LA}{YD}\right)_t$$

$$+ \underset{(3.54)}{0.32313}\left(\frac{TYDR}{YDR}\right)_t - \underset{(3.71)}{0.0047}\,(RPD)_t - \underset{(2.19)}{0.00082}\,(RPD)_{t-2} \tag{1.91}$$

$\underset{(5.9)}{\rho = 0.813}$, $S = 0.006$, $S/ME = 0.007$, $\chi^2_2(9) = 13.98$, $\chi^2_3(1) = 1.44$,

$F(1,13) = 0.48$

with $\chi^2_2(K)$ being an asymptotically valid test of the independence of the chosen instruments and the error term, based on a comparison of the SSR of the OLS estimate and the SSR of the IV estimate with $K = (q - k)$ degrees of freedom, where q is the number of instruments used and k the number of parameters estimated. Sixteen instrumental variables were used: lagged values of all six variables in the equation, the predetermined variable $(RPD)_{t-2}$, the constant and eight additional predetermined or exogenous variables from the rest of the model ($(YD)_{t-3}$, $(PCD)_{t-1}$, $(PCD)_{t-2}$, $(UNER)_{t-1}$, $(IPR)_{t-1}$, $(BR)_{t-1}$, $[(GDPR)_{t-1} - (GDPR)_{t-2}]$, $[(GDPR)_{t-2} - (GDPR)_{t-3}]$). (For definition of variables see Chapter 8.)

MODEL SELECTION

A preferred estimated relationship should first of all make economic sense. (For an entertaining illustration of how easy it is to formulate a 'nonsense' regression which, nevertheless, performs spectacularly on the basis of standard statistical criteria, see Hendry, 1980.) Explicit specification of the size and sign of particular parameters, including linear and non-linear restrictions, the steady state of endogenous variables and whenever possible the lag structure at a pre-estimation stage helps greatly in model selection. When the estimation results are available tests or measures of the validity of restrictions, the explanatory and predictive power of the regression, the stability of the parameters, the size and pattern of residuals, etc., are criteria used to choose between rival specifications. The development of more recent tests has rendered the old practice of choosing between relationships merely in terms of the size of R^2 obsolete. It is by now well known that a high R^2 does not establish causality. In addition to the fact that R^2 is just a single criterion in a comparative exercise it also suffers from serious limitations. A high R^2 can easily be achieved especially when the variables are of an aggregate nature - most macro variables are trended and are bound to be markedly correlated.

As mentioned in the preceding section, R^2 (the coefficient of determination) measures the percentage of the variance in the dependent variable explained by the particular relationship, that is

$$R^2 = 1 - \frac{\Sigma e_t^2}{\Sigma y_t^2} \tag{1.92}$$

where $\Sigma e_t^2 = \Sigma(Y_t - \hat{Y}_t)^2$ and $\Sigma y_t^2 = \Sigma(Y_t - \bar{Y})^2$

Adding extra regressors would result in an increase in R^2 irrespective of their relevance or significance. In the case of two regressors, for example,

$$\Sigma e_{t1}^2 = \Sigma(Y_t - \hat{\alpha} - \hat{\beta}_1 X_{1t} - \hat{\beta}_2 X_{2t})^2$$

where the OLS estimators, α, $\hat{\beta}_1$, $\hat{\beta}_2$, are those that minimise Σe_{t1}^2. With an extra regressor we have

$$\Sigma e_{t2}^2 = \Sigma(Y_t - \hat{\alpha} - \hat{\beta}_1 X_{1t} - \hat{\beta}_2 X_{2t} - \hat{\beta}_3 X_{3t})^2$$

and $\Sigma e_{t2}^2 < \Sigma e_{t1}^2$ since the latter can be thought of as the outcome of minimising Σe_{t2}^2 subject to the constraint $\hat{\beta}_3 = 0$. This is not so, however, when Σe_t^2 and Σy_t^2 are replaced by unbiased estimates of the variances of e_t and Y_t, that is

$$\text{Var}(e_t) = \frac{\Sigma e_t^2}{n - k} \text{ and } \text{Var}(Y_t) = \frac{\Sigma y_t^2}{n - 1}$$

so that we have an adjusted R^2:

$$\bar{R}^2 = 1 - \frac{\Sigma e_t^2/(n - k)}{\Sigma y_t^2/(n - 1)} \tag{1.93}$$

or

$$\bar{R}^2 = 1 - (1 - R^2)\frac{n - k}{n - 1} \tag{1.94}$$

where k is the number of estimated parameters. This could fall if the rise in R^2 is more than offset by the fall in $(n - k)/(n - 1)$ as k increases. If 1.92 and 1.93 are rearranged so as to give

$$\Sigma e_t^2 = (1 - R^2)\Sigma y_t^2 \tag{1.95}$$

and

$$\frac{\Sigma e_t^2}{n - k} = (1 - R^2)\frac{\Sigma y_t^2}{n - 1} \tag{1.96}$$

we can see that in the case of two different regressions with the same R^2 or $\bar{R}^2$ the value of Σe_t^2 or $\Sigma e_t^2/(n - k)$ will depend on the value of Σy_t^2 and $\Sigma y_t^2/(n - 1)$; the higher the variation in the dependent variable, the higher the value of Σe_t^2 will be expected to be. It should therefore be clear that in comparing relationships explaining different variables a higher R^2 should not be taken as an indication of smaller residuals either in absolute terms or relative to the level of Y_t. This can be illustrated by the following example:

Y_{1t} :	10	15	11	18	14	16	19	24	29	34
e_{1t} :	1	2	0	-3	-2	-1	-2	-2	3	4

$\bar{Y}_1 = 19$, $\Sigma(Y_{1t} - \bar{Y}_1) = \Sigma y_{1t}^2 = 546$, $\Sigma e_{1t} = 0$, $\Sigma e_{1t}^2 = 52$

$\bar{R}_1^2 = 0.905$, RMSPR = 0.111, S/ME = 0.134

Y_{2t} :	15	15	16	17	18	19	19	22	24	25
e_{2t} :	-1	0	1	1.12	-0.5	1	-1	-1.12	1.5	-1

$\bar{Y}_2 = 19$, $\Sigma(Y_{2t} - \bar{Y}_2) = \Sigma y_{2t}^2 = 105$, $\Sigma e_{2t} = 0$, $\Sigma e_{2t}^2 = 10$

$\bar{R}_2^2 = 0.905$, RMSPR = 0.052, S/ME = 0.059

where RMSPR = $\sqrt{(1/n)\Sigma(e_t/Y_t)^2}$ is the root-mean square percentage residual, S = $\sqrt{\Sigma e_t^2/(n - k)}$ is the standard error of estimate and ME = $\bar{Y}$. It should be clear that despite the same arithmetic mean, $\bar{R}^2$, n and k, the residuals are much higher in the case of Y_1. Thus for comparison among different relationships the latter two measures are preferable to $\bar{R}^2$. But for different specifications of the same relationship a rise in R^2 always results in a fall in Σe_t^2.
In the Appendix, where the OLS structural form estimates appear, we report values for R^2, S and S/ME. R^2 is not provided for IV and restricted form estimates since its interpretation and properties are different from those applied to OLS estimates.

Finally, the level of R^2 is lower when first differences are used, instead of the absolute values of the dependent variable. This can be illustrated using the following example:

$$Y_t = \beta_0 + \beta_1 X_{1t} + \beta_2 Y_{t-1} + u_t \qquad (1.97)$$

or

$$Y_t - Y_{t-1} = \beta_0 + \beta_1 X_{1t} + \beta_3 Y_{t-1} + u_t \qquad (1.98)$$

where $\beta_3 = -(1 - \beta_2)$.

The two coefficients for these regressions are, respectively,

$$R_1^2 = 1 - \frac{\Sigma e_t^2}{\Sigma(Y_t - \bar{Y})^2}$$

and

$$R_2^2 = 1 - \frac{\Sigma e_t^2}{\Sigma[(Y_t - \bar{Y}) - (Y_{t-1} - \bar{Y}_{-1})]^2}$$

so that $R_1^2 > R_2^2$, that is, the R^2 for the equation in first differences, equation 1.98, is lower than the R^2 for the equation in levels, equation 1.97.

The next statistic always quoted in regression results is the t-statistic. In practice it is very often used to decide whether a regressor should be retained or dropped from a relationship. A theoretically developed relationship is expected to provide significant coefficients. But lack of significance in the case of a regressor should not always lead to a new specification excluding the particular regressor. Instead, one should explore the possibility that the lack of significance may be caused by various types of mis-specification (for a specific example, see Rao and Miller, 1971, pp. 37-40) and/or measurement errors. In estimating the relationships that constitute the model of this study we have often followed such a procedure. As a result, but for a very few exceptions, relationships contain only statistically significant coefficients. A process of experimentation is common practice in economic modelling given the inexactitude of economic hypotheses, the uncertainty about the true specification, and the presence of measurement problems. The value of χ_1^2 is of great help in such a process as a test of the validity of the initial specification. Its contribution in choosing the final specification is, of course, greater when quarterly or monthly data are used because it is under such circumstances that the choice of the lag structure becomes more important.

Sometimes a modification of a specification may be dictated by the unusual or theoretically unacceptable size of a coefficient. This can be illustrated by the following example of arbitrary regressions:

$$Y_t = 10 + 0.5I_t + 0.5G_t + 1.5Y_{t-1} \qquad (1.99)$$

$$Y_t = 10 + 0.5I_t + 0.5G_t - 0.5Y_{t-1} \qquad (1.100)$$

Assuming that investment (I_t) and government expenditure (G_t) are independent of income (Y_t), 1.99 implies a negative equilibrium value of Y while 1.100 implies an unacceptably low multiplier. The equilibrium value (Y^e) of Y is obtained as the solution to each equation for $Y^e = Y_t = Y_{t-1}$. In the first case we have

$$Y^e = (10 + 0.5I_t + 0.5G_t)/(-0.5) \tag{1.101}$$

and in the second

$$Y^e = (2/3)(10 + 0.5I_t + 0.5G_t) \tag{1.102}$$

with -2 and 2/3 as the respective multipliers.

The first response to such outcomes would be to look for possible mis-specifications which, when corrected, would remove the problem. A left-out variable which is highly correlated with Y_t and Y_{t-1} could lead to a distortion of the true coefficient of Y_{t-1}. Including the missing variable would restore the latter to its proper size, that is, the value reflecting the influence of Y_{t-1} alone.

Looking at the residual series may lead to legitimate modifications of the initial specification which will improve its explanatory performance. Unusually large residuals may be the result of one-off events such as strikes, weather conditions, tax changes, elections, etc. Dummy variables are commonly used to account for their influence on the dependent variables. Such considerations are more frequently met when quarterly data are used. In our annual model dummy variables have been used in explaining changes in public expenditure and inflation - in the first case to distinguish between Labour and Conservative governments and in the second to account for the influence of incomes policies. Such events cause disturbances which do not impair the validity of the structure of the relationship. There are, however, changes which affect the nature of the relationship on a more permanent basis - usually called 'structural breaks'. Important institutional changes, interchange of governments of significantly different political and/or economic persuasion, introduction of influential social measures, changes in customs and social codes, new legislation regulating aspects of production and exchange, all could render structural relationships obsolete. Such transformations may be gradual or abrupt. In the former case the performance of a particular relationship will tend to deteriorate when long time series are used and it may go unnoticed when observations over relatively short periods are employed accompanied by *ad hoc* and relatively minor modifications of the basic specification of the underlying structure. In the latter case, however, the performance of a relationship will tend to decline rather suddenly alter the structural break. Usually an F-test is used to detect a structural shift in a relation. The Chow test is based on a comparison of the sum of the squares of the residuals of two different estimates of the same equation. The first estimate is based on observations before the occurrence of the assumed structural break, while the second encompasses the whole period. In the absence of a break one would expect a uniformity of the residuals, and thus a significantly different residual structure is taken as evidence of a structural change. A test of the null hypothesis that the observations after a certain point obey the same relation experienced before is given by the ratio

$$\frac{(SSR - SSR_1)/m}{SSR_1/(n - k)} \qquad (1.103)$$

which follows the F-distribution with (m, n - k) degrees of freedom. SSR and SSR_1 are the sums of the squares of the residuals from the regression fitted, first through all n + m observations and second on the first n observations; k is the number of parameters estimated. For a value of F higher than the critical value obtained from the F-distribution table for the given degrees of freedom and the chosen probability level we reject the null hypothesis.

The Chow test has been estimated and is reported for each preferred regression as F mainly for illustration purposes. It tests whether the 1978 data obey the relationship estimated for 1957-77. To test for just one period is of course unsatisfactory, but this has been dictated by the need to preserve degrees of freedom given the short length of our sample period. Although its importance, in this instance, is clearly limited, it so happens that its value is, in most cases, insignificant at the 95 per cent probability level. It should be emphasised, however, that a significant value of F does not necessarily imply a structural break unless we are certain that the specification used is the true relationship for part of the whole period. But more often the failure of a relationship is the result of mis-specification. We may, for example, have a case where for a considerable period of time a left-out variable is relatively stable so that it either has a relatively minor effect on the dependent variable or its effect is successfully captured by another regressor with which it is highly correlated. This may come to an end when the left-out factor undergoes unusual changes which are not reflected by changes in any of the other regressors, with the result that the explanatory power of the regression declines substantially. This seems to be the case with consumption-function specifications, which up to the early 1970s did not incorporate an inflation variable. With the advent of the new inflationary era in the early 1970s omission of inflation effects seemed to matter very much. Thus while simple specifications were doing well until 1971-2, they completely failed to predict the rise in the saving ratio from 1973 onwards.

In economic modelling we are interested in stable relationships. By stability in this context we mean relative constancy of the estimated parameters of an equation over time. One way of testing for this is to divide the whole sample period into two or more sub-periods and obtain estimates by running separate regressions of the same specification on each sub-period. The test involves comparison of the different estimates. A special case of this is the F-test given in 1.103 which is frequently used when one of the two sub-periods is very short. If, however, the number of observations corresponding to each sub-period is sufficiently large, the following F-test can be used:

$$F = \frac{[SSR - (SSR_1 + SSR_2)]/k}{(SSR_1 + SSR_2)/(n_1 + n_2 - 2k)} \tag{1.104}$$

where SSR, SSR_1, SSR_2 are the sums of the squares of the residuals from the whole period, the first and the second sub-periods, respectively, with $(n_1 + n_2)$, n_1 and n_2 as the corresponding observations and k the number of estimated parameters. A stricter test is the post-sample parameter stability test, which is obtained as follows: n - m of the available observations are used for estimation of the relationship with the last m observations used to obtain *ex post* 'predictions' of the dependent variable by substitution in the estimated equation. These 'predictions', which are based on the actual rather than the predicted values of the regressors, are subsequently subtracted from the actual values of the dependent variable to obtain 'prediction' errors. The test is based on a comparison of these errors with the sample residuals according to the expression

$$Z(m) = \sum_{t=n-m+1}^{n} (f_t/\hat{\sigma})^2 \tag{1.105}$$

which is distributed as χ^2 in large samples if the parameters remained constant, with m = degrees of freedom, f_t = the prediction error and $\hat{\sigma}$ = the standard error of estimate ($\hat{\sigma} = \sqrt{\Sigma e_i^2/(n - m - k)}$). For a Z(m) greater than its critical value the null hypothesis of constant parameters is rejected. It should be clear that this is a comparative test and that it provides no clue as to the absolute value of the residuals. To illustrate the use of this test, we have re-estimated our preferred equations on 1957-77 data retaining the 1978 observations for a post-sample parameter stability test. It should therefore be made clear that this statistic, reported as χ_3^2, does not refer to the reported regressions but to their counterparts estimated for the shorter (by one year) 1957-77 period. The comments made earlier on in relation to F also apply here.

We have noted before that in estimating macroeconomic relationships it is not difficult to obtain regressions with high R^2 and significant coefficients, and we concluded that this, by itself, should not be considered as satisfactory evidence on the explanatory performance of the relationship. A more important criterion is to examine the stability of each estimated relationship on the basis of appropriate tests such as 1.103 to 1.105. It is our view that most of the econometric work of the last twenty years would have considerable difficulty in passing such tests. We feel that the establishment of an expanded and expanding set of tests marks real progress in economic modelling in that it increases considerably the rate of failure of competing hypotheses. The importance of extensive testing is succinctly expressed by one of the best British practitioners of econometric modelling: 'The three golden rules of econometrics are test, test and test' (Hendry, 1980). Davidson *et al.* (1978) suggest that another criterion of a good model is its ability to explain relevant findings obtained in previous studies. This is frequently a very demanding criterion which nevertheless is expected to contribute greatly towards greater efficiency in empirical macroeconomics research. Finally, the ultimate criterion of the performance of a model is very often considered to be its predictive record. All the tests discussed so far do not ensure that a model will predict well. They make it more likely, however, that predictions will be more accurate than they would otherwise have been. The present model is not used for *ex ante* forecasting. Unlike the model in this book, forecasting models are bigger, estimated on the basis of quarterly data and continuously updated so as to incorporate recent developments in the economy.

In building our annual model for 1957-78 we have been constrained by the availability of only a small number of observations available for estimation. We decided that we could not afford to allow a shrinkage of our estimation period for the purpose of retaining observations for a post-sample parameter stability test. The same applies with regard to F-tests for structural breaks. We cannot therefore claim that our model is stable in an econometric sense. Given, however, that our model is not put forward as a rival to existing fully fledged large quarterly forecasting models (which anyway have not yet adopted the complete panoply of new tests) but is mainly a pedagogic exercise, we do not consider this as a major deficiency.

In this chapter we have not dealt with the problems encountered in evaluating the performance of multi-equation models. This is done in Chapter 9, where simulation of the model is undertaken and explained and policy exercises carried out and commented upon.

2

Consumers' Expenditure

Consumers' expenditure constitutes the biggest aggregate component of total domestic expenditure. Measured at constant prices it accounts, over the period 1950-78, for between 60 and 65 per cent of gross national product. Furthermore, it is the most stable element of national expenditure and certainly much more predictable than investment or imports. Following Keynes's treatment of consumption[1] as a component of effective demand in his general theory of income determination, as well as the development of appropriate econometric techniques for the estimation of economic relationships, and given the early availability of reasonably reliable time-series data of an aggregate nature, it is not surprising that empirical studies of the consumption function have been popular among economists.

The importance given to consumption in economic analysis can be further illustrated by the following two contrasting views on the matter. First, the view that consumption is the 'sole end and purpose of all production' underlies most contemporary neoclassical economic analysis;[2] following this the explanation of a society's economic activity is significantly based on how people strive to achieve an optimum consumption pattern and maximise their utility; also in contemporary economic 'growth theory' savings constitute the main driving-force of the determination of output and accumulation. In contrast to this, Marxist analysis puts the emphasis on production. It is assumed that capitalists are motivated by their fanatical pursuit of accumulation and as a result they force 'the human race to produce for production's sake' (Marx, 1976, p. 739). It is this incessant drive for accumulation in combination with insufficient expansion of consumption that leads to the so-called 'underconsumption' crises.

In this chapter we develop a model which attempts to explain changes in the aggregate propensity to consume over the last twenty years. But before we proceed to do that we shall consider the following questions, the answers to which will provide useful background information concerning consumers' expenditure in the United Kingdom: (i) the main characteristics of the aggregate propensity to consume since 1950, (ii) changes in the composition of consumers' expenditure, (iii) the distinction between durables and non-durables, and (iv) measurement problems.

AGGREGATE PROPENSITY TO CONSUME

We define the aggregate propensity to consume (APC) as the ratio of total consumers' expenditure to total personal disposable income,[3] which is equivalent to the average propensity to consume for the economy as a whole. This ratio has been declining since 1950, when it stood at 99 per cent, reaching a little over 85 per cent in 1978. The downward trend which was in full swing in the 1950s and in relative abeyance in the 1960s accelerated rapidly in the period 1972-3. That there has been a downward trend in APC is clear from the linear trend equation estimated from annual data from 1950-77 and given below:

$$\frac{C}{Y_d} = \underset{}{0.9866} - \underset{(11.6)}{0.0046T} \qquad R^2 = 0.842$$

where C = consumers' expenditure, Y_d = personal disposable income, T = 0, 1, ..., 27.

The second related issue to be examined is the view that the APC tends to decline during the upswing of the business cycle and to rise during an economic recession. We think that the most appropriate variable with which the APC should be compared in an attempt to check whether the sample data conform with this hypothesis is personal disposable income rather than gross domestic product. These two variables are imperfectly related because of changes in direct taxation, public transfers and the functional distribution of income. Using percentage deviations from trend for both APC and disposable income we can clearly discern an inverse relationship (Figure 2.1). Despite the fact that a complete conformity of APC to a countercyclical pattern is not what we observe (compare, for example, the movements in the two variables in 1964-5 and 1974-5) the evidence is strong enough to suggest that the ratio C/Y_d is systematically related to the cyclical movements of Y_d. As we shall see later, the inverse relationship between the two can be explained in terms of either a habit-persistence hypothesis or a permanent income hypothesis. Defining, for example, $\bar{Y}$ as permanent income, which can be approximated by the trend or steady-state income, we can assume that consumers want to maintain the ratio $C/\bar{Y}$ constant, *ceteris paribus*. It then follows that C/Y_d should be positively related with $\bar{Y}/Y_d$. This will be so irrespective of the cause of the deviation of $\bar{Y}/Y_d$ from 1.0.

The third variable indicated in Figure 2.1 is the marginal propensity to consume (MPC). It can be seen that unlike the APC the MPC is not characterised by a downward trend - probably one exception on which we will have to say more later on, is the period 1967-74.

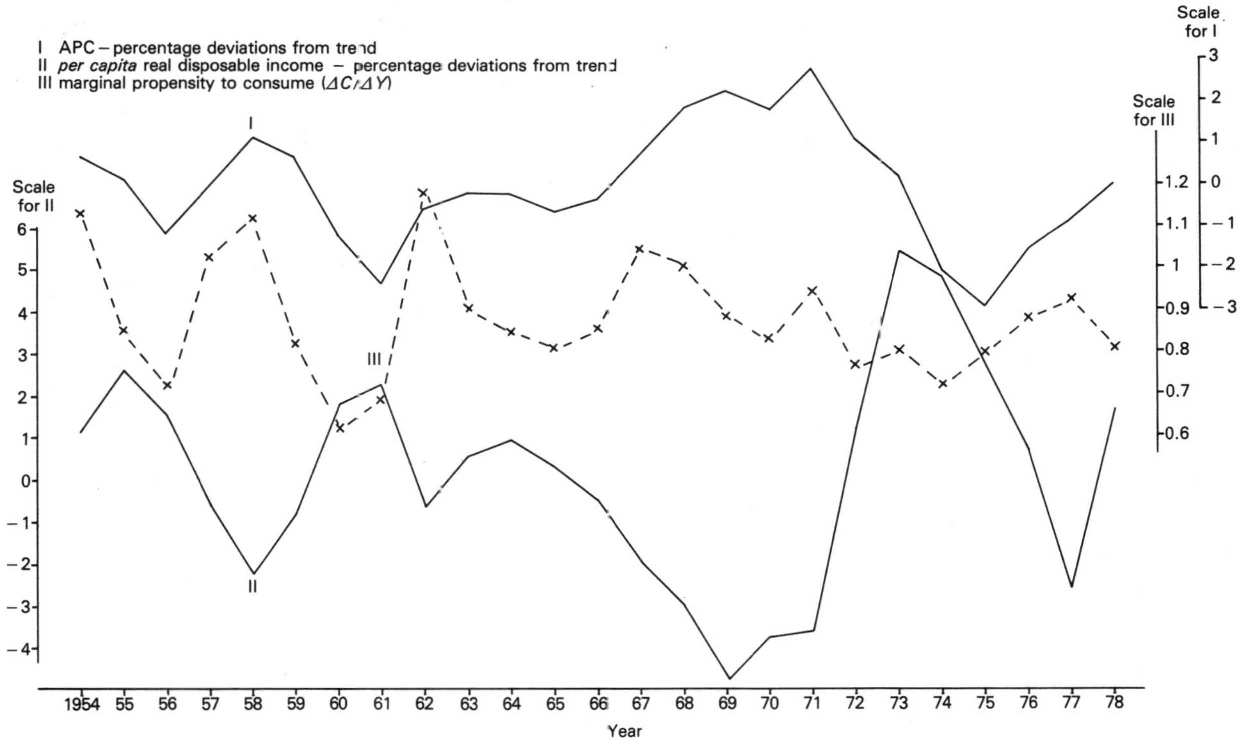
I APC – percentage deviations from trend
II per capita real disposable income – percentage deviations from trend
III marginal propensity to consume (ΔC/ΔY)
Scale for I
Scale for II
Scale for III
I
II
III
Year
1954 55 56 57 58 59 60 61 62 63 64 65 66 67 68 69 70 71 72 73 74 75 76 77 78

Figure 2.1

It so happens that the latter period coincides with a clear break of the counter-cyclical pattern of MPC. Another difference between APC and MPC is that the variability of the latter is much greater, its value ranging between 1.190 and 0.626. The decline in APC can be explained by the fact that the average value of MPC over each business cycle since 1950 has been consistently lower than the corresponding value of APC.

While the cyclical fluctuations in APC constitute a pattern of change consistent with expectations about movements in APC based on early observations in more than one country, the UK postwar downward trend of the same propensity does not fulfil any specific anticipation for such a development. The new theories of the consumption function which originated in the USA have been markedly influenced by the observation of a long-run constancy of the APC in that country. Although they have been so formulated so as to be consistent with this observation, they do not seem to be incompatible with the presence of a trend. It is interesting that these theories have been developed as replacements of the absolute-income hypothesis, usually associated with Keynes's views on consumption, according to which there are reasons to expect 'a greater proportion of income being saved as real income increases' (Keynes, 1964, p. 97). It is clear from the data we use that the postwar UK experience so far seems to be closer to the Keynesian prediction of a falling APC rather than the expectation of a long-run constancy. In a recent study of the UK personal savings ratio Coghlan and Jackson (1979) suggest that the personal savings ratio should be expected to grow with real personal disposable incomes; they argue that there is substantial evidence in support of this old proposition and that the failure of forecasting models to predict saving behaviour in the 1970s is the consequence of their short-term nature - they use estimates based on relatively small samples - and, therefore, their lack of historical perspective.

The next important aspect of consumers' expenditure is its relation with gross national product (GNP). When both variables are measured at current prices the ratio C/GNP, like APC, declines throughout the period 1950-78. But when valuation at constant prices is adopted a different picture emerges. There is no discernible trend for the whole period, though a gradual but slight decline is suggested by the data after 1963, despite an upward trend in the share of disposable income in GNP. The observed difference in the evolution of the two ratios corresponding to a different type of valuation indicates that the average rate of growth of consumers' goods and services' prices has been on the whole lower than the corresponding rate for the rest of the GNP components.

It has been argued that the importance of the evidence on the long-run development of consumers' expenditure in relation to GNP lies in its relevance for the empirical validity of the underconsumption theories (Bleany, 1976). It is one of the basic tenets of these theories that there is an inherent tendency of the growth in the demand for consumption to fall behind the growth in national output.

It is argued by the exponents of the underconsumption thesis - mostly Marxist economists - that because of the interdependence of consumption and investment and despite the incessant drive of capitalists to expand surplus value the increasing gap is not closed by increasing investment, with the consequence of a chronic depression or recurrent crises. As it has been indicated above in the case of the UK economy the postwar experience consists of a falling APC but a less definite decline in the share of consumers' expenditure in GNP. Although useful, this evidence is not sufficient to make one pass judgement on this theory. For a pronouncement one would want to combine the above with, among other things, developments in public-sector consumption and the extent to which the latter crowds out private consumption.

COMPOSITION OF CONSUMERS' EXPENDITURE

An examination of the composition of consumers' expenditure shows that the downward trend of APC is in the first instance associated with a significant decline, over the whole period, in the percentage of real disposable income spent on food and services. The percentage of income spent on food alone declined from 29.4 in 1951 to around 16.0 in 1977. This is, of course, a confirmation of Engel's law, according to which the proportion of expenditure devoted to food decreases as the standard of living of the household increases. Over the whole period the income elasticity of the demand for food has been consistently less than 1.0. On the other hand, that the relative importance of expenditure on services should decline is not so obvious. But it has been suggested that this development is partly the result of the tendency according to which as people's standard of living increases they prefer to buy the durable goods which provide the required services rather than purchase the services direct through the market (Gershuny, 1979). Examples of such durable goods, which tend to reduce the amount of marketed services, are private cars, television sets and video systems, washing-machines, hi-fi and tape-recording systems, do-it-yourself equipment, etc. Furthermore, a considerable amount of services such as medical care, education, and refuse clearance are provided by the state as non-marketed goods. There are three more categories of consumers' goods, clothing, footwear and alcoholic drinks, on which spending, as a percentage of total spending, has either declined or remained relatively constant. In contrast to the above categories of expenditure, spending on housing, motor-cars and motor-cycles, durable goods and 'other goods' have risen in importance, with the highest increase recorded in the case of housing.[4]

CONSUMERS' EXPENDITURE ON DURABLES AND NON-DURABLES

From all the categories of consumers' expenditure the distinction between durable and non-durable goods plus services has attracted a great deal of interest. This has not been incidental. It has been argued that consumption proper should be identified with expenditure on non-durable goods and services - including service known as the 'use' definition of consumption, has been generally accepted by the new theories of the consumption function. Furthermore, it has been suggested that expenditure on durables, a category that accounts for a considerable part of consumers' expenditure, from the point of view of the individual might more appropriately be treated as savings or capital expenditure. This definition has been criticised on the grounds that the distinction should be made 'not on the basis of the physical properties of the assets involved, but in the light of their economic function, i.e. depending on whether they enter consumption as "final goods" or serve as means of production contributing thus to an increase of output in the subsequent period' (Baran, 1968, p. 327). In addition to this the problems associated with a satisfactory measurement of consumption, when adopting the 'use' concept of this term (mainly the value imputation of services accrued from durable goods, the correct identification of these goods as well as the durability of some services), have led in the case of many empirical studies to the adoption of consumers' expenditure rather than consumption as the variable to be explained.[5]

Notwithstanding the reservations as to the functional usefulness of the 'use' definition of consumption, this is a characteristic example of the problem which arises when the available data (on consumers' expenditure in this case) do not conform to the theoretical categories which they purport to measure (consumption).

MEASUREMENT PROBLEMS

It is customary to measure savings of the personal sector as the *residual* of personal disposable income left over after allowing for the whole of consumers' expenditure. At the same time there is an alternative and broadly independent method that provides an estimate of personal saving. According to this second method, saving is *identified* as the sum of personal-sector capital formation, capital transfers and identified financial transactions. What is important is that, despite the fact that conceptually the two measures are identical, in practice they provide significantly different results. It has been observed, for example, that over the period 1952-70, while residual saving as a percentage of personal disposable income increases, identified saving as a proportion remains fairly constant. The discrepancy between the two can be explained on the basis of two types of errors: (i) the omission from identified saving of certain financial loans, and (ii) inaccuracies in the measurement of each of the items entering into the estimation of both residual saving and identified saving.

Given the difference between the two alternative series, what is relevant for the present study, which uses national accounting data, is that to the extent that the correct one is identified saving, either personal disposable income or consumers' expenditure (or both) must be incorrectly measured. Possible sources of measurement error are: (i) the difficulty in allocating accurately certain financial items, such as rent and transfers, between the personal and the company sectors, and (ii) the need to impute the value of a certain amount of disposable income such as income received in kind and the rental value of owner-occupied housing - for a full discussion see Odling-Smee (1967, 1973) and *Midland Bank Review* (1977).

A related problem is a recent suggestion according to which during inflationary periods the national accounting measure of personal income is overstated. Given that the personal sector is a substantial net creditor, it is argued that when inflation is high a substantial part of interest revenue should not be considered as income as it only constitutes a compensation for wealth losses in the form of a reduction in the real value of financial assets. Assuming that this effect is substantial, it can be shown, for example, that, *ceteris paribus*, during inflationary periods the conventionally measured APC declines. (For a detailed discussion of this problem see Taylor and Threadgold, 1979; Hendry and Ungern-Sternberg, 1980; Siegel, 1979.) The problem with this suggestion is that as soon as we accept the principle of allowing changes in wealth to enter our measurement of income we cannot confine our adjustments of national accounting income to the one referred to above. Acceptance of this principle leads effectively to the adoption of the concept of permanent income - the particular adjustment is then seen as a very partial solution in the light of the permanent income hypothesis. The consumption function used in the empirical work contained in this chapter originates from the permanent income principle and should therefore be seen as a more general formulation than the one based on the particular suggestion explained above - although, in practice, as long as the measurement of permanent income is based on national accounting income, the problem persists.

THREE MAJOR THEORIES OF CONSUMERS' BEHAVIOUR

Most of the empirical work on the consumption function in the last thirty years is based on specifications implied by three major theories of consumers' behaviour put forward by American economists. (For a comprehensive review of such empirical studies see Mayer, 1972.) These are the permanent income hypothesis, the relative income hypothesis and the life-cycle income hypothesis. All three theories claim to be consistent with the following stylised facts (at least as far as the US economy is concerned) on the relation between consumption and income: (i) the long-run constancy of the percentage of personal disposable income consumed (APC) when using time-series data, (ii) the decline of the same percentage with rising income when using cross-section data, and (iii) the cyclical fluctuation of the same variable.

In what follows we describe the main features of each one of the above theories. The basic tenets of the permanent income hypothesis (PIH) can be summarised as follows:

$$C_p = k\ (i, w, u)\ Y_p \qquad (2.1)$$

$$Y = Y_p + Y_T \qquad (2.2)$$

$$C = C_p + C_T \qquad (2.3)$$

where C_p = permanent consumption, Y_p = permanent income, Y_T = transitory income, C = measured consumption, Y = measured income, C_T = transitory income, k = propensity to consume permanent income, i = the rate of interest, w = the ratio of non-human wealth to total wealth, u = error term. The hypothesis is supplemented by the following assumptions:

(a) $E(Y_T) = E(C_T) = 0$

(b) $\text{Cov}(C_p, C_T) = \text{Cov}(Y_p, Y_T) = 0$

(c) $\text{Cov}(C_T, Y_T) = 0$

One of the implications of equation 2.1 is known as the proportionality assumption. According to this assumption, given the values of i, w and u consumption is a constant proportion of (permanent) income irrespective of the level of this income. This is expected to apply whether one uses time-series or cross-section data. This particular hypothesis goes against both the Fisherian and Keynesian views on the matter, according to which consumption is expected to be a declining proportion of income as income increases. But according to equation 2.1, k, the coefficient of proportionality, does not have to be constant over time. Its value depends (i) on the rate of interest, which determines the time pattern of individual consumption - the latter being allocated over time so that the marginal rate of substitution between, for example, this year's consumption and next year's consumption is equal to the rate of interest; (ii) on the ratio of non-human wealth to total wealth: since non-human wealth is much more liquid than human wealth a higher ratio provides the individual with more security, being a contingency reserve in a world of uncertainty and non-price rationing of finance, and thus a lesser motive for undertaking more savings; (iii) on changes in tastes or preferences, indicated by the presence of the u term.

As this theory is formulated primarily in terms of an unobservable variable in the form of permanent income, defined at the theoretical level as the total return on wealth in a prescribed period, a measurement problem arises. Friedman's suggestion and subsequent practice has been to measure permanent income by an exponentially weighted average of past incomes with geometrically declining weights, including a trend component. One consequence of this crude estimation scheme is, of course, the introduction of an additional assumption (namely, that permanent income is correctly measured by the suggested scheme) arising from the need for empirical implementation of the hypothesis. In the context of the permanent income hypothesis and in the light of the rational expectations literature a recent contribution suggests that we can easily and without loss do away with the need to have a measure of permanent income (Hall, 1978). It is in effect argued that since actual consumption in a certain period is solely determined by a 'rationally expected' permanent income, consumption in a subsequent period should be the same except for a historical trend and the inevitable 'white noise'. In other words, consumption, being proportional to permanent income, is the best proxy we can have for the latter. It is therefore suggested that the simple autoregressive scheme $C_t = bC_{t-1} + u_t$ is sufficient and that 'under the pure life cycle-permanent income hypothesis a forecast of future consumption obtained by extrapolation of today's level by the historical trend is impossible to improve' (Hall, 1978, p. 986). This is certainly a very bold claim which, however, has already been shown to be contradicted by an analysis of the UK data (Daly and Hadjimatheou, 1981).

The assumptions that (i) permanent income and transitory income and (ii) transitory consumption and transitory income are uncorrelated, as indicated by the zero covariances in assumptions (b) and (c) above, have attracted a great deal of interest and have been repeatedly criticised. It has been shown, for example, that the first of these assumptions is inconsistent with the convention by which permanent income is measured as a weighted average of past incomes and a trend. A further criticism of the same assumption is based on the observation that within a certain time period permanent income will have to be adjusted to take into account changes in wealth, and therefore the extra yield arising this way, which result from unanticipated transitory income. Let it be reminded that assumptions (b) and (c), in combination with equation 2.1, imply that consumption is completely independent of transitory income or, in other words, all transitory income is saved. This is considered by commentators (Holmes, 1971, for example) as an unduly restrictive assumption; it is widely assumed, instead, that although the correlation between consumption and transitory income is significantly lower than the correlation between consumption and permanent income, nevertheless it is significantly different from zero. Expressed in a different way, it is argued that the propensity to consume out of transitory income is lower than the propensity to consume from permanent income.

One of the earliest attempts to formulate a model of consumers' expenditure in accord with the stylised facts was the relative income hypothesis developed by Duesenberry (1949). This hypothesis is based on two main propositions. (1) A household's consumption is determined by the household's position in the income distribution. Low-income households trying to keep up with their richer neighbours, friends or acquaintances are expected to have a higher average propensity to consume than high-income households. Even when a household's absolute income increases, its average propensity to consume will not be affected as long as its position in the income distribution does not change. It can be shown then that, assuming the income distribution remains constant, aggregate consumption is proportional to aggregate income.

(2) In addition to relative income a household's consumption is influenced by the past pattern of consumption and more specifically by that particular past consumption level which corresponds to the previous peak income. The purpose of this proposition is to provide an explanation for the cyclical fluctuation of APC. Since Duesenberry subsequently accepted that 'it seems reasonable to make consumption depend upon a moving average of past incomes rather than on the income of a single past year' (Duesenberry, 1958, pp. 177-8), this proposition makes APC a function of the ratio $\bar{Y}/Y$, where $\bar{Y}$ is an average of past incomes, and it could therefore be thought of as a conventionally measured permanent income. But as initially formulated this proposition categorises the relative income theory as a habit-persistence theory rather than a wealth theory - no consideration is given to expected income or wealth.

The main difference between the permanent income hypothesis and the relative income hypothesis lies in their explanation of cross-section data. Specifically, the relative income hypothesis rejects the proportionality assumption in the cross-section context by asserting that the APC declines as income decreases.

The third of the consumption theories is the life-cycle hypothesis. According to this hypothesis, the individual maximises his utility function

> subject to the resources available to him, his resources being the sum of current and discounted future earnings over his lifetime and his current net worth. As a result of this maximization the current consumption of the individual can be expressed as a function of his resources and the rate of return on capital with parameters depending on age (Ando and Modigliani, 1963, p. 56).

Total consumption of a person of age T is given by the following function:

$$C_t^T = \lambda_t^T \left[y_t^T + W_{t-1}^T + \sum_{\tau=T+1}^{N} \frac{y_t^{eT\tau}}{(1 + r_t)^{\tau-T}} \right]$$

where λ_t^T is a proportionality factor which will depend on the specific form of the utility function, the rate of return on assets, and the present age of the person, but not on total resources, given by the sum inside brackets; y_t^T is the current non-property income; $y_t^{eT\tau}$ is the non-property income an individual of age T expects to earn in the τth year of his life; W_{t-1}^T is the existing stock of wealth; finally N stands for the earning span and r_t for the rate of return on assets. This is the life-cycle version of the proportionality assumption on the micro level. Defining average annual expected income as

$$y_t^{eT} = \frac{1}{N - T} \sum_{\tau=T+1}^{N} \frac{y_t^{eT\tau}}{(1 + r_t)^{\tau-T}}$$

we can rewrite the individual consumption function as

$$C_t^T = \lambda_t^T \left[y_t^T + W_{t-1}^T + (N - T)\, y_t^{eT} \right]$$

The aggregate counterpart of this is

$$C_t = \alpha_1 Y_{1t} + \alpha_2 Y_{1t}^e + \alpha_3 A_{t-1}$$

where Y_{1t} = current non-property or labour income; Y_{1t}^e = expected annual non-property income and A_{t-1} = net worth. Ando and Modigliani (1963) suggest a number of schemes by which expected non-property income is approximated by observable variables. One such scheme results in the following formulation:

$$C_t = b_1 Y_{1t} + b_2 \left(\frac{L_t}{E_t} \right) Y_{1t} + b_3 A_{t-1}$$

where L_t denotes the total labour force and E_t the number of persons engaged in production. For a constant L_t/E_t and A_{t-1}/Y_{1t} the APC is also constant; changes of L_t/E_t over the cycle produce the cyclical fluctuations in C/Y_{1t}. Furthermore, the observed non-proportionality between consumption and income in cross-section studies can be explained in the context of the life-cycle hypothesis by the following reasoning. In a cross-section sample high-income households are more likely to be at the stage when they earn more than their lifetime average earnings and are therefore expected to save proportionately more than low-income households, who are more likely to be earning less than their lifetime average earnings and are therefore expected to be saving proportionately less.

An assumption which is usually considered to be an integral part of the life-cycle hypothesis is that households save only for the sake of consuming later in their lifespan, but not for the sake of passing wealth on to their heirs. This is one of the differences between this theory and the permanent income hypothesis. One implication of this assumption is that net saving in a static economy is equal to zero. But for a steady-state growth of population and/or technology net saving becomes positive and a constant proportion of income. Another important difference between the two theories is that for the permanent income hypothesis assets are only implicitly taken into account - as a determinant of permanent income; and it also relies on unobservable aspects of income - 'permanent' and 'transitory' income. The life-cycle hypothesis, on the other hand, relies more on observable income components which are separated into labour income and the value of assets. One could therefore argue that the life-cycle hypothesis might be more useful to econometric model-builders and forecasters since it explicitly takes into account measured income and assets to explain consumption.

Mayer (1972, p. 48) proposes a 'very heavily toned down version of the permanent income theory and the life cycle hypothesis', based on the presumption that the truth lies between the wealth theories and the measured income theories, by abandoning the restrictive assumptions of the permanent income hypothesis: first, the proportionality assumption, the rejection of which is rationalised by assuming (i) lack of perfect foresight, (ii) existence of capital rationing and (iii) the probable significance of psychological time preference; second, it is asserted that the income elasticity of consumption is greater for permanent income than for transitory income but it is neither unity for the former nor zero for the latter. It is claimed that this theory is 'consistent with all the valid empirical evidence which has been adduced both for and against the wealth theories' (Mayer, 1972, p. 49).

A common characteristic of all the above theories is the abandonment of measured or current income in favour of a broader concept of income. Although the main concern of these theories has been the relation between consumption and income, other possible determinants of consumption have also been discussed. In empirical work, in addition to various approximate measures of the appropriate concept of wealth and/or income, other variables have also been used such as the distinction between types of income, liquid assets, capital earnings, the rate of interest, the rate of inflation, the rate of unemployment, etc.

A MODEL OF THE AVERAGE PROPENSITY TO CONSUME

In recent years there have been attempts to look yet again at the relationship between aggregate disposable income and aggregate consumers' expenditure, perhaps because existing models failed to predict the peculiarly high levels of the personal saving ratio since 1972.[6] A number of explanations have been put forward for this 'paradox of personal saving'. In the *Midland Bank Review* (1977) it is suggested that the high saving ratio may be largely attributed to a 'squeeze' exerted by companies and nationalised industries on the trade credit available to the personal sector, while in the *Bank of England Quarterly Bulletin* (1978) it is argued that increases in contractual savings accounts contributed substantially to the increase. It has also been proposed that unanticipated inflation may have had a major role to play (Deaton, 1977; Davidson *et al.*, 1978; Howard, 1978); another suggestion refers to a desire to maintain the real value of liquid assets (Townend, 1976; Howard, 1978) or wealth (Bean, 1978) which has been eroded by high inflation rates. A somehow different interpretation is that a significant structural break may have taken place which existing theories were ill-prepared to anticipate (Walters, 1978). The studies by Hadjimatheou (1979) and Arestis and Hadjimatheou (1982) argue that some of the major factors suggested by the above studies constitute only a subset of the determinants of consumers' behaviour. It is because we would like to contribute to the discussion of the determinants of the average propensity to consume that in this chapter we postulate and estimate the latter, rather than an aggregate consumption function.

The way we tackle the APC relationship is to develop a simple conventional model of consumers' behaviour based principally on

Friedman's (1957) permanent income hypothesis (PIH) and drawing heavily on Hadjimatheou (1979) and Arestis and Hadjimatheou (1982), which attempt to explain the recent UK experience of unusual changes in consumers' expenditure. The PIH postulates that

$$C = K\,(i,w,u)\,Y_p \tag{2.4}$$

where, following Friedman (1957), measured consumption (C) is assumed to be a reasonably good approximation of permanent consumption (C_p). Dividing throughout by measured income (Y) we have

$$\frac{C}{Y} = K\,(i,w,u)\,\frac{Y_p}{Y} \tag{2.5}$$

The variable Y_p is usually approximated by a weighted average of present and past values of measured income with geometrically declining weights, which provides a measure of income that exhibits much less variability than observed national accounting income. As a result of this procedure the ratio Y_p/Y follows a cyclical pattern with its value increasing during the downswing of the business cycle and decreasing during the opposite phase of the cycle. A convenient measure of this ratio as cyclical indicator is obtained if permanent income is calculated as a weighted average of present and past trend values of measured income in the following way:

$$Y_{pt} = W_o \sum_{j=o}^{n} W^j\, \bar{Y}_{t-j} \tag{2.6}$$

where $\bar{Y}_t$ = trend value of personal disposable income. Given, however, that

$$\bar{Y}_t = (1 + a)^j\, \bar{Y}_{t-j}$$

it follows that equation 2.6 can now be written as

$$Y_{pt} = \left[W_o \Sigma \frac{W^j}{(1 + a)^j} \right] \bar{Y}_t$$

or

$$Y_{pt} = m\, \bar{Y}_t \tag{2.7}$$

which we can proceed to substitute in 2.5 to yield

$$\frac{C}{Y} = K\,(i,w,u)\,\frac{m\,\bar{Y}_t}{Y_t} \tag{2.8}$$

Equation 2.8 incorporates what is known as the proportionality hypothesis feature of the permanent income theory according to which, although K in 2.8 is not a constant for all individuals or for all time periods, it is, nevertheless, assumed to be independent of permanent income. This proportionality hypothesis, however, has been shown to have been refuted by a large number of empirical tests (Mayer, 1972, esp. pp. 10-12, 347-8). In view of these findings, and given that we would like to retain C/Y as the variable to be explained, we utilise a linear approximation of equation 2.8 for estimation purposes.[7] The relationship to be explained is thus written as follows:

$$\frac{C}{Y} = b_0 + b_1 i + b_2 w + b_3 \frac{\bar{Y}}{Y} + u \tag{2.9}$$

Estimation of equation 2.9 is difficult due to the non-availability of a consistent series of wealth.[8] The importance of the latter variable can be highlighted by referring to the balance-sheets of the personal sector for 1966-76 (*Economic Trends*, January 1978, pp. 97-107). According to this valuable information, net wealth of households, after a rise of 67.5 per cent between 1970 and 1973, declined by just over 1 per cent in 1974. As a multiple of personal disposable income (PDI) net wealth rose rapidly during 1971-3 but fell substantially in the succeeding two years. The exceptional increase in the early 1970s is mainly due to above-average increases in the price of dwellings, land and other buildings, assets which amount to over 70 per cent of all physical assets of the personal sector. The subsequent stabilisation of housing and land prices has meant that this component of wealth hardly changed over the next two years. As regards financial assets, the rapid rise in their value recorded in 1971-2 was reversed by actual decreases in 1973-4 caused by the marked fall of share prices. Liquid assets, the component of wealth most frequently associated with consumers' expenditure, as a percentage of PDI fell substantially in 1974-5.

Looking at the liability side of the balance-sheets we observe that total liabilities as a percentage of net wealth rose slightly in 1971-3 and significantly so in 1974. The increase in the latter year was mainly due to the fall in wealth rather than a rise in liabilities. As a percentage of PDI liabilities rose to a high level in 1972-3, from which they fell gradually in subsequent years.

From the above observations it is firmly established that the unusually high volume of savings relative to disposable income in 1974-5 coincides with a decline of the ratio of wealth to disposable income. Although it is possible that this may be a mere coincidence, it seems unwise to treat it so in the knowledge that wealth, human and non-human, plays a large part in the theoretical explanation of consumption. The poor forecasting of the saving ratio in 1974-5 is very probably the result of the failure of the models employed to provide for the wealth effect on consumption. (As suggested earlier, the fact that the substantial changes in wealth were observed at the time of the emergence of a period of high inflation rates is not a mere coincidence.) The reason for this shortcoming stems, at least partly, from the shortage of data on wealth. But even if such a series of data was available its use could be severely questioned, for

> The historical path of household wealth results from: (a) planned accumulation, the consequence of the very saving behaviour that wealth is supposed to help explain, (b) unexpected gains or losses due to changes, actual or expected, in the capacity of the economy's capital stock to earn income for its owners, and (c) unexpected gains or losses due to changes in the discount rates at which the market capitalizes prospective earnings. These sources of change in wealth should not be expected to have identical effects on consumption (Tobin and Dolde, 1971, p. 102; see also Coghlan and Jackson, 1979).

In fact, the Central Statistical Office's balance-sheets of the personal sector show that fluctuations in relative prices of assets, for example the rapid increase in house prices in 1971-3 and the tremendous fall in share prices in 1973-4, result in considerable changes in the value composition of wealth. Total financial assets accounted for 63 per cent of total net wealth in 1966 but only 45 per cent in 1976; at the same time, total liabilities as a percentage of financial assets increased from 20 per cent in 1966 to 29 per cent in 1976 - 32 per cent in 1974. It is reasonable to assume that consumers' expenditure in relation to income has not been independent of these changes; indeed, the use of a single figure in the form of total net wealth which does not take into consideration this kind of development is an unsatisfactory procedure in applying a consumption function like equation 2.9.

For all these reasons the alternative adopted for the purposes of this study is to approximate w by the ratio of liquid assets to income. The importance of liquid assets in influencing consumers' expenditure has been rationalised on various grounds: (i) as a proxy for wealth inasmuch as liquid assets are the most important component of wealth in determining consumers' expenditure, (ii) as an independent determinant of various types of consumers' expenditures, (iii) as a reservoir for imminent purchases, and (iv) as a reserve for emergencies. In Friedman's permanent income hypothesis the ratio w is utilised as a determinant of the value of K since, in his opinion, non-human wealth is a more satisfactory form of reserve than human wealth; it is also argued that the use of liquid assets is an attempt to provide for the fact that all forms of non-human wealth are not equally satisfactory as a reserve for emergencies. Friedman, however, argues that no distinction between forms of wealth is 'as pervasive and fundamental as the distinction between human and non-human wealth' (Friedman, 1957, pp. 16-17).

In this study we adopt the view that there is a desired ratio of liquid assets to income (LA/Y), and that if the actual ratio falls short or exceeds the desired or equilibrium ratio, then consumers' expenditure will either be constrained or expanded until equilibrium is reached again. Furthermore, it is assumed that any deviations of the actual from the desired ratio (LA/Y) last for some time. This assumption is especially valid if changes in the actual ratio are dominated by unanticipated changes in income. It can be argued, for example, that the decline in this ratio in the 1970s was mainly due to the rapid increases in nominal disposable income. It can in turn be suggested that consumers reacted by saving more, partly in an attempt to restore the liquid assets ratio to its desired level.[9] (It should be recognised, however, that the extent to which the present specification is consistent with Friedman's formulation depends on whether liquid assets is a good proxy for non-human wealth.)

The rate of interest used for estimation is the long-term, 2½% Consol rate. What is important is the *a priori* sign of the interest-rate variable, for it is possible to advance arguments in favour of either a positive or negative sign: a change in interest rates is associated with a negative substitution effect - higher interest rates induce people to save more, thus decreasing their consumption;[10] and a positive income effect - if people save for a given monetary return higher interest rates increase consumption, for it is now possible to provide for the given income by a smaller amount of savings. A negative coefficient implies a stronger substitution effect (Hamburger, 1967; Taylor, 1971; Boskin, 1978), whereas a positive coefficient implies a stronger income effect (Weber, 1970, 1971, 1975). Nevertheless, the majority of opinion would favour a negative coefficient (Taylor, 1971, p. 393, n. 16).[11]

Another problem concerning the interest-rate variable is whether one should be employing nominal interest rates or real interest rates. It can be justifiably argued that in a period of increasing instability of the general price level and high rates of inflation, nominal interest rates fail to reflect the real cost of borrowing. There are two alternative ways of taking this into account: first, one can use a measure of a real rate of interest obtained from the nominal rate after provision is made for inflation. The implication of the assumption that the real rate of interest is the relevant variable is that consumers do not suffer from money illusion. More specifically, it is assumed that such changes in the nominal rate of interest and the rate of inflation which leave the real rate unchanged will have no direct effect on consumption. A way by which we can avoid imposing any restrictions on the coefficients is to use the rate of inflation as an autonomous explanatory variable in addition to the real rate of interest.

The final specification used for estimation is as follows:

$$(\mathrm{APC})_t = a_0 + a_1[(\mathrm{RL})_t - (\mathrm{RPD})_t] + a_2(\mathrm{RPD})_{t-i} + a_3\left(\frac{\mathrm{LA}}{\mathrm{YD}}\right)_t + a\left(\frac{\mathrm{TYDR}}{\mathrm{YDR}}\right)_t \qquad (2.10)$$

where APC is the average propensity to consume defined as CON/YD, i.e. the ratio of total consumers' expenditure to total personal disposable income, RL is the 2½% Consol rate, RPD is the percentage change in the GDP price deflator, LA is selected liquid assets of the personal sector and TYDR is a five-period moving average of real personal disposable income (YDR) (see below, equations 2.15 and 2.16). In addition the following are complementary equations which, with equation 2.10, constitute the part of the model relating to consumers' expenditure:

$$(CON)_t = (APC)^*_t \, (YD)_t \tag{2.11}$$

$$(CONR)_t = \left(\frac{CON}{PCD}\right)_t \tag{2.12}$$

$$(PCD)_t = b_0 \, (PD)_t \tag{2.13}$$

$$(LA)_t = c_0 + c_1 \left[\frac{(M3)_t + (M3)_{t-1}}{2}\right] + c_2 \left[\frac{\Delta(GS)_t + \Delta(GS)_{t-1}}{2}\right] \tag{2.14}$$

$$(TYDR)_t = [(YDR)_t + (YDR)_{t-1} + (YDR)_{t-2} + (YDR)_{t-3} + (YDR)_{t-4}]/5 \tag{2.15}$$

$$(YDR)_t = \left(\frac{YD}{PCD}\right)_t \tag{2.16}$$

2.11 and 2.12 are identities defining consumption in nominal terms (CON) and in real terms (CONR), with PCD being the price deflator for consumers' expenditure which is assumed to be related to the GDP price deflator (PD) via equation 2.13. Equation 2.14 relates liquid assets to the money supply (M3) and changes in total government debt, Δ(GS); the latter two variables are divided by two for consistency purposes since the variable LA refers to mid-year changes. Both equations 2.14 and 2.13 are simply convenient assumptions, the sole purpose of which is to endogenise PCD and LA and link the latter with money supply and government borrowing. As they are not behavioural equations but aim only at capturing certain associations for LA and PCD, we do not report detailed diagnostics for these two variables in Table 2.1 below. Equation 2.15 defines TYDR, which is equivalent to $\bar{Y}$ above, while equation 2.16 defines real disposable income (YDR), with YD being disposable income in nominal terms.

EMPIRICAL EVIDENCE

The estimated forms of equations 2.10, 2.13 and 2.14 are reported in Table 2.1, where the technique of instrumental variables is utilised. In this table the appropriate regression for APC is the restricted form for a first-order autoregressive scheme indicated by the significance of the autocorrelation coefficient (ρ) and the validity of the autoregressive restrictions confirmed by the low and insignificant value of χ^2_1. The independence of the instruments used with the error term is also confirmed by the low and insignificant value of χ^2_2; we also note the low values for χ^2_3 and the F-Chow test - for what they are worth. The standard error of estimate for this equation is around 0.7 per cent of the mean value of the dependent variable, indicating very small over-all residuals. This is illustrated by the size of the individual residuals, given in Table 2.2, where with the exception of 1958, when it is just

Table 2.1

---

1. $$(APC)_t = \underset{(3.94)}{0.473} - \underset{(3.13)}{0.004}\,[(RL)_t - (RPD)_t] - \underset{(3.71)}{0.005}\,(RPD)_t$$

$$+ \underset{(2.95)}{0.214}\left(\frac{LA}{YD}\right)_t + \underset{(3.54)}{0.323}\left(\frac{TYDR}{YDR}\right)_t - \underset{(2.19)}{0.001}\,(RPD)_{t-2}$$

$\rho = \underset{(5.90)}{0.813}$, $S = 0.006$, $S/ME = 0.007$, $\chi^2_2(9) = 13.98$,

$\chi^2_3 = 1.44$, $F(1,13) = 0.48$

2. $$(CON)_t = (APC)_t \times (YD)_t$$

3. $$(CONR)_t = \left(\frac{CON}{PCD}\right)_t$$

4. $$(PCD)_t = \underset{(70.86)}{0.938}\,(PD)_t$$

$\rho = \underset{(6.14)}{0.815}$

5. $$(LA)_t = \underset{(1.95)}{6.489} + \underset{(15.64)}{1.153}\left[\frac{(M3)_t + (M3)_{t-1}}{2}\right]$$

$$+ \underset{(1.77)}{0.345}\left[\frac{\Delta(GS)_t + \Delta(GS)_{t-1}}{2}\right]$$

$\rho = \underset{(6.30)}{0.854}$

6. $$(TYDR)_t = [(YDR)_t + (YDR)_{t-1} + (YDR)_{t-2} + (YDR)_{t-3} + (YDR)_{t-4}]/5$$

7. $$(YDR)_t = \left(\frac{YD}{PCD}\right)_t$$

---

over 1 per cent, the largest of them is 0.007.

What is especially encouraging is that there is no systematic overestimation in the 1970s - the usual fall in APC in 1974-5 is completely explained by the model. The coefficient on the rate of interest is negative and significant; the negative coefficient is consistent with the expected effect of changes in interest rates according to the permanent income hypothesis. These results are also consistent with the views that the nominal rate of interest is (i) a proxy for the degree of liquidity or credit availability on

Table 2.2 Actual and fitted values of APC and residuals from regression equation

	Actual	Fitted	Residuals
1958	0.960	0.946	0.0140
1959	0.952	0.954	0.0018
1960	0.929	0.935	-0.0063
1961	0.914	0.921	-0.0069
1962	0.926	0.924	0.0025
1963	0.925	0.925	-0.0003
1964	0.920	0.923	-0.0034
1965	0.912	0.918	-0.0062
1966	0.909	0.914	-0.0052
1967	0.915	0.917	-0.0020
1968	0.921	0.919	0.0023
1969	0.919	0.917	0.0022
1970	0.911	0.905	0.0055
1971	0.915	0.908	0.0074
1972	0.895	0.896	-0.0009
1973	0.883	0.881	0.0020
1974	0.859	0.860	-0.0013
1975	0.847	0.848	-0.0012
1976	0.854	0.853	0.0012
1977	0.856	0.860	-0.0042
1978	0.856	0.854	0.0022

the ground of the 'package-deal' approach to monetary restrictive measures, and (ii) an indicator of capital gains and losses on gilts. Bean's (1978) recent results, based on quarterly data with a different model and a different definition of the real rate of interest, are inconclusive on the importance of the latter on consumers' expenditure, though in two out of three cases the coefficient on the rate of interest is negative. In a recent study of personal saving behaviour and the rate of inflation in Canada, West Germany, Japan, the United Kingdom and the USA, Howard (1978) finds that a long-run nominal interest rate appears with a positive and significant coefficient in an equation explaining UK personal saving. A significant interest-rate effect is also found by Coghlan and Jackson (1979, p. 318).

The results in Table 2.1 suggest that the immediate effect of a rise in the price level is a decline in the APC. These results are consistent with the findings of recent studies by Deaton (1977), Davidson *et al.* (1978) and Bean (1978). A negative response of consumption to a rise in prices can be explained in more than one way (Deaton, 1977); it has been suggested, for example, that a falling APC while inflation increases can be explained in terms of Deaton's theory of sequential purchasing and expectations on inflation which lag behind reality. According to this view, in periods of accelerating inflation consumers misconceive changes in the absolute price level as increases in relative prices affecting the items they intended to buy. As a result they substitute future consumption for present consumption. But, as Coghlan and Jackson (1979, p. 313) observe:

> The implication of this is, however, that as soon as the rate of inflation is anticipated, or stops accelerating, or falls, this process must stop and might even be expected to reverse itself. It is difficult, therefore, to apply this explanation to the continued existence of a high savings ratio in a period of falling rates of inflation.

Other views on how inflation exerts a negative effect on consumption suggest that inflation (i) creates a feeling of uncertainty and pessimism about the future - especially the development of real incomes, (ii) erodes the real value of nominal assets and, to the extent that the personal sector is a net creditor, results in a reduction of net real household wealth, (iii) assuming it is unanticipated, can cause a redistribution of income in favour of people with a relatively low propensity to consume - this is the case when redistribution is from creditor to debtor and from employee to employer. For a depressing effect of inflation on consumers' expenditure in the United Kingdom see Davidson *et al.* (1978). Howard (1978) in his comparative study fails to find significant coefficients for both anticipated and unanticipated inflation in the UK case; however, he finds that changes in unemployment, liquid assets and, as we have already mentioned, a nominal long-run rate of interest are all significant regressors in explaining savings. Furthermore, he suggests that the rate of interest may capture the effects of long-run inflation expectations.

The liquid assets ratio and the cyclical indicator always appear with positive and statistically significant coefficients, in accordance with expectations. All in all the explanatory performance of the APC equation seems to be particularly satisfactory. Using this equation we can now explain why the APC in 1975 was by 6.8 percentage points lower than its value in 1971. A 4.6 percentage point rise caused by the fall in the real rate of interest was more than offset by a 11.4 point decline due to the combined negative effects of changes in the rest of the explanatory variables. Of the latter the rate of inflation was responsible for 75 per cent of this decline, and the liquid assets ratio for the rest. This by itself illustrates the significance of inflation in explaining the unusual fall in APC over this period.

Finally, it is worth mentioning that a number of slightly different specifications have been tried. The results, however, were always inferior to those reported. First, the rate of unemployment and, subsequently, the ratio of disposable income to a weighted moving average of disposable income were used in place of the cyclical indicator finally chosen. Also, in a number of specifications the coefficient of variation of disposable income over a three-year period was used as a proxy for the degree of uncertainty facing the consumer as income-earner. Second, bank advances to the personal sector, excluding loans for house purchases, plus hire-purchase loans, were used instead of the rate of interest. It has been usual practice, especially in the United Kingdom, to include a similar variable in consumption functions (Garganas, 1975; Cuthbertson, 1980) on the grounds, not always spelt out, that the volume of lending is on a permanent basis supply-determined (see, however, Cuthbertson, 1980). In other words it is assumed that non-price rationing of lending to the personal sector is a permanent feature of the lending policy of financial institutions. As it turns out, in this study this variable nearly always fails the 5 per cent significance test. Third, when the logarithms of the variables are used in place of their absolute values the explanatory performance of the relationship declines considerably and some of the coefficients lose their significance.

CONCLUSIONS

The main implications of this chapter are the following:

(a) The recent UK experience of unusual changes in consumers' expenditure in relation to income can be adequately explained by a simple conventional model of consumers' behaviour. Although the derivation of the model has been based mainly on the permanent income hypothesis, its specification can also be easily rationalised on many other grounds.
(b) The failure of forecasting models to anticipate the substantial decline in APC was the consequence of using relationships from which theoretically significant variables were omitted.
(c) The estimation results suggest that monetary policy could be used to influence in a significant and direct way consumers' expenditure through changes in interest rates.
(d) A wealth variable, in this case in the form of liquid assets, seems to play a significant role in explaining the observed fluctuations of APC over the period 1958-77.
(e) In accordance with other recent evidence the rate of inflation exercises an over-all negative influence on APC; more specifically it seems to be the most significant single factor in explaining the fall of APC in the 1970s.
(f) In contrast to other studies of the British consumption function the present investigation implies that liquid assets, the rate of inflation and the interest rate are all significant explanatory factors of consumers' behaviour.

The usual criticisms can, of course, be made with respect to the reliability of these results: the sample is rather small, the regressors may be highly correlated and there are measurement problems. It seems that these and other problems, including different specifications and sample periods, may be the reason for the divergence of the results obtained by different researchers.

It should be clear by now, however, that it is not the purpose of this book to provide a model-selection exercise on the basis of a comparative study.

3

Investment and Stockbuilding

Fixed investment in the private sector is considered by most economists as the most important component of aggregate private expenditure in the determination of national output. This is so despite the fact that consumers' expenditure constitutes a much higher share of GDP than private investment. For the period 1955-78, for example, the size of the latter was never more than a fifth of consumers' expenditure. The main reason for this view on investment is the prevailing hypothesis that consumers' expenditure is a relatively more stable percentage of GDP than investment. More specifically, it is generally assumed that the decision to invest is not as dependent on the level of income as the decision to consume. The high degree of autonomy of investment expenditure is very probably the result of the crucial importance of expectations in investment decisions. This importance was strongly emphasised by Keynes in the *General Theory* when suggesting that

> It is important to understand the dependence of the marginal efficiency of a given stock of capital on changes in expectation, because it is chiefly this dependence which renders the marginal efficiency of capital subject to the somewhat violent fluctuations which are the explanation of the Trade Cycle (1964, pp. 143-4).[1]

Another important factor which partly explains the autonomous nature of investment is technical progress and innovation - a determinant of the investment decision which was repeatedly emphasised by Shackle (1970) using the concept of *novelty*: 'business success depends, in its most dramatic forms, on the exploitation of *novelty*, and novelty is that which has been unknown until now' (Shackle, 1970, p. 30).[2]

The importance of the degree of fixed capital expansion does not only derive from the crucial role of investment in explaining the business cycle (Hicks, 1950). It also derives from the realisation that it is through positive net investment that the productive capacity of the economy can expand in the long run.[3] It is not therefore surprising that the relatively low rate of fixed capital accumulation in the United Kingdom has been often blamed for the observed relatively low rates of growth of national output.

Investment is therefore clearly an important factor in an analysis of both the secular growth of output and the cyclical movements around a long-run trend. Moreover, post-Keynesians consider investment as a primary determinant, not only of output and employment, but also of the distribution of national output between labour and capital (Kregel, 1979).

Before we embark on a discussion of the various hypotheses on the determination of investment expenditure, it is worth noting the main changes in the relative volume and composition of fixed private investment in the last twenty years.

VOLUME AND COMPOSITION OF INVESTMENT AND STOCKBUILDING

The UK ratio of real gross domestic fixed capital formation (GDFCF) in the private sector to GDP has been consistently lower than the corresponding ratios in other EEC countries. Viewed in terms of its own development in the last twenty years, however, it seems to be characterised by an upward trend.[4] From around 8 per cent in the mid-1950s it rose gradually to above 11 per cent and above 12 per cent in the 1960s and 1970s respectively (see Table 3.1). This observation led Matthews (1968) to suggest that an explanation of the significant rise in the ratio of fixed capital formation in the postwar period, in comparison with the interwar period, lies at the heart of the explanation of the rise in the level of economic activity:

> What have been the reasons for the high level of investment? This subject is a relatively unresearched one. Economists have been so preoccupied with explaining why investment in this country has been low compared with other countries that they have devoted little attention to considering why investment has been so much higher relatively to national income than it has ever been before in this country (Matthews, 1968, p. 960).

Matthews's tentative suggestion was that the main factor for the observed high rate of capital formation was the rise in the marginal efficiency of investment schedule - the investment demand function - due to the pressure of a high effective demand on productive capacity rather than the effect of government policy (mainly fiscal policy).

Some ten years later, despite the fact that the level of private investment relative to income is even higher, the level of economic activity is considerably lower. This casts some doubt on the adequacy of Matthews's approach in explaining changes in the level of economic activity. Its main defect lies with its neglect of changes in the other components of final expenditure; for example, while in the 1960s the average propensity to consume was relatively stable, in the 1970s it declined at a rapid pace (Hadjimatheou, 1979). In these circumstances a rising ratio of investment,

Table 3.1 Composition of real private gross domestic fixed capital formation by type of asset (percentages of total) plus fixed investment and stockbuilding as percentages of real GDP

	Vehicles, ships and aircraft	Plant and machinery	Dwellings	Other new buildings and works	Fixed investment	Stock-building
1955-60	15.1	37.0	21.0	26.9	9.10	1.16
1961-4	12.7	33.6	21.4	32.1	10.82	1.05
1965-8	12.6	35.5	21.8	30.2	11.36	1.19
1969-73	14.5	36.1	21.0	28.7	12.58	1.12
1974-8	14.7	39.8	17.4	28.1	12.35	0.53

relative to income, could coexist with a static or even decreasing level of investment expenditure.

Related to the above issue is the changing composition of GDFCF. Looking at the four main components of private investment (see Table 3.1), i.e. vehicles, ships and aircraft, plant and machinery, dwellings, and other new buildings and works, it becomes clear that, unlike consumers' expenditure, there does not seem to exist any significant discernible trend. It seems, however, that the relative importance of investment in plant and machinery has risen since the early 1960s at the expense of other new buildings and works. On the other hand, the relative importance of each one of these four categories of investment seems to alter in the course of the business cycle. One of the major causes here is the lack of uniformity of the speed of adjustment of actual to desired capital in the four cases. Furthermore, fluctuations in housing investment tend to lead to fluctuations in the level of general economic activit This is mainly due to the relative importance of finance in house-building activity and house-buying in conjunction with the pattern of change in the cost and availability of finance over the cycle (Hadjimatheou, 1976).

Looking at the breakdown of total GDFCF by industry groups, the main developments in the 1970s have been the rise in the relative importance of investment in petroleum and gas, mining and quarrying and a decline in the relative importance of investment in electricity and water, transport and communication and social and other public services.[5] Finally, for the whole of the postwar period, investment in manufacturing follows a downward trend, while investment in other service industries follows an upward course. The latter is a common experience of industrially developed countries and it gives rise, in combination with a number of related developments, to the notion of the 'post-industrial' society (Gustafsson, 1979).

The second major variable to be considered in this chapter is the value of physical increases in stocks and work in progress (stock-building). This is the smallest and the least stable component of GDP: over the period 1955-78 as a percentage of GDP it has fluctuated within the range -1.57 to 3.18. Stocks are usually distinguished as materials and fuel, work in progress and finished products. In mainstream economics firms are supposed to decide on an optimum level of stocks on the basis of the requirements of a smooth production process, the anticipated fluctuation in demand and the cost of holding stocks. In an environment of uncertainty, however, actual stocks are likely to differ from planned ones. If, for example, actual output in a period turns out to be smaller than planned output and actual demand and sales are higher than anticipated, stocks will bear the brunt of adjustment, and given their relatively small size in relation to both output and sales their decline may be substantial. This may have important implications for the duration of the business cycle. As Matthews (1959, p. 90) observes:

If the desired level of inventories does vary with output, and at the same time there is a lag in the response of output to sales, the combination of the two potential sources of disturbance will strengthen the tendency to fluctuations ... Planned inventory investment will rise through most or all of the upswing, but actual inventory investment will persistently fall short of the planned amount because of the passive inventory reduction resulting from the change in sales.

Increases in output may therefore continue for a period after the decline in sales. In the same way, following an accumulation of stocks during the downswing, output may go on declining for a period following the turning-point in the cycle for sales.

The above considerations have led to the view that, despite the relative unimportance of stocks as a constituent of GDP, changes in stocks (stockbuilding or inventory investment) are very important in explaining fluctuations in GDP (Meltzer, 1941). This can be illustrated by the following examples: in 1975 GDP at constant prices declined by £818m, of which £743m was a decline in stocks; also of the £2,968m for which GDP rose in 1973 £1,321m was the result of a rise in stocks.

In a disaggregated study changes in each of the main categories of stocks should be studied separately. It should be expected, for example, that stocks of finished products are directly affected by unanticipated changes in demand, while stocks of unfinished products are more closely associated with changes in the volume of output. In the present study, however, an aggregate stockbuilding function will be estimated; the reason, of course, is simply to keep the model as small as possible, a practice followed in all other chapters where no disaggregation in any of the variables is undertaken at all.

Figure 3.1 provides a visual comparative picture of fluctuations in the ratio of stockbuilding to GDP, the rate of growth of GDP, the rate of growth of industrial production and the index of capacity utilisation. Fluctuations in the first three variables seem to be closely associated with peaks and troughs coinciding in nearly every case.[6] Cycles of capacity utilisation, on the other hand, seem to follow the rest with, on average, a year-long lag. Given that we deal throughout with annual observations, shorter lags are not investigated. Finally, none of the four series exhibits a discernible time trend.

DETERMINATION OF FIXED INVESTMENT EXPENDITURE

All theories of investment are based on prior theories of the determination of the optimum stock of capital. Investment flow can, in general, be considered as a process through which the actual stock of capital can be adjusted towards the optimum stock. The problem of the determination of the speed of adjustment has given rise to the development of a series of distributed-lag schemes which in turn have been used in other areas of empirical work including research on consumers' expenditure on durables.

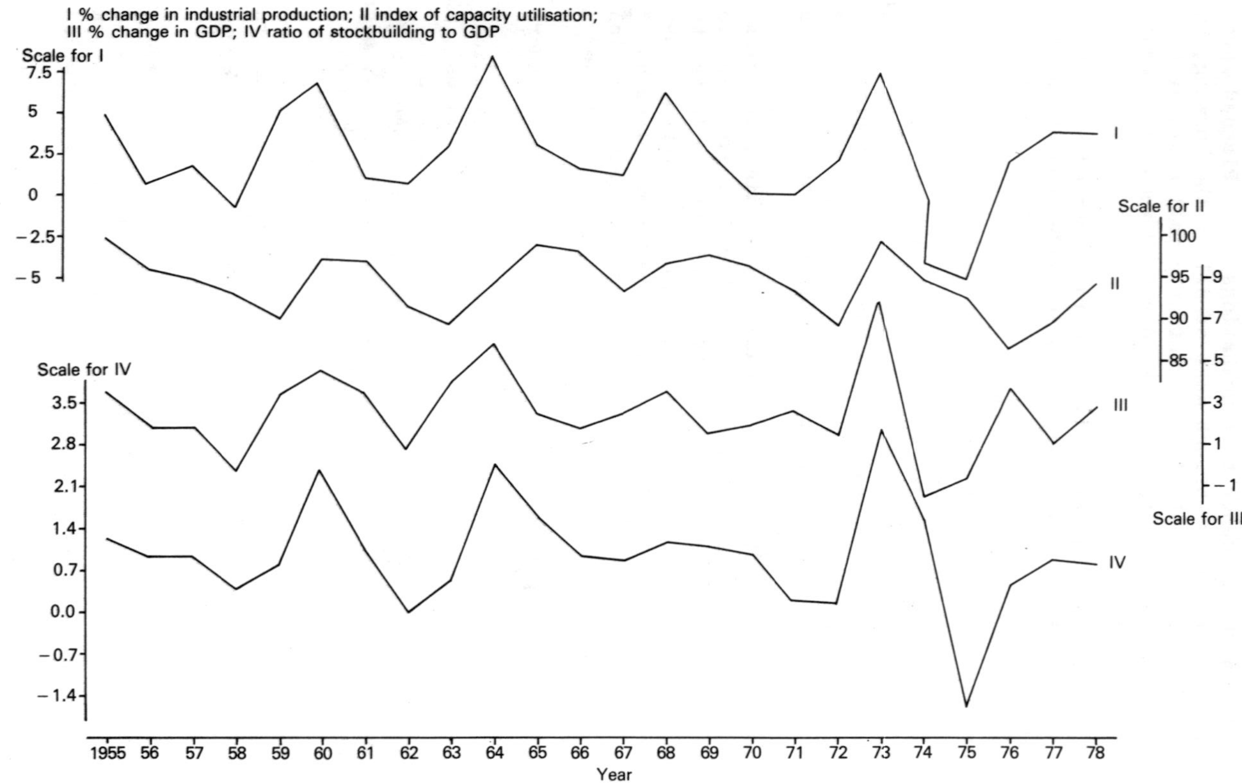
I % change in industrial production; II index of capacity utilisation;
III % change in GDP; IV ratio of stockbuilding to GDP
Scale for I
7.5
5
2.5
0
−2.5
−5
Scale for IV
3.5
2.8
2.1
1.4
0.7
0.0
−0.7
−1.4
Scale for II
100
95
90
85
9
7
5
3
1
−1
Scale for III
I
II
III
IV
1955
56
57
58
59
60
61
62
63
64
65
66
67
68
69
70
71
72
73
74
75
76
77
78
Year

Figure 3.1

One of the most popular hypotheses of the investment decision is the *accelerator principle*. According to this principle, entrepreneurs attempt to maintain an optimum relationship between capital stock and output, i.e.

$$K_t^* = cY_t \tag{3.1}$$

where K^* denotes the desired capital stock, which is assumed to be the same as actual capital stock, in the sense that any discrepancy between the two is automatically adjusted, and Y equals output. It therefore follows that a change in output will necessitate a change in capital stock:

$$I_t = \Delta K_t^* = c\Delta Y_t \tag{3.2}$$

A more general formulation of this idea which focuses on the time structure of investment is the flexible accelerator model. According to this, capital is adjusted towards its desired level by a constant proportion of the difference between desired and actual capital, K^* and K respectively, i.e.

$$I_t = (1 - \lambda)[K_t^* - K_{t-1}] \qquad 0 < \lambda < 1 \tag{3.3}$$

which is the so-called partial adjustment hypothesis with $1-\lambda$ being known as the partial adjustment coefficient (for $\lambda = 0$ the adjustment is completed within one time period, while for $\lambda = 1$ no adjustment takes place at all). Given 3.1, the latter equation can be expressed as

$$I_t = (1 - \lambda)\ cY_t - (1 - \lambda)\ K_{t-1}$$

Alternatively, given that $I_t = K_t - K_{t-1}$, 3.3 can be written as

$$K_t = (1 - \lambda)\ K_t^* + \lambda K_{t-1} \tag{3.3a}$$

which after repeated substitutions for K can be expressed as

$$K_t = (1 - \lambda)\ K_t^* + \lambda(1 - \lambda)\ K_{t-1}^* + \lambda^2(1 - \lambda)\ K_{t-2}^*$$
$$+ \lambda^3(1 - \lambda)\ K_{t-3}^* + \ldots$$

or

$$K_t = (1 - \lambda)\sum_{r=o}^{\infty} \lambda^r K_{t-r}^* \tag{3.4}$$

so that

$$I_t = K_t - K_{t-1} = (1 - \lambda)\sum_{r=o}^{\infty} \lambda^r(K_{t-r}^* - K_{t-r-1}^*) \tag{3.5}$$

Given 3.2 the above can be written as

$$I_t = (1 - \lambda)\ c\Sigma\lambda^r(Y_{t-r} - Y_{t-r-1}) \tag{3.6}$$

which is the standard distributed-lag model with geometrically declining weights. A more general scheme is one which does not constrain the coefficients:

$$I_t = \alpha \sum_{r=o}^{\infty} \beta_r (Y_{t-r} - Y_{t-r-1}) \tag{3.7}$$

The partial adjustment hypothesis 3.3a can be derived from minimising a quadratic cost function

$$C = c_1 (K_t^* - K_t)^2 + c_2 (K_t - K_{t-1})^2 \tag{3.8}$$

with respect to K_t; total cost consists of the cost of being out of equilibrium, $c_1(K_t^* - K_t)^2$, and the cost of adjustment, $c_2(K_t - K_{t-1})^2$. The first-order condition for minimisation is

$$\frac{dC}{dK} = - 2c_1 (K_t^* - K_t) + 2c_2 (K_t - K_{t-1}) = 0$$

or

$$c_1 (K_t^* - K_t) = c_2 (K_t - K_{t-1})$$

and solving for K_t we have

$$K_t = \frac{c_1}{c_1 + c_2} K_t^* + \frac{c_2}{c_1 + c_2} K_{t-1}$$

which for $\lambda = c_2/(c_1 + c_2)$ is the same as 3.3a.

All the above specifications refer to net investment. A specification for gross investment can be obtained by assuming that replacement is proportional to actual capital stock, so that

$$I_t = \sum_{r=o}^{\infty} \beta_r (Y_{t-r} - Y_{t-r-1}) + \delta K_{t-1} \tag{3.9}$$

The flexible accelerator has remained a popular empirical formulation of aggregate investment behaviour, mainly because it seems to perform rather well in comparison with alternative schemes. Despite this, however, efforts have been made either to find an alternative hypothesis to replace the flexible accelerator or to modify it so as to overcome some of its shortcomings. It was felt that the theoretical validity of the accelerator model rests with the acceptance of the following implicit assumptions:

(a) Expectations about future levels of aggregate demand are static: expected future output is equal or proportional to its current level.
(b) Existing productive capacity is fully utilised.
(c) There are no financial constraints.
(d) The capital-output ratio is not affected by the user cost of capital.
(e) The process of capital formation is symmetrical for upward and downward changes in output.

Kalecki (1971), as far back as 1943, dismissed the accelerator principle on both theoretical and empirical grounds. He suggested that fixed investment expenditure is determined, with some lag, by the gross savings of firms, the rate of interest, the rate of change of aggregate profits, the rate of change in the stock of capital, fluctuations of share yields and technical progress.

The first three of these variables have been used extensively in empirical work. The relevance of these factors has been rationalised on a number of grounds. It has been suggested, for example, that changes in profitability affect in a direct way expectations about future profitability, while internal funds are assumed to be less costly than external funds due to imperfections in the market for borrowed funds, arising from differences in information about the riskiness of new projects. The rate of interest is considered an important determinant of the cost of capital. It plays a crucial rôle in Fisher's (1930) theory of capital and Keynes's theory of investment. Keynes defined the marginal efficiency of a capital-asset as 'that rate of discount which would make the present value of the series of annuities given by the returns expected from the capital-asset during its life just equal to its supply price' (Keynes, 1964, p. 135). In the expression

$$C = \frac{R_1}{(1 + r)} + \frac{R_2}{(1 + r)^2} + \dots + \frac{R_n}{(1 + r)^n} \tag{3.10}$$

where C is the cost of a capital-asset and R_i is the expected annual return (annuity) in period i, r is the marginal efficiency of investment and it is only when r exceeds the rate of interest that it is profitable to invest. In chapter 11 of the *General Theory* Keynes developed a downward-sloping investment demand schedule on the basis that

> the marginal efficiency of that type of capital will diminish as the investment in it is increased, partly because the prospective yield will fall as the supply of that type of capital is increased, and partly because, as a rule, pressure on the facilities for producing that type of capital will cause its supply price to increase (1964, p. 136).

But in chapter 12 ('The State of Long-term Expectations') the stability of this schematic construction is forcefully questioned on the basis of the unpredictability of expectations: 'The outstanding fact is the extreme precariousness of the basis of knowledge on which our estimates of prospective yield have to be made' (1964, p. 149). And in a passage which clearly underlies Shackle's views on uncertainty we are reminded that

> human decisions affecting the future, whether personal or political or economic, cannot depend on strict mathematical expectation, since the basis for making such calculations does not exist; and that it is our innate urge to activity which make the wheels go round, our rational selves choosing between the alternatives as

best we are able, calculating where we can, but often falling back for our motive on whim or sentiment or chance (1964, p. 163).

We believe that this should set the tone and spell out the rationale for the cautiousness with which estimated investment functions should be treated.

The accelerator model proper and its variants obtained by introducing additional explanatory variables have been criticised on the ground that they are *ad hoc* formulations. They are not based on the neoclassical principle that the optimal combination of factor inputs should be a function of their relative prices. As in so many other areas of economic theory, here, too, the neoclassical approach, as exemplified by Jorgenson's work on the study of investment decisions, emphasises substitution effects and thus changes in relative prices at the expense of changes in income, effective demand and availability of finance - factors which are central to the work of Keynes and Kalecki and in studies based on the accelerator principle.

Assuming a constant elasticity of substitution (CES) production function,[7] the marginal productivity conditions give the equilibrium solution to the cost-minimisation problem for given output as

$$K^* = \frac{AY}{c^{\sigma}} \tag{3.11}$$

where K^* = desired capital stock, c = user cost of capital, i.e. the net cost of holding a unit of capital stock for one period, Y = output and σ = elasticity of substitution. c is the implicit rental value of capital services and it is measured as a composite variable (a shadow cost rather than a market price) which increases with the price of capital equipment, the rate of interest, the rate of depreciation, the rate of taxation, the rate of capital loss, and decreases with any rise in tax allowances for depreciation, interest payments and capital losses. Assuming further that replacement investment is proportional to the existing capital stock, and introducing a lag structure, we can derive an equation in gross investment:

$$I_t = b(L)\Delta\left(\frac{Y}{c^{\sigma}}\right) + \delta K_{t-1} \tag{3.12}$$

where δ = rate of depreciation and b(L) = function in the lag operator L. For $\sigma = 1$ we have Jorgenson's model (Jorgenson, 1963) with a Cobb-Douglas production function, while for a fixed coefficient production, i.e. $\sigma = 0$, we obtain the simple flexible accelerator model. (The use of the CES instead of the Cobb-Douglas production function does not affect the main features of the neoclassical model as expounded by Jorgenson.)

The neoclassical theory of capital accumulation has been criticised on a number of grounds. It has been argued that:

(a) The level of investment is made to depend on changes in desired capital stock - which means that persistence of disequilibrium over a number of periods largely caused by partial adjustment is ignored, whereas in practice the introduction of a distributed lag on output is an *ad hoc* device.

(b) The assumption of proportional depreciation reduces replacement to a mechanistic procedure and ignores the effect of technical progress and the existence of different vintages of capital-assets.

(c) The critique of the aggregate production function by the Cambridge School, arising from the problem of measuring capital, argues that because capital is heterogeneous, contrary to the homogeneity assumption of the neoclassical model, any measurement of it requires knowledge of the relative values of the individual units comprising capital. This, in turn, requires knowledge of the price vector of the economy and of the rate of profit. Since the latter must be known already, no theory of the rate of profit and distribution exists within this tradition (Robinson, 1954).

(d) The derived investment function is a demand function; supply considerations - capacity constraints, for example - and in particular their effect on short-term dynamics are ignored.

(e) The effect of each of the components of the user cost of capital on investment is constrained to be the same both for the time structure of the response and the size of the response.

(f) The assumption of complete capital malleability, i.e. a putty-putty model, and a perfect capital-goods market. The putty-putty assumption refers to the smooth substitutability between capital and labour, both *ex ante* (before the instalment of capital) and *ex post* (after its instalment).

Brainard and Tobin (1968) and Tobin (1969) suggest, in a portfolio-balance approach, that capital formation is significantly affected by the ratio of the market value of a firm to the replacement cost of its assets. A rise in this ratio above 1.0 would mean that the absolute value of the firm would increase by investing in more capital. The value of this ratio is of course expected to reflect expectations about the future profitability of the particular firm and it should therefore be related with changes in those variables which generate expectations about future returns. The adoption, however, of this indicator in empirical work of a macro nature raises problems of measurement, especially regarding replacement cost. Attempts to model investment behaviour on the basis of this factor have not met with great success (Clark, 1979; Latter, 1979, p. 33).

Most of the empirical work on the aggregate investment function is of an eclectic variety. Burman (1970), in a study of the determinants of fixed investment, using accelerator models of the stock-adjustment type, found that capacity utilisation seemed to explain most of the variation of investment in manufacturing industry with an average lag of seven to eight quarters. When the model was extended to an aggregate of all industries, for which capital-stock figures were available, a cash-flow variable and a long-term rate of interest were also significant regressors. Hines and Catephores

(1970), using a modified flexible accelerator model, found that income and the long-term rate of interest are important factors in explaining investment decisions in manufacturing industry. The level of profits was not a significant regressor. Lags were long; the average lag between a change in the interest rate and its impact on investment had been of the order of nine quarters. In the case of output the lag had been, on average, around six quarters. In the study by Burman, although the length of the average lag was smaller, individual lags up to seven quarters were significant. Bean (1979), using a series of specifications, found that apart from output the rate of interest, lagged by five to six quarters, was significant in explaining manufacturing investment up to 1975. He does not attempt to develop a measure of the cost of capital, *à la* Jorgenson, on the grounds that definitional problems regarding individual components of such a complex shadow price are so serious as to make the task unproductive. Although a measure of capacity utilisation is found to be statistically significant, it was omitted from his preferred equation on the basis that its inclusion results in a deterioration of post-sample performance, and the lags involved are difficult to reconcile with the lags on output. On the basis of a Cox-statistic test suggested by Pesaran and Deaton (1978) Bean finds that, although his model is amenable to improvement in specification, it performs better than a flexible accelerator model, a neoclassical model and two more specifications based on the work by Hines and Catephores (1970) and Nadiri and Rosen (1969). The use of distributed lags has played an important role in the development and estimation of investment functions. Boatwright and Eaton (1972) developed a neoclassical model to explain the level of fixed investment in plant and machinery in manufacturing industry which constituted the basis for the particular investment function in the London Business School model. They estimated the model using three different types of distributed-lag schemes: the Almon technique (Almon, 1965), the Pascal distribution (Griliches, 1967), and the Gamma distribution (Tsurumi, 1971). Their main conclusion is that the Almon technique seems to perform better than the other two and that their results are consistent with a CES production function with an elasticity of substitution which lies between 0.4 and 0.7.

Feldstain and Flemming (1971) developed a generalised neoclassical investment function by assuming that (i) the price elasticity of the desired capital may be different for the various components of the user cost of capital, and (ii) the time patterns of each price response and of the response to increased output may also be different. They concluded that 'both the accelerated depreciation allowances and the use of differential taxation to induce the retention of corporate profits had substantial and significant impacts on investment behaviour' (1971, p. 431).

Finally, Bischoff (1971) and Clark (1979) adopt a comparative approach in carrying out empirical work on the determination of fixed investment in the USA. By using a number of different investment models they expect to overcome the problem of 'model dependence' in their analysis. Five alternative models of business fixed investment are estimated on the basis of quarterly data and are subsequently used for post-sample prediction. Although the models used in the two studies are almost identical the conclusions arrived at by the two researchers are different. Clark's study makes use of an extended sample covering the period 1954-78 to estimate and test the following models: accelerator, cash flow combined with accelerator, neoclassical, modified neoclassical, and securities values based on the portfolio-balance approach. On the basis of goodness of fit and *ex post* forecasting performance the accelerator model seems to out-perform the alternatives, with output as the primary determinant of non-residential fixed investment. The rental price of capital services is not found to be helpful in explaining quarterly data on business fixed investment in 1954-79. Clark concludes that the

> primary implication of these results for economic policy is that there is no quick and easy way to channel aggregate demand toward non-residential fixed investment. The response of investment to direct incentives may be both slower and weaker than was indicated by Bischoff's model. In the short run, at least, the best way to keep investment spending up is to keep capacity utilization high (1979, p. 104).

Despite the increasing complexity of the investment-determination models the following empirical and theoretical issues are far from being satisfactorily resolved:

(a) The measurement of capital.
(b) Dealing with choice under uncertainty and expectations.
(c) The time response of real investment to changes in the determinants of desired capital.
(d) The degree of substitution between capital and labour.
(e) The importance of internal finance in the presence of market imperfections.
(f) The level of disaggregation in empirical work.
(g) The treatment of replacement investment.

The neoclassical approach to investment decisions, despite its apparent sophistication and its explicit appeal to optimisation principles, merely attempts to deal with (d) - as usual *ad hoc* assumptions are employed in dealing with the rest of the issues. Bean (1979, p. 1) remarks that 'investment relationships have been regarded with a certain amount of suspicion by model-builders and much weight has been laid on survey information when producing forecasts of investment'.

It should of course be clear that it is not the purpose of this book to attempt to tackle these difficult problems. But their presence and importance should guide appreciation of empirical work on the investment function. Given our concern with the size of the model we have decided to use a highly aggregate function which explains the whole of real GDFCF in the private sector. Our specification is based on the accelerator hypothesis, amended so as to provide for influences on the basis of the critique of the accelerator principle. The dynamic specification used for estimation can be thought of as an approximation of a function derived in the following way:

$$K_t - K_{t-1} = c(K^*_t - K_{t-1})$$

or

$$K_t = cK^*_t + (1 - c)K_{t-1}$$

and

$$K_t - K_{t-1} = c(K^*_t - K_{t-1}) + (1 - c)[K_{t-1} - K_{t-2}]$$

or

$$I_{Nt} = (1 - c)I_{Nt-1} + c\Delta K^*_t \quad (3.13)$$

where I_{Nt} = net investment.

Next, assume that

$$\Delta K^*_t = b_1 r_t + b_2 \Delta Y_{t-1} + u_t \quad (3.14)$$

where r_t = real rate of interest and Y = real output. Combining 3.13 and 3.14 we have

$$I_{Nt} = cb_1 r_t + cb_2 \Delta Y_{t-1} + (1 - c)I_{Nt-1} + w_t \quad (3.15)$$

The extra regressors used in estimation, i.e. capacity utilisation and internal funds flow, are included in an effort to provide for the likelihood of persisting disequilibrium, especially when $K^*_{t-1} < K_{t-1}$, and the presence of imperfections in the market for capital finance. Furthermore, following conventional practice according to which gross, rather than net, investment is the dependent variable, we have modified our equation to allow for the effect of capital consumption. For this we used the series on net real capital stock as an additional regressor. A number of specifications were tried with either net investment or gross investment as the dependent variable and various lags on the explanatory variables. The estimated regression given below, with capital consumption instead of capital stock and gross rather than net investment as the dependent variable, seems to give the best results.

The instrumental-variables estimate of the chosen investment function is as follows:

$$IP_t = \underset{(3.58)}{-2.969} + \underset{(2.39)}{0.085}\,[(GDPR)_{t-1} - (GDPR)_{t-2}] + \underset{(2.49)}{0.022}\,(CU)_t$$

$$+ \underset{(11.65)}{0.420}\,(IF)_t + \underset{(4.30)}{1.565}\,(CC)_t + \underset{(3.21)}{0.411}\,(IP)_{t-1}$$

$$- \underset{(3.50)}{0.031}\left[(RL)_{t-1} - \frac{(RPD)_{t-1} + (RPD)_{t-2} + (RPD)_{t-3}}{3}\right]$$

ρ = -0.554, S = 0.103, S/ME = 0.021, χ_2^2 (6) = 8.22,
(1.92)

χ_3^2 (1) = 11.77, F(1,12) = 6.90

Investment is therefore a function of the change in real GDP lagged once, the level of capacity utilisation (CU), the internal funds of the corporate sector (IF), real capital consumption (CC), a proxy for the real rate of interest, obtained as the difference between the 2.5% Consol rate (RL) and a three-year moving average of the change in the GDP implicit price deflator (RPD) - lagged twice - and lagged investment. The significance of capacity utilisation and of the cash-flow variable indicates that the degree to which investment responds to an expected change in demand depends on the extent to which the existing productive capacity is utilised and also on the availability of internal funds. (The capacity-utilisation index used refers to the end of the first quarter of each year.)

Although all the coefficients are statistically significant and bear the expected signs, it must be noted that the size of the influence of the change in real income and the rate of interest are unusually low. On the other hand, the coefficient on CC suggests that discarded capital is more than replaced in one period; also, the coefficient on IF suggests that the size of internal funds is very important in determining the level of investment.

The high coefficient on CC may be interpreted in a number of ways. It may, for example, indicate an underestimation of the real replacement cost of capital or a tendency of the organic composition of capital, meaning capital per man employed, and measured by the capital-output ratio, to rise. It could also simply be the result of the fact that a high replacement investment programme is expansionary, especially in the case of net investment. Finally, it could easily arise as a result of mis-specification or spurious correlation between CC and IP, with both of them being influenced by the same variables.

It should finally be noted that in all specifications we failed to find a higher coefficient for the change in real GDP or significant coefficients for longer lags of the same variable, i.e. $\Delta GDPR_{t-j}$ for j > 1.

DETERMINANTS OF STOCKBUILDING

As already mentioned earlier, stockbuilding or inventory investment is the most volatile component of national output. This volatility spreads over all major types of stocks, i.e. materials, finished products and work-in-progress. In order to find out the determinants of the level of this type of investment it is necessary to examine the motives for holding inventories. Some inventories are held as a result of the nature of the production process - in a modern productive system at any point in time an amount of raw materials, work-in-progress and finished products will inevitably be in the hands of producers. It is also reasonable to assume that the level of this category of inventories is a function of the scale of production. Since there is a cost in holding inventories firms are usually assumed to hold an optimum stock which minimises the over-all cost. This optimum will therefore be influenced by the desire of producers, wholesalers and retailers to ensure an uninterrupted level of production and satisfaction of demand for their products. It follows, therefore, that the expected level of sales is another determinant of the level of inventories. The final major reason for changes in inventories is speculation. Expected changes in prices or the availability of products may be such so as to make profitable the accumulation or decumulation of inventories. In all cases, of course, changes in the cost of holding inventories will affect the optimum or desired amount of stocks.

In reality changes in inventories are not always consistent with planned or desired stockbuilding. Passive inventory change may result for a number of reasons:

(a) Errors in anticipations concerning future sales.
(b) Production smoothing, according to which stocks act as a buffer protecting output from fluctuations in sales.
(c) Unanticipated changes in output.

Although inventory investment is a very small percentage of GDP - it never exceeded 3 per cent in the whole of our sample period - when compared with changes in the latter it becomes very significant. The need to adjust upwards the level of inventories during the upswing of the business cycle and the failure of production at the same time to keep pace with increases in demand, leading to a sub-optimal level of inventories, result in an increase in both the amplitude and duration of the cycle.[8]

The greater instability of inventory investment in comparison with fixed investment is mainly due to (i) the greater ease and quicker pace with which inventories can be adjusted, and (ii) the fact that very often changes in inventories, which is the residual between output and sales, is subject to errors of anticipation regarding both output and sales.

In explaining the determination of the level of inventory investment frequent use is made of the accelerator principle and the partial (stock) adjustment hypothesis (for a useful survey see Evans, 1969, ch. 8). Lovell (1964) uses a specification which is based on the accelerator principle modified to provide for anticipation errors:

$$\Delta I_{if} = c[(I^*_{if})_t - (I_{if})_{t-1}] + \lambda[(S^e_f)_t - (S_f)_t] \qquad (3.16)$$

where I_{if} = inventories in the finished-goods sector, I^*_{if} = desired level of inventories, and S^e_f = anticipated level of sales. It is also assumed that $(I^*_{if})_t = b(S^e_f)_t$. The second term in equation 3.16 allows for the presence of anticipation errors. When λ, the 'production adaptation' coefficient, is equal to 1.0, production fails completely to respond to anticipation errors and planned changes in inventories deviate from actual changes by the total of the difference between actual and anticipated sales. For $\lambda = 0$ production responds so that planned changes in inventories equal actual changes. Writing equation 3.16 as

$$\Delta I_{if} = cb(S^e_f)_t - c(I_{if})_{t-1} + \lambda(S^e_f)_t - \lambda(S_f)_t \tag{3.17}$$

and assuming that $\lambda = -cb$ we have

$$\Delta I_f = c[b(S_f)_t - (I_{if})_{t-1}]$$

meaning that production was adapted so as to eliminate completely the influence of anticipation errors on inventory investment. Lovell suggests the following function for the anticipation of sales (we drop the subscript f for convenience):

$$S^e_t = \rho S_{t-1} + (1 - \rho)S_t \tag{3.18}$$

so that for $\rho = 1$, $S^e_t - S_{t-1}$; $\rho = 0$, $S^e_t = S_t$.

Substituting 3.18 in 3.17 we have

$$\Delta I_i = cb\rho S_{t-1} + cb(1 - \rho)S_t + \lambda\rho S_{t-1} + (1 - \rho)S_t - \lambda S_t - cI_{it-1}$$

$$= cbS_t - (cb + \lambda)\rho\Delta S_t - cI_{it-1}$$

which forms the basis for estimation.

In this book an aggregate function is used for the total of stockbuilding. We recognise that aggregation implies approximation: different components of stockbuilding are influenced both by common factors and different factors at varying degrees. An aggregate function does not allow for this. We select three conventional determinants - scale of production, changes in sales and the cost in terms of forgone interest-yield - that seem to contribute significantly in explaining stockbuilding as a whole. Preliminary observation (Figure 3.1 above) shows that stockbuilding moves in conformity with the rate of change of industrial production and the rate of change of real GDP. For estimation purposes, contemporaneous and lagged changes in both these variables were used in conjunction with the rate of growth of the volume of total retail sales and the measure of the real rate of interest used for the investment function. The preferred equation is given below:

$$\begin{aligned}(STB)_t = {} & \underset{(7.06)}{0.090}[(IPR)_t - (IPR)_{t-1}] + \underset{(3.65)}{0.060}[(IPR)_{t-1} - (IPR)_{t-2}] \\ & + \underset{(3.08)}{0.068}(GSA)_{t-1} \\ & - \underset{(2.25)}{0.040}\left[(RL)_{t-1} - \frac{(RPD)_t + (RPD)_{t-1} + (RPD)_{t-2}}{3}\right]\end{aligned}$$

D-W = 2.24, S = 0.172, S/ME = 0.459, $\chi^2_2(6) = 3.05$, $\chi^2_3(1) = 0.93$,

$F(1,16) = 0.43$

where STB = stockbuilding (1970 prices), IPR = index of industrial production (1970 = 100), GSA = rate of growth of sales.

Although the explanatory power of the equation is, in absolute terms, far from satisfactory, in comparison with other estimates of the same function, and taking into account the very high variation of the dependent variable, these estimation results seem acceptable. That the goodness of fit of the equation for inventory investment is both relatively and absolutely low is a well-known fact to model-builders. We agree with Budd (1979, p. 13) that 'one should be highly suspicious ... of a well fitting equation for stockbuilding' (see also Ormerod, 1979b, p. 119).

DETERMINANTS OF CAPACITY UTILISATION AND INDUSTRIAL PRODUCTION

One of the consequences of using the levels of capacity utilisation and industrial production to explain fixed and inventory investment is that our model should be expanded so as to provide an explanation of the determination of both these variables - given that later on the model will be used for policy evaluation exercises, it seems preferable that capacity utilisation and industrial production should be treated as endogenous rather than exogenous variables. On the basis of Figure 3.1 we have developed and estimated the following simple regressions - using instrumental variables for industrial production (IPR) and ordinary least squares for capacity utilisation (CU) - which seem to provide a reasonable explanation:

$$(IPR)_t = \underset{(3.80)}{2.589} \left[(GDPR)_t - (GDPR)_{t-1}\right] + \underset{(120.3)}{0.993} (IPR)_{t-1}$$

$$D\text{-}W = 1.84,\ S = 1.595,\ S/ME = 0.017,\ \chi^2_2(3) = 3.01,\ \chi^2_3(1) = 0.19,$$

$$F(1,18) = 0.17$$

$$(CU)_t = \underset{(6.35)}{64.101} + \underset{(6.35)}{84.574} \left[\frac{(IPR)_{t-1} - (IPR)_{t-2}}{(IPR)_{t-2}}\right] + \underset{(2.43)}{0.299} (CU)_{t-1}$$

$$\rho = \underset{(2.87)}{-0.586},\ S = 2.361,\ S/ME = 0.025,\ \chi^2_1(1) = 0.09,$$

$$\chi^2_3(1) = 0.17,\ F(1,16) = 0.13$$

The first equation indicates that changes in industrial production are highly correlated with changes in real GDP, while the second equation suggests that capacity utilisation tends to vary directly with changes in industrial production lagged once. These are simple instrumental relationships reflecting an observed pattern of temporal change rather than fully fledged structural equations.

4

The Trade Balance

The UK economy is a very open economy with imports and exports constituting considerable components of GDP. The data given in Table 4.1 can be used to illustrate this and to discuss the main developments in exports and imports in the period 1955-78. It can be seen, for example, that the degree of openness of the economy, measured by the ratio of imports to GDP, at constant prices, has been increasing for the whole of the postwar period, with most of the rise occurring since the 1967 devaluation. When current prices are used, however, the same ratio tends to decline for the period up to 1967, indicating that import prices were rising less rapidly than domestic prices. This is further illustrated by comparing the corresponding ratios of exports to imports for the two sub-periods. It is clear that Britain enjoyed the benefits of rising terms of trade - while the volume of imports in 1955-67 increased by 60 per cent, the volume of exports rose by a mere 43 per cent, without a concomitant deterioration in the balance of trade. Nevertheless, this pattern came to an end with the 1967 devaluation and, especially, the dramatic surge of import prices in 1973-4. Thus, whereas the ratio of exports to imports at current prices in 1972-4 declined by 15.3 per cent, its volume counterpart rose by 6 per cent. In empirical work on the determinants of exports and imports it is frequently assumed that the import ratio tends to fluctuate in a pro-cyclical way, while the export ratio tends to fluctuate counter-cyclically, i.e. a higher pressure of domestic demand on productive capacity leads to an acceleration of the flow of imports and a deceleration of the flow of exports. It is therefore expected that the ratio of exports to imports should move in a counter-cyclical manner. Figure 4.1 constitutes a preliminary attempt to examine this hypothesis. The picture presented, with two cyclical indicators and the export-import ratio, is not sufficient to establish the validity of this hypothesis, which is further investigated later in the context of modelling imports and exports.

Table 4.1 Exports (X), imports (Q), capacity utilisation (CU) and GDP

	1975 prices					Current prices		
	X/GDP	Q/GDP	X/Q	% ΔGDP	CU	X/Q	X/GDP	Q/GDP
1955	0.201	0.228	0.884	3.6	99.9	0.932	0.247	0.265
1956	0.206	0.224	0.920	1.8	96.0	1.010	0.251	0.249
1957	0.208	0.226	0.921	1.9	95.0	1.012	0.249	0.246
1958	0.205	0.229	0.896	-0.4	93.1	1.027	0.233	0.227
1959	0.204	0.236	0.865	3.4	90.2	0.994	0.229	0.230
1960	0.206	0.252	0.817	4.6	97.4	0.928	0.228	0.245
1961	0.205	0.242	0.849	3.6	97.2	0.977	0.222	0.228
1962	0.206	0.245	0.844	0.9	91.8	0.983	0.218	0.222
1963	0.208	0.246	0.848	4.0	89.6	0.978	0.218	0.223
1964	0.205	0.258	0.795	5.1	94.7	0.915	0.213	0.232
1965	0.209	0.253	0.826	2.7	98.9	0.957	0.213	0.223
1966	0.214	0.254	0.841	2.2	98.1	0.989	0.216	0.218
1967	0.210	0.265	0.793	2.6	93.6	0.943	0.212	0.224
1968	0.227	0.272	0.834	4.5	97.1	0.964	0.240	0.249
1969	0.245	0.276	0.887	1.8	98.1	1.023	0.256	0.250
1970	0.253	0.285	0.888	2.1	96.4	1.037	0.265	0.256
1971	0.265	0.302	0.874	2.6	93.4	1.070	0.263	0.245
1972	0.264	0.314	0.838	1.5	89.2	0.995	0.248	0.249
1973	0.273	0.325	0.841	8.2	99.3	0.912	0.270	0.296
1974	0.295	0.332	0.888	-1.4	94.8	0.843	0.312	0.370
1975	0.290	0.310	0.935	-0.9	92.9	0.935	0.290	0.310
1976	0.305	0.311	0.981	3.7	87.1	0.963	0.321	0.334
1977	0.322	0.309	1.042	1.5	89.9	1.029	0.349	0.339
1978	0.321	0.314	1.023	2.4	94.5	1.046	0.335	0.321
		1955-60	0.884			0.984		
		1961-4	0.834			0.963		
		1965-8	0.824			0.963		
		1969-73	0.866			1.007		
		1974-8	0.974			0.963		

Source: *Economic Trends: Annual Supplement, 1980.*

IMPORT PENETRATION

The upward trend in the degree of economic openness and import penetration[1] is not a phenomenon confined to the UK economy. Other industrialised countries have become increasingly more open to foreign trade in the postwar period. There has been a number of explanations of this trend. Krause (1968) suggested that increasing import penetration in 1957-64 was the result of trade liberalisation and extensive specialisation within different manufacturing

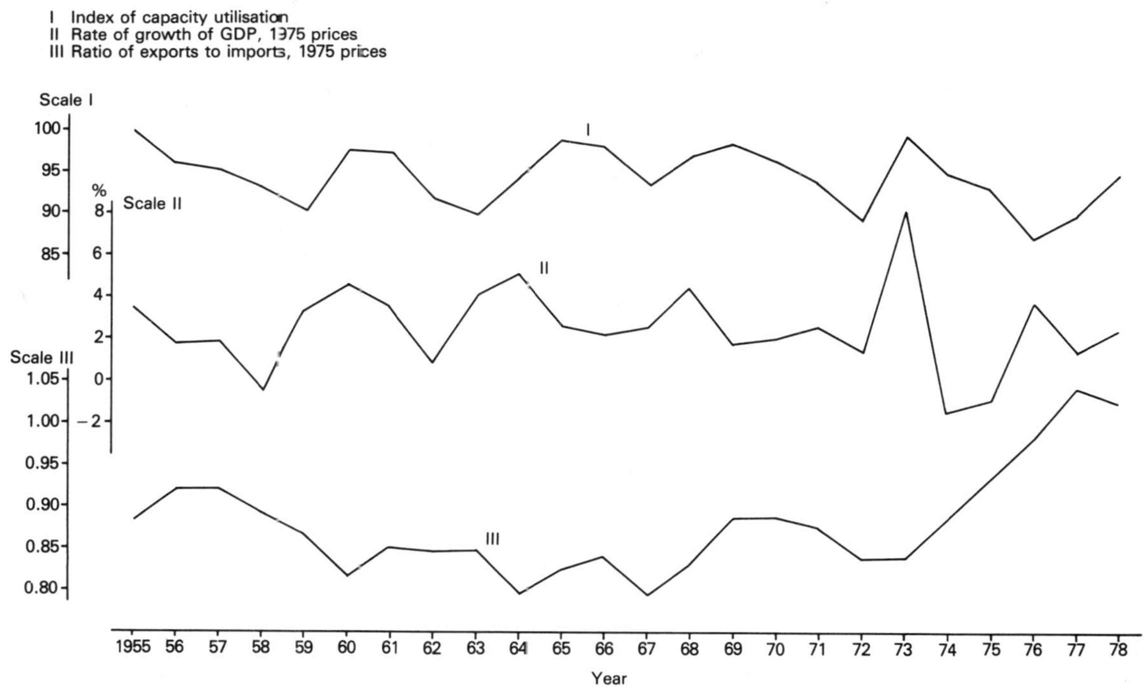

I Index of capacity utilisation
II Rate of growth of GDP, 1375 prices
III Ratio of exports to imports, 1975 prices
Scale I
100
95
90
85
%
Scale II
8
6
4
2
0
−2
Scale III
1.05
1.00
0.95
0.90
0.85
0.80
I
II
III
1955
56
57
58
59
60
61
62
63
64
65
66
67
68
69
70
71
72
73
74
75
76
77
78
Year

Figure 4.1

industries. Barker (1977, p. 65) advanced the 'variety' hypothesis according to which 'as incomes increase, purchasers tend to buy more varieties of a product; and since a greater number of these varieties is available from abroad than from home sources, the share of imports in demand tends to increase'.

But what is considered more significant for the UK economy is the evidence that its income elasticity for imports is higher in relation to other industrialised countries. According to Panić (1975) and Humphrey (1976), the difference is mainly the result of a higher import income elasticity for manufactures in the UK case.[2] They argue, especially Panić, that neither the degree of specialisation in production nor trade liberalisation or the rising variety of products demanded can explain this difference. They suggest, instead, that the main cause is a structural disequilibrium or structural deficiency arising from the failure of the UK economy to adjust to the relatively rapidly changing patterns of both domestic and international demand as quickly as its competitors. The structural deficiency is expressed in terms of an (effective) supply structure and productive capacity of the economy which are out of balance with effective demand. It is made possible because of slow responses of production and output patterns to changes in prices - the slow responses themselves being explained in terms of imperfect competition and obstacles to high mobility of capital and labour. The realisation and special significance of this type of disequilibrium in the case of the United Kingdom is attributed to the low rates of growth of the UK economy. It is furthermore argued by Humphrey (1976, p. 295) that this weakness should be expected to have unfavourable repercussions on the export performance of the economy, and is thus likely to explain the relatively low world income elasticity for UK exports found by Houthakker and Magee (1969) and Meyer-zu-Schlochtern and Yajima (1970). The combination of a high import and a low export income elasticity is held responsible for the severe problems of an external payment imbalance of the economy.

Evidence on import penetration is also produced by Hughes and Thirlwall (1977, 1979), who conclude that deviations of the imports penetration ratio from its upward trend are significantly explained in terms of the degree of pressure of demand in the labour market - imports tend to rise more rapidly than usual when the labour market is tight. A further conclusion, albeit tentative, is on the presence of a ratchet effect according to which a more than average import penetration during the upswing of the cycle is not reversed on the downturn. But Whitley and Wilson (1979) criticise these results mainly on methodological grounds and produce alternative evidence, based on a more complete specification of the import function, according to which aggregate demand and relative competitiveness are capable of explaining most of the changes in import penetration, with capacity variables playing a very minor role. Similar results are obtained by Barker (1979, p. 68), who, while dealing mainly with mis-specification errors of estimated import functions, concludes that 'the interpretation of the upsurge [in imports] is not so much a cyclical effect as a long-term activity effect associated with the increase in demand rather than the increase in the pressure of demand' (see also Whitley, 1979).

Notwithstanding these differences, it is widely accepted that the structure of the UK economy is such as to give rise to frequent trade deficits. Thirlwall (1978) carries further the argument by suggesting that the poor performance of the UK economy should be explained in terms of its tendency to run into serious balance-of-payments problems even before full employment is achieved. In other words, the combination of import and export income elasticities is compatible with a problem-free balance of payments only at a relatively low growth of output. A congruent explanation of the stop-go cycle which emphasises the importance of the balance of payments in explaining changes in fiscal policies is offered by Matthews (1971, p. 14):

> the chief reason why steps were sometimes taken that had a destabilising character was that stabilisation of the level of activity was not as such the objective. For most of the post-war period, a better summary description of the objective would be achievement of as high a level of economic activity as was compatible with the state of the balance of payments. Pursuit of this objective meant that courses were changed as changes occurred in the balance of payments and the authorities' expectations about it.

But the balance of payments as a constraint to growth does not seem to be very widely supported. Paish (1970, p. 170), for example, takes a different view:

> The worsening of the balance of payments as the result of the rise in imports usually causes the Government to introduce its first tentative measures to check the rise in incomes. These measures frequently accompany the slowing down in the rise of output caused by the exhaustion of the margin of unused potential. The check to output is therefore popularly attributed to the balance of payments difficulties, although in fact the rapid rise could not have continued for long even in their absence (see also pp. 138-42).

These alternative views on the timing of the 'stop' policies have different implications for economic policy. According to the latter view, measures to improve the balance-of-payments position would not significantly affect the over-all level of growth, which is mainly determined by the productive capacity of the economy. The former view, on the other hand, suggests that the real constraint is the balance of payments, which, if successfully removed by appropriate policy measures, would allow the economy to run at a level of activity nearer to its full-capacity potential. It is in this context, and in the light of increasing import penetration of UK domestic markets, that advocacy of import controls by the Cambridge Economic Policy Group (Godley and Cripps, 1980) has gained momentum in the trade-union movement and the Labour Party in the late 1970s and early 1980s.

Despite the fact that exports and imports constitute higher percentages of GDP in the 1970s than in earlier periods, it is true that the United Kingdom has suffered a major decline in its world trade position. Although the commodity composition of UK exports has changed little at the aggregate level, the UK share of manufactured exports in world trade has declined (Brown and Sheriff, 1979). At the same time import penetration in a wide spectrum of industries, especially in the form of finished manufactures, has risen substantially (Wells and Imber, 1977; Hughes and Thirlwall, 1977).

These adverse trends of the UK economy are very often associated with the relatively low rates of expansion of productive capacity which lead to low productivity rates and lack of competitiveness in world markets. It has been suggested (e.g. Beckerman, 1966; Moore and Rhodes, 1976) that the United Kingdom suffers from a vicious circle of cumulative decline. Losses in market shares prevent a fast growth of demand at the same time as an unfavourable balance of trade is experienced. Slow growth of the domestic market, then, results in slow growth of domestic industries and a slow improvement in productivity - which in turn leads to further losses in market shares. Thus the relationship between economic growth and trade is subject to mutual causation, with structural deficiency being the cause of trade imbalances and the latter being the cause of slow growth and the lack of structural adjustments (see Kaldor, 1966).

The above analysis is criticised by Beenstock and Warburton (1980), who develop and test a model according to which (i) the increasing import penetration of major economies is the result of international trade liberalisation, (ii) the long-run import income elasticity for the United Kingdom is unity, and (iii) there is nothing exceptional about UK import performance relative to developments in the world as a whole. They therefore argue that the UK trade balance is not subject to a structural deficiency and that arguments for import controls are misguided. The observed higher growth of imports in relation to national income in most industrial countries is the syndrome of the adjustment process towards the new equilibrium of openness following a phase of trade liberalisation. In this process the United Kingdom lags behind the other EEC members, as it joined at a later stage than other countries. It is therefore predicted that in contrast to the short-run income elasticity for imports which is expected to be high during the adjustment period the long-run elasticity is expected to be unity.

MODELLING IMPORTS AND EXPORTS

In this section we are concerned with the determination of exports and imports of goods and services as they appear in national expenditure accounting. These constitute by far the largest part of the current account of the balance of payments, which, in addition, incorporates public- and private-sector transfers including interest, profits and dividends. In the following formulation of the current-account identity

$$CB = (XR)\ (PXD) - (QR)\ (PQD) + (OCB) \qquad (4.1)$$

exports of goods and services at constant prices (XR), and likewise imports (QR), as well as the index of export prices (PXD), are determined by the model, while the index of import prices (PQD) and other current balance items (OCB), mainly transfers, are exogenously determined. The role of current balance (CB) in the government's budget constraint, as well as the determination of the balance-of-payments capital account (investment and capital transactions) are discussed in Chapter 5.

IMPORTS

In the case of an individual traded product i the volume of imports can be expressed as follows:

$$QR_i = D_i\ (GDPR,\ P_i,\ P) - S_i\left(\frac{P_i}{C_i}\right) \qquad (4.2)$$

i.e. imports is the difference between total demand (D_i) and total supply (S_i); demand is assumed to be a function of income (GDPR), the price of the product (P_i) and a price vector (P) of substitutes, complementary goods, etc.; supply is a function of a profit margin or mark-up (P_i/C_i), where C_i is the cost of production. Combining demand and supply we can express the import function in an alternative way, i.e.

$$QR_i = Q\ (GDPR,\ P_i,\ P,\ C_i) \qquad (4.3)$$

in which case the coefficient on P_i is the difference between the demand and supply coefficients; it is expected to be negative since the demand coefficient is expected to be negative and the supply coefficient is expected to be positive. This specification has to be modified in a number of ways to obtain an aggregate import function (some of the problems of aggregation and the resulting bias in the case of import functions are discussed in a study by Barker (1970), to which a further reference is made later in this section).

(a) P_i is replaced by an aggregate import price index which is assumed to be exogenous, while P disappears because we now consider all tradeable goods.
(b) We assume a constant mark-up, in which case C_i is approximated by an aggregate domestic price index; the actual index used covers the whole economy, thus implying the same mark-up for tradeables and non-tradeables.
(c) It is frequently assumed that when the pressure of demand on domestic capacity is high bottlenecks in domestic supply are encountered which result in suppliers being in difficulty to meet their share in incremental demand, and therefore additional imports are sucked in (Rees and Layard, 1971).

(d) In addition to (c) it has been suggested that unanticipated changes in stocks in one period will have a significant influence on the volume of imports in the subsequent period; for example, a sudden depletion of stocks due to an unanticipated rise in demand is expected to enhance total demand in subsequent periods. In practice, however, since data on unanticipated stock changes are not available a proxy of this variable, usually lagged values of stockbuilding, are used in estimation.

The basic estimating equation for imports can then be written as

$$(QR)^d = f\ [(GDPR,\ PD,\ PQD,\ CU,\ (STB)_{t-1})] \tag{4.4}$$

where QR = volume of imports, GDPR = real GDP, PD = index of home prices, PQD = index of import prices, CU = index of capacity utilisation and STB = stockbuilding. Furthermore, as actual imports may adjust to demand with a lag, an adjustment is specified to the effect that imports change in period t according to the difference between demand for imports in period t and the actual value of imports in period t - 1:

$$\Delta(QR)_t = (QR)_t - (QR)_{t-1} = \delta[(QR)_t^d - (QR)_{t-1}] \tag{4.5}$$

and δ is the adjustment coefficient lying between zero and unity. When $(QR)_t^d$ is substituted as above, we obtain a dynamic specification with $(QR)_{t-1}$ as an additional regressor.

Various specifications based on these variables were tried with the following regression, based on the instrumental-variables estimation technique, giving the best results:

$$(QR)_t = \underset{(1.75)}{-\ 4.118} + \underset{(2.3)}{0.231}\ (GDPR)_t + \underset{(2.33)}{3.647}\ (PD)_{t-1}$$

$$-\ \underset{(2.7)}{2.695}\ (PQD)_{t-1} + \underset{(2.6)}{0.416}\ (QR)_{t-1}$$

$$\rho = \underset{(3.02)}{0.659}\ ,\ S = 0.257,\ S/ME = 0.025,\ \chi_2^2(9) = 15.6$$

$$\chi_3^2(1) = 3.96,\ F(1,14) = 1.75$$

The long-run (i.e. when $(QR)_t = (QR)_{t-1}$) mean-income and mean price elasticities are 1.56, 0.65 and -0.52 respectively. A summary of income elasticities obtained in previous studies is given in Table 4.2. The differences can be explained in terms of different sample periods, aggregation levels, equation specifications and varying definitions of the variables used. It has been suggested that instead of using the whole of GDP as the main income variable one should employ the sum of expenditures on importables, thus excluding spending on services, distribution, transport, water and construction; another alternative is to distinguish individual marginal propensities to import by including different types of demand expenditures as separate explanatory variables - the purpose being to provide for the effect of changes in the composition of total expenditure (Barker, 1970). The main problem with this approach, however, is that some of the components of total final expenditure tend to be highly correlated, thus giving rise to the multicollinearity problem. On the other hand, however, when using an aggregate import function with a single demand variable one should be aware of possible aggregation errors arising from changes in the composition of domestic aggregate demand and total imports either in the long run or over the business cycle (Barker, 1970).

Table 4.2 Income elasticities for imports*

Houthakker and Magee (1969)	1.66	
Barker (1970)	1.12	
Rees and Layard (1971)	1.80	- semi-manufactures
Rees and Layard (1971)	2.10	- consumer goods
Taplin (1973)	2.61	- total manufactures
Panić (1975)	1.82	
Kahn and Ross (1975)	1.83	
Barker (1976)	1.64	
Humphrey (1976)	2.20	
Deppler and Ripley (1978)	1.32	
Whitley (1979)	4.12	- finished manufactures
Treasury (1979)†	1.10	
Fetherston and Coutts (1979)	2.00	
NIESR (1979)	1.90	
London Business School (1980)	1.00	

* These elasticities refer to total imports unless otherwise stated: for money income elasticities of the demand for imports at a highly disaggregated level see Thirlwall (1980).

† For the derivation and correct interpretation of the last four entries see Beenstock and Warburton (1980).

There are also problems with respect to price indices used in estimation. It seems preferable, for example, that an index of domestic prices of import substitutes or importables should be used instead of the GDP price deflator. Ideally the weighting of individual prices in compiling such an index should provide for the compositional pattern of total imports, especially as affected by various import-control schemes. Import prices are usually represented by either the import price deflator or the unit value index for imports. In addition to the observation that these indices may not fully provide for quality change over time, it has been suggested (Morgan, 1975) that tariff changes should appear as a separate price variable. When tariffs are very effective, in that they are near prohibitive, their abolition may result in a substantial increase in imports, not fully captured by the corresponding reduction in the import price index. In recent empirical work Humphrey (1976) finds that nominal tariffs is a significant explanatory variable in the case of imports of manufactures, while Whitley (1979) fails to find a separate tariff effect.

Pressure of internal demand is included in import functions in a number of ways; the level and/or rate of change of capacity utilisation seems to be a popular variable, though alternative indicators have been employed. Rees and Layard (1971) have also used zero-unity dummy variables to distinguish periods of below-average and above-average pressure of demand based on responses from a questionnaire of manufacturing firms. A ratchet effect is also incorporated in their regressions according to which expansion of imports caused by a high pressure of demand is not reversed when the pressure of demand subsides. However, most of these measures have proved to be of limited success. Trivedi (1976) used an excess-demand variable measured by the volume of imports minus changes in stocks, while others used a deviation of output (or demand) from its trend value (e.g. Barker, 1979). In the same study Barker shows that because of the interdependence of measures of economic activity, capacity utilisation and trend, omission of any one of them could lead to apparently significant results for the included variables.[3] As a result erroneous conclusions can be drawn on the relative importance of the regressors used and the size of elasticities. It should therefore not be surprising that different income elasticities are obtained from specifications which differ in terms of the set of regressors they use. Including a time trend leads invariably to a lower income elasticity.

Meaningful comparison of our results with previous findings is limited by the fact that the level of disaggregation usually adopted in other studies contrasts with the highly aggregative nature of our model. Another difference is that we have opted for a linear function whereas most of the recent studies are based on logarithmic transformations of exponential relationships. The obvious consequence of our choice, of course, is that we assume constant propensities and variable elasticities. But the explanatory power of the preferred equation is satisfactory and the magnitude of elasticities and set of regressors are consistent with the findings of a subset of earlier studies.

EXPORTS

On the micro level the allocation of the output of a profit-maximising firm between the home market and the foreign market can be examined with the help of a diagram (see Figure 4.2). Assuming that the firm is a price-taker in the foreign market and that it operates in an imperfectly competitive market at home, with an upward-sloping marginal cost curve, it will sell $0Q_H$ of its output internally at P_H and Q_HQ abroad at P_F. According to this simple model a rise in home demand, indicated by a shift in the AR_H to the right, will lead to a shift of sales from the foreign market to the home market, while a rise in P_F will raise both total output and exports. This diagram, however, fails to describe more complex and more realistic alternatives: the level of output may be determined by productive

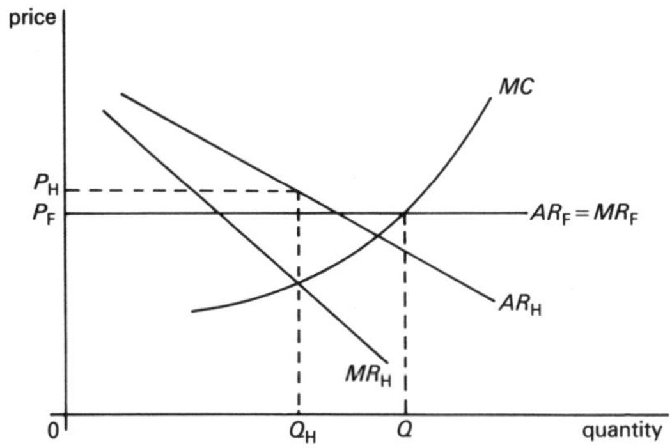

Figure 4.2

capacity rather than an upward-sloping marginal cost curve; non-price factors such as length of delivery time, credit terms and after-sales servicing may be important determinants of foreign demand; and a large firm may have considerable influence on world prices.

On a macro level the following identity could form the starting-point for the discussion of the determinants of the volume of total exports:

$$(O + M) - D = X + \Delta(STB) \tag{4.6}$$

where O = domestically produced output, M = imports, D = aggregate domestic demand, X = exports and Δ(STB) = unplanned changes in stocks. The demand for exports function can be expressed as

$$X^d = f\ (WD,\ P_d,\ P_f,\ Z) \tag{4.7}$$

where WD = world demand for exportables, P_d, P_f = home and world price indices for exportables, and Z = a vector of non-price indicators of the degree of competitiveness of domestically produced exportables. As long as $[(O^f + M) - D] > X^d$, where O^f = full-capacity output, there does not seem to be any quantitative constraint in satisfying the demand for exports. It is widely assumed, however, that in periods of a rapid expansion in domestic demand not accompanied by a commensurate increase in imports the pressure on domestic productive capacity would result in a reduction in non-price competitiveness. It is for this reason that a number of researchers use the pressure of domestic demand as a proxy for Z in estimating the demand for exports function.

So far we have treated exports as a residual; it is implicitly assumed that domestic demand is satisfied first, even at the expense of exports. This may be so only if selling at home is at least equally profitable as exporting. This is an assumption frequently, albeit usually implicitly, made in empirical work. It would be useful, however, to assume explicitly the presence of a supply function of the following simple form:

$$X^s = g\ (P_f,\ D,\ C,\ CU) \tag{4.8}$$

where C = cost of production, assumed to be proportional to home prices, and CU = capacity utilisation. It therefore follows that a problem arises when $X^s < X^d$, in the sense that the lack of an equilibrium prevents the proper identification of demand. Hutton and Minford (1975), in an attempt to resolve this problem, have developed a model according to which demand and supply functions of UK manufacturing exports are separately estimated. The essence of their method, which is based on Fair and Jaffee's (1972) work on estimating demand and supply functions for markets in disequilibrium, lies in utilising information to divide the sample period into periods of excess demand and periods of excess supply. Subsequent to this, data from excess-supply periods are used to estimate the demand function and data from excess-demand periods are used to estimate the supply function. The information used to divide the whole period into sub-periods was based mainly on the level of capacity utilisation (CU), so that quarters for which CU < 95 are classified as excess-supply periods. It should be obvious that the validity of this procedure depends on whether the resulting classification of periods - based on a rather *ad hoc* criterion - corresponds to the actual state of the economy.

Given the constraints of the present study, especially in this particular case the small number of observations available for estimation, we have opted for a conventional aggregate export function:

$$XR = f\ (WD,\ WP,\ PXF,\ CU) \tag{4.9}$$

where XR = volume of exports, WD = world demand, WP = index of world prices, PXF = index of UK export prices in foreign currency, and CU = index of capacity utilisation. Estimation of various versions of the above specification failed to produce a significant coefficient for the latter variable.[4] This is not entirely surprising given the aggregate nature of the export function employed. In the context of previous empirical work on the determinants of export volumes it has been noted that the coefficient on capacity utilisation may be indeterminate. This is so since this variable is likely to be positively related to the level of world demand, domestic production, imports and exports. It is also consistent with the view that the volume of exports for most of the sample period has been supply-constrained so that an expansion of domestic production is directly related to exports. To overcome this problem Ball *et al.* (1966) use the UK export share, rather than export volume, as their dependent variable, which they find to fluctuate cyclically around a linear trend moving inversely with the pressure of internal demand. What would also be true is that the ratio of imports to exports would tend to be positively related to the growth and the pressure of domestic demand. The following estimated regression, used in this study, seems to provide a satisfactory explanation of the export-determination process:[5]

$$XR_t = \underset{(6.8)}{5.951} + \underset{(34.2)}{0.037}\ (WD)_t + \underset{(1.77)}{0.009}\left[\frac{(WP)_t + (WP)_{t-1}}{2}\right]$$

$$+ \underset{(3.4)}{0.024}\left[\frac{(WP)_{t-1} + (WP)_{t-2}}{2}\right] - \underset{(2.5)}{2.799}\ (PXF)_{t-1}$$

$$- \underset{(3.0)}{4.685}\ (PXF)_{t-2}$$

$D\text{-}W = 2.35$, $S = 0.142$, $S/ME = 0.013$, $\chi_1^2(3) = 2.12$, $\chi_3^2(1) = 0.72$,

$F(1,14) = 0.24$

The mean elasticity of exports with respect to world demand is around 0.75; the corresponding elasticities with respect to world prices and domestic export prices are 0.4 and 0.7 respectively. These are reasonable statistics and the export demand elasticity conforms with the long-run decline of UK exports in world trade. The higher own price elasticity is not surprising since PXF is a more reliable measure of the opportunity cost of UK exports than WP, which refers to world export prices in general. The latter is a measure of the cost of a product-mix which is different from the composition of UK exports.

Table 4.3 provides estimates of export demand elasticities obtained in earlier studies.[6] The consensus is that the UK income elasticity of exports is below unity. Furthermore, it also seems that there is agreement that the UK elasticity is smaller than those obtained for other industrialised countries (Deppler and Ripley, 1978; Houthakker and Magee, 1969; Meyer-zu-Schlochtern and Yajima, 1970). Given the different specifications of the export functions used for estimation, the different sample periods and estimation techniques, the range of elasticity values is not large.

A special feature of empirical work on imports and exports is the lack of uniformity in the measurement or definition of most of the relevant explanatory variables. This problem is especially difficult when aggregate functions are used. Most of these problems are the result of the non-availability of data, but lack of appropriate theoretical work has also been a contributing factor. Ideally the measure of the world demand variable needed in estimating the UK exports function should encompass only those countries which

Table 4.3 World income elasticities of UK exports

Houthakker and Magee (1969)	0.86
Duffy and Renton (1970)	1.00
Hutton and Minford (1975)	0.60
Winters (1976)	0.64
Deppler and Ripley (1978)	0.90
Enoch (1978)	0.53-0.88

constitute potential customers of the United Kingdom; it should also be weighted on the basis of UK specialisation in production of exportables.

A given increase in world demand will have a different impact on UK exports depending on its composition; changes in favour of products for which the United Kingdom has a comparative advantage will be more beneficial. It can be argued, for example, that the declining UK share in world trade could be the result not so much of the lack of competitiveness but simply of an expansion of world demand and trade away from goods and services produced in the United Kingdom. Thus an unstable commodity structure of world demand will imply an unstable income elasticity of UK exports when an unqualified aggregate world demand variable is used.

Another problem arises with regard to the selection of indicators for UK price competitiveness. In a comprehensive study of this problem Enoch (1978) concludes, on the basis of empirical performance, that the best price variable is the relative unit labour cost adjusted for cyclical variation.

IMPORT PRICES AND EXPORT PRICES

In this section so far we have dealt with quantity equations. Given the use of the model for simulation purposes in Chapter 9 some treatment of import and export prices is in order. In common with most models import prices are treated as exogenous. On the other hand, export prices are endogenised on the basis of the simple assumption that they are highly associated with internal costs. We therefore assume that the export price deflator in foreign currency is a function of the GDP price deflator as follows (where the lags are determined empirically):

$$(PXFD)_t = \underset{(19.5)}{0.573} + \underset{(3.8)}{1.083}\,(PD)_t - \underset{(2.6)}{1.245}\,(PD)_{t-1} + \underset{(2.4)}{0.566}\,(PD)_{t-2}$$

$$\text{D-W} = 1.85,\ S = 0.038,\ S/ME = 0.035,\ \chi_2^2(1) = 0.011,$$

$$\chi_3^2(1) = 1.65,\ F(1,\ 16) = 0.62$$

In disaggregated studies of export prices Winters (1976) and Ormerod (1980) find that the other major determinant is world prices. Given the highly aggregative nature of our model and the high correlation between world and domestic prices we feel that the link between domestic costs and export performance is, for our purpose, satisfactorily ensured by the above equation.

Data for PXFD are generated according to the following equation:

$$PXFD = (PXD)\ (ER) \tag{4.10}$$

where PXD is the implicit price deflator for UK exports of goods and services and ER is the sterling effective exchange rate, which is treated as an exogenous variable in this model. Although the adoption of a flexible exchange-rate system in 1971 and the 1970s' experience of marked fluctuations in sterling's exchange rate render the exogeneity assumption rather unreasonable, it should be noted that for the largest part of the sample period a fixed exchange-rate regime was in operation. It is nevertheless true that the role of the exchange rate in the present model is rather limited, and that in this respect there is considerable room for improvement.

5

The Monetary Sector

In any real economy where the monetary authorities[1] can hope to influence economic behaviour in a predictable way via changes in the money supply, there are a number of preconditions that have to be fulfilled. The most important of these preconditions is that the monetary authorities should be able to control that set of assets which constitute the 'money stock', and that the latter should itself influence the rest of the economy. Professor Shackle (1971, p. 32) is quite explicit on this point: 'If the controlling of money is to provide a means of controlling the economy, money has to be something which passes two tests. It must itself have, or it must transmit, powerful effects on the economy; and it must itself be susceptible to control in appropriate respects.' Whether these preconditions are satisfied in the case of the UK economy has been the subject of a good deal of debate and controversy. And not surprisingly so: 'These two requirements give us, perhaps, a sort of map-maker's fix on the definition of money. Neither requirement alone is sufficient, and, of course, there is no presumption that such a "money" can be identified or shown to exist' (Shackle, 1971, p. 32). Central to the debate, therefore, is the question of a proper definition of the 'money stock', and we begin this chapter with a discussion of this.

DEFINITIONS OF MONEY

In general there are four approaches to defining money: the conventional approach, the Chicago approach, the Gurley and Shaw approach, and the central bank approach.

The conventional approach views money by its distinguishing functional characteristic as a medium of exchange. According to this view (Latane, 1954), the theory of the demand for money is a theory of the demand for an asset that is a generally acceptable means of exchange and also happens to be a store of value. It goes on to argue that a nation's money stock consists of currency (coins and legal tender paper money) as well as demand deposits (current-account deposits). Unlike demand deposits, which are readily transferable by cheque, time deposits, savings deposits and so forth are not means of exchange. Another argument (Pesek and Saving, 1967) put forward to support this approach says that demand deposits represent net wealth to the community even though they are the liabilities of commercial banks whose owners are members of the economy, whereas time deposits and the liabilities of other financial institutions do not represent net wealth. This is so because the banking sector does not pay interest on demand deposits, while at the same time it charges interest on the debts they create; thus, the argument goes, banks earn an excess profit whose discounted value is reflected in the capital of banks. So the existence of the banking system itself involves an increase in wealth in the form of shares which bear interest. It is argued that the principal means by which monetary policy works is the wealth effect and that the proper empirical definition of money is confined to currency plus demand deposits, since it is only changes in the real quantity of these assets that represent changes in the community's wealth.

The Chicago approach, associated with Milton Friedman and other University of Chicago monetary theorists (Friedman, 1956), defines the function of money more broadly as 'a temporary abode of purchasing power'. This approach includes in its definition of money not only currency and demand deposits but also time deposits, which are interest-bearing deposits with commercial banks. This definition of money is, obviously, in conflict with the conventional definition because commercial bank time deposits are not directly spendable. They do not function, therefore, as a medium of exchange. The owner of a time deposit who wants to use it to buy a car, for example, must exchange this deposit for currency or a demand deposit before being able to make the payment for the purchase. The Chicago approach, however, is based on the theoretical criterion of defining as a single good those things which are perfect substitutes for one another. It is argued that since time deposits are such close substitutes for currency and demand deposits, it is fruitful to treat them as if they were perfect substitutes. The relatively timeless and costless ease of transferring time deposits into demand deposits and currency, as well as the notion that a time deposit is actually 'money in the bank', provide support for the close-substitutability arguments. In the case of the United Kingdom Shackle's remarks on this point are quite convincing:

> In Britain at least, the distinction of availability between demand and time deposits (current and deposit accounts) is practically negligible. A note to my bank will transfer money at any moment, at a loss of seven days' interest. I cannot write a cheque on my deposit account, but I can write one on my current account which, even if that account is empty, will be honoured if covered by my deposit balance. No holder of accounts in a British bank would make any distinction between the two sorts of account in regard to their readiness of availability, as opposed to the question of loss of interest (Shackle, 1971, p. 33).

However, one could not possibly go as far as to argue that they are perfect substitutes, for if they were, a satisfactory answer would have to be given to the awkward question of why anyone would wish to hold non-interest-bearing demand deposits or currency when there is interest to be earned on time deposits.

The Gurley and Shaw approach owes its name to a major theoretical contribution by Gurley and Shaw (1960), who argue that currency and demand deposits are not unique assets (except as a medium of exchange) but are instead just two amongst many in the family of claims against financial intermediaries. Furthermore, they particularly stress the close substitution relationships between currency, demand deposits, commercial bank time deposits, savings bank deposits, and so on, all of which are viewed by the public as alternative liquid stores of value.

This approach seems to be very similar to the Chicago approach. They are in fact similar in their objective, for both attempt to define money to include all those assets that are means of payment plus those assets which are close substitutes for the means of payment. They differ, however, in their analysis. Whereas the Chicago approach considers only time deposits to be close substitutes for the means of payment, Gurley and Shaw expand the number of substitutes to include deposits of, and claims against, all types of financial intermediaries. The Gurley and Shaw analysis does raise the important question of how to account for the substitution relationships when defining the money stock. Gurley (1960) suggests that the money supply should be defined as a weighted sum of currency, demand deposits and their substitutes, with weights being assigned on the basis of the degree of substitutability.

Finally, there is the central bank approach, the approach to money taken by many monetary authorities. In this case the tendency is to view money in its widest possible concept - to the point, in fact, that money is used as if it were synonymous with credit.[2] This is really quite understandable once we note that the main interest of this approach is not monetary theory as such, but rather monetary *policy* - thus there is the notion of 'total credit availability' in the USA as the key monetary-policy variable for regulating the economy, and in the United Kingdom we have the notion of the 'liquidity' of the economy as it was popularised by the Radcliffe Committee (Radcliffe Committee, 1959, ch. 6) and subsequently clarified by Sayers (1960). More recently, however, monetary authorities have started pursuing policies which imply defining money less broadly. So we have the US Federal Reserve System concentrating on M1 - the conventional approach - though supplementary targets are set for M2 - the Chicago approach. In the United Kingdom the target is for the M3 definition of money - a definition which is broader than M2 but not as wide as the Gurley and Shaw definition.

A summary of the definitions currently used for money in the United Kingdom (and the USA) is provided in Table 5.1. It is obvious that even the same definition may differ from country to country, reflecting differences in the institutional set-up. In particular, the M1 definition in the United Kingdom is slightly broader than the

Table 5.1 Alternative definitions of the money supply

	UK M1	US M1	US M2	UK M3 (US credit proxy)	£M3
Notes and coin	Yes	Yes	Yes	Yes	Yes
Private-sector demand deposits in native currency*	Yes	Yes	Yes	Yes	Yes
Private-sector interest-bearing sight deposits in native currency	Yes	No	Yes	Yes	Yes
Public-sector deposits in native currency	No	No	No	Yes	Yes
Public-sector deposits in foreign currency	No	No	No	Yes	No
Private-sector interest-bearing 'retail' deposits in native currency (time deposits less than $50,000)	No	No	Yes	Yes	Yes
Private-sector interest-bearing wholesale deposits, in native currency					
Certificates of Deposit in native currency	No	No	No	Yes	Yes
Private-sector deposits with native banks in foreign currency	No	No	No	Yes	No
Non resident deposits in native currency	No	No	Yes	No	No

*That is, sterling for the United Kingdom, dollars for the USA.
Note: Fuller definitions of M1 and M3 can be found in the June 1970 issue of the *Bank of England Quarterly Bulletin*; and the full definition of sterling M3 is in the Treasury's *Economic Progress Report* for January 1977.
Source: Gowland (1978, appendix B).

one used in the USA, in that some private-sector interest-bearing deposits are included in M1. Furthermore, in the case of the United Kingdom, where the M2 series are no longer published, there are two definitions for M3. There is £M3 and simply M3. The latter is broader in that it includes private and public deposits in foreign currency. In this study we make use of the M3 definition in our attempt to model the UK monetary sector; given the recent concern of the monetary authorities with the £M3 definition, and also that deposits in foreign currency are of crucial importance owing to Britain's position in the international financial scene, our choice in terms of M3 becomes obvious enough.

However, regardless of what particular definition of money one cares to utilise there still remain the problems of (i) whether the authorities can in fact control the stock of money, and (ii) how money supply changes influence the rest of the economy, which we deal with first.

THE TRANSMISSION MECHANISM OF MONETARY POLICY

There are basically two views on the transmission mechanism. The Keynesian view emphasises the importance of interest rates as a link between changes in the money supply and its impact on the rest of the economy. The monetarist view, on the other hand, postulates a direct link between monetary and real phenomena in an economic system.

We may begin by assuming that the economy is at equilibrium, and that the monetary authorities proceed to increase the money stock by, say, open-market operations. What are the channels through which this increase is expected to influence the level of economic activity as measured, for example, by the level of national income?

In Keynesian analysis the assumption is made that financial assets, short-term liquid assets in particular, are close substitutes for money, whereas goods and real assets are viewed as not being such close substitutes. The increase in the money stock will therefore be spent on these substitutes, thus raising their price and lowering their yield. This, in turn, causes further purchases of somewhat less liquid assets, so that eventually the price and yield of long-term financial assets are affected, causing the cost of capital to diverge from the return on capital. This divergence will, of course, affect investment and the level of economic activity. In addition to these cost-of-capital effects there are also 'availability' and 'wealth' effects (Goodhart and Crockett, 1970, p. 162). Interest-rate rigidities, such as that introduced by the Building Societies Association's practice of infrequent adjustments in mortgage rates, are responsible for the 'availability' effects, while wealth effects come about because changes in interest rates alter the present value of the existing volume of wealth which can affect expenditure behaviour.

In the monetarist tradition, money is viewed as a substitute, not just for financial assets, but for all assets alike, real and financial (Friedman and Meiselman, 1963, p. 217; see also Goodhart and Crockett, 1970, p. 164). The increase in the money stock will therefore be spent uniformly on financial assets as well as on real assets. There would thus be an initial increase in prices and a reduction in yields of financial assets. This immediate negative response of interest rates would stimulate investment and other forms of expenditure, and hence income and employment. The latter would also be influenced in the same direction by the initial increase of money spending on physical assets. In the meantime interest rates would tend to drift back to their initial level as the expansionary effects of monetary policy spread through the economy. What is observed, so the monetarist argument goes, is a nearly proportionate relationship between money and incomes, but none between money and interest rates.

To summarise, Keynesian analysis implies a negative relationship between interest rates and money stock, i.e. an increase in money supply would result in a lower interest rate in the new equilibrium. The implication of this analysis is that monetary policy could be undertaken with greater certainty by acting directly to influence and to control interest rates rather than by seeking to control the money stock. Monetarist analysis, on the other hand, does not postulate such a relationship; indeed, the only observed relationship is one of proportionality between money and incomes. The monetarist policy instrument, therefore, is that of money supply, which can register the thrust of monetary policy, unlike interest rates, which although changing initially, are expected to reverse back to their original position at the next equilibrium. Thus, for the monetarists, using interest rates as the instrument of monetary policy would be misleading. In this monetarist prescription for the proper conduct of monetary policy it is evident that the stability of the demand for money function is of paramount importance.

These propositions are in fact testable. This is done by calculating the 'interest elasticity of the demand for money', which purports to show the percentage change in the money stock associated with a given percentage change in interest rates on alternative financial assets. A high interest elasticity means that a large percentage increase in money balances would be associated with a small percentage fall in interest rates on alternative financial assets. Such a result would imply a high degree of substitution between money and alternative financial assets, and this empirical finding should therefore help to settle the theoretical difference between the Keynesian transmission mechanism and that of the monetarists. The evidence produced on this issue has been voluminous and it clearly suggests 'that there is a significant negative relationship between movements in interest rates and money balances... but that the interest-elasticity of demand appears to be quite low' (Goodhart and Crockett, 1970, p. 168). These empirical findings, a summary of which is provided in Table 5.3 below, do not provide support for the extreme forms of Keynesian and monetarist theories. The estimated interest elasticities are far too low to provide support for the extreme Keynesian contention that substantial changes in the money supply would simply cause a small and ineffectual variation in interest rates. Similarly, the monetarist postulate of zero interest elasticity of demand for money, so that changes in money supply would only affect money incomes, leaving interest rates unaffected, after full adjustment has taken place, is again rejected. And while this evidence refers to the period up to early 1970s, the situation since then has been even more damaging for the monetarist propositions. As we have indicated above, the stability of the demand for money is central to the monetarist prescriptions for the best conduct of monetary policy. The evidence that has been produced on the demand for money for this period seems to indicate that this relationship has been unstable with the exception, perhaps, of those cases where the M1 definition of money is utilised (Goodhart, 1981). In Coghlan's (1978) study a stable demand for money for the M1 definition is identified, while Hacche (1974) and Artis and Lewis (1974, 1976) have produced evidence of unstable demand for money functions since 1971 - the year of the introduction of 'Competition and Credit Control' (see, however, Courakis, 1978, and Hendry and Mizon, 1978). The evidence of instability, however, has to be interpreted with some care, since, as Hendry (1979) has demonstrated, it could very well arise from a mis-specification of this particular function, especially of its dynamic structure.

It is true to say that ever since the end of the Second World War, but with decreasing emphasis after 1968, the UK monetary authorities have pursued policies geared to the Keynesian perception of the transmission mechanism (Radcliffe Committee, 1959; Norton, 1969; Crockett, 1970; Goodhart, 1973a). Emphasis was placed on the role of credit and interest rates in influencing expenditure; the stock of money was never an explicit concern of the authorities. In the period before 1971 the authorities turned increasingly to direct control of bank lending to the private sector. This took the form of 'requests' - informing the banks and a growing circle of non-bank financial intermediaries during periods of squeeze what they might and might not do - which were occasionally supported by 'special deposits' - deposits lodged with the Bank of England, at Treasury Bill rate, by the commercial banks. These policies did not seem to have been effective. Norton (1969) and Goodhart (1973a) provide results to show that the effects of such 'requests' upon the granting of credit by the banks to the private sector and the calling of 'special deposits' were not very large. Norton (1969, p. 493) concludes that

> It is tempting on the basis of the foregoing to argue that the authorities would be advised to abandon requests and deposits and rely instead on more flexible interest rates and possibly a stricter control of the money supply. The official argument against more flexible rates has asserted amongst other things that the market is unstable. But the finding of this paper suggests that this is essentially a short-term phenomenon and may well be due to the way the authorities operate in the market. If this is correct, then a large part of the case for official policy disappears.

In May 1971 the monetary authorities did just that, by announcing new techniques of monetary control. These 'Competition and Credit Control' (CCC) proposals and the particular form in which they were to be implemented are set out in three basic papers (*Bank of England Quarterly Bulletin*, 1971b, 1971c, 1971d). In addition, an address by the Governor of the Bank of England (*Bank of England Quarterly Bulletin*, 1971a) is also useful in understanding the new system, as it constitutes an official statement of the economic thinking which underlies the changes.[3] The principal aim of the CCC proposals was to introduce greater flexibility in interest rates, thus enabling the market mechanism to work. Clearing banks were to be encouraged to compete with one another in the terms and services they offered to the public, and all lending requests were abolished, while all banks, not just clearing banks, were to adhere to a 12.5 per cent minimum reserve asset ratio.[4] All these, so it was assumed, would give the authorities more room for manoeuvre in their attempt to control the volume of credit, which was to be achieved through the market mechanism of interest rates. The then Governor of the Bank was quite specific on this point: 'Basically what we have in mind is a system under which the allocation of credit is primarily determined by its cost [and in which] we expect to achieve our objectives through market means' (*Bank of England Quarterly Bulletin*, 1971a). The implementation of CCC was followed by a period of rapid monetary expansion as banks aggressively, and successfully, attempted to increase their business in the 'parallel' money markets from which they had been previously excluded. More important, perhaps, rising interest rates failed to check the very rapid growth of the broadly defined money stock, thus raising 'doubts as to whether the interest-elasticity of the demand for credit was sufficiently high to enable the new system of attempting to regulate bank lending by the cost of credit rather than by lending requests and advances ceilings to operate smoothly' (Savage, 1979, p. 48). Not surprisingly in December 1973 the Bank of England introduced, against the spirit of CCC, the 'supplementary special deposits' scheme (*Bank of England Quarterly Bulletin*, 1974), which has come to be known as the 'corset'. This scheme aimed at penalising banks by requiring them to lodge interest-free deposits with the Bank of England when the growth of their liabilities exceeded a specified limit; it was thus seen as an effective way of moderating monetary expansion without imposing upward pressures on interest rates to 'unacceptable' levels. Two further elements of this scheme were the reintroduction of 'terms control' on hire purchase and, more significantly, the adoption of explicit money supply targets. Clearly the latter element represented a major change in official attitudes regarding the conduct of monetary policy. A number of arguments have been put forward for this change (Gowland, 1978, pp. 123-4). It was seen as a method of curbing public spending and represented a belief amongst Treasury and Bank of England circles that the financial community is 'monetarist' and that therefore money supply targets inspire confidence. The Chancellor was also convinced that control of the money supply was a necessary if not a sufficient condition for control of the rate of inflation. Finally, there is the argument that the IMF impressed the need for money supply targets on the UK authorities.

Our position on the transmission mechanism is that the adjustment from one equilibrium to another, following a monetary disturbance, falls on financial assets. We therefore ascribe to the Keynesian transmission mechanism and postulate, therefore, that the demand for money is related to the short-term rate of interest (RS). Since the M3 definition of money is utilised throughout this book, we include an 'own rate' of interest (ROB). This is the term employed to define the rate of interest on money; for example, the rate of interest on interest-bearing deposits - which are included in the M3 definition - would be the 'own rate'. In fact it has been argued (Goodhart, 1981) that the instability in the M3 demand for money could very well be due to mis-specification inasmuch as the estimated equations do not include an 'own rate'. In addition, the level of nominal income (GDPN) is included because of the consideration of the store of value function of money, in addition to that of the medium of exchange, which makes money an asset alternative to other assets, and justifies the treatment of the demand for money as an application of portfolio analysis. In this context the role of income is that of a constraint in a maximisation problem. The inclusion of income in the demand for money could also be rationalised on the grounds that it is the main determinant of the transactions demand for money. In other words, people are assumed to hold money for their everyday transactions and the amount of money required for this purpose would obviously depend on the number of transactions undertaken. The latter is expected to depend on the level of income, so that a positive relationship between the demand for money and the level of income is expected to be observed.

We may thus write the demand for money as follows:

$$M^d = N\ (RS, ROB, GDPN) \qquad (5.1)$$

THE CONTROLLABILITY OF MONEY STOCK

The central question of this section is whether the money supply is an exogenous variable, that is, under the control of the monetary authorities in the sense that it is purely determined by their decisions, or whether it is an endogenous variable determined by factors completely or partly outside the authorities' control. The usual textbook analysis makes the assumption that money supply is in fact exogenous. In this approach one begins with the definition of the money supply, in our case M3, as follows:

$$M3 = C_p + D \qquad (5.2)$$

where C_p = currency held by the public, and D = total deposits (see Table 5.1 above).

We may now introduce a new variable, monetary base (BA), which is the sum of currency held by the public plus bank reserves (R):

$$BA = C_p + R \qquad (5.3)$$

Bank reserves may be defined as a fraction (r) of deposits; these r reserves are held by banks in the form of cash and deposits with the Bank of England - what is usually termed as 'Bankers Deposits'. So

$$R = rD \qquad (5.4)$$

The public is now assumed to hold a fraction of total deposits in the form of currency (C_p): we may therefore write

$$C_p = cD \qquad (5.5)$$

Dividing 5.2 by 5.3 we have

$$\frac{M3}{BA} = \frac{C_p + D}{C_p + R}$$

and utilising relationships 5.4 and 5.5 we have

$$\frac{M3}{BA} = \frac{cD + D}{cD + rD} = \frac{(1 + c)D}{(c + r)D}$$

$$M3 = \frac{1 + c}{c + r} \quad (BA)$$

$$M3 = m(BA) \qquad (5.6)$$

It is usually argued that if the money multiplier (m) is reasonably constant, then an increase in the monetary base is necessarily accompanied by a multiple expansion in the money supply. Furthermore, a fall in either the reserve ratio (r) or the currency (c) will increase the value of the money multiplier and will therefore lead, *ceteris paribus*, to an increase in the money supply. Sheppard (1971) has produced evidence to show that, over the period 1881-1962, changes in the monetary base accounted for 92 per cent of the change in the money supply, while 8 per cent was accounted for by changes in the money multiplier - with changes in the currency ratio being more important than changes in the reserve ratio.

It follows, therefore, that to the extent that the c ratio is constant and also to the extent that r and BA are under the control of the monetary authorities, then the latter could have a firm control over the money supply. In this case the money supply can be considered as an exogenous variable. The strength of the above analysis, of course, depends on the constancy of the monetary multiplier. A cursory look at the data clearly reveals that this ratio is not a constant during the period covered in this study; its range of fluctuation is between -4 per cent and +19 per cent. A number of explanations can be offered for the non-constancy of m. Consider the c ratio first. One can hypothesise that this ratio depends on the rate of interest. As interest rates go up, the currency ratio falls due to the inducement to hold more interest-bearing deposits in relation to currency. Similarly, the reserve ratio could be thought of as a function of the rate of interest. Banks could very well hold reserves above those legally required as a precaution against unexpected withdrawals by the public. Should this happen banks would be forced to sell some of their interest-bearing assets, perhaps at a loss. The higher the volume of reserves, the lower the danger of losses in view of unexpected withdrawals; the higher the reserves, however, the higher is the opportunity cost - namely, the interest banks could earn on interest-bearing assets. This argument is particularly important in the case of the UK economy, where under the existing institutional arrangements - introduced in 1971 - banks are not obliged to adhere to a formal cash ratio, with the exception of balances with the Bank of England, which are in any case very small in relation to total eligible liabilities. It follows, then, that the reserve ratio is also negatively related to the rate of interest. Furthermore this ratio could also be related to Bank Rate/Minimum Lending Rate (BR). Banks could always sell first-class bills, i.e. bills accepted by the Bank of England at a discount, through discount houses, to the Bank of England for cash if need be. The higher the cost of doing so, i.e. the higher BR, the more reluctant banks would be to use this particular facility - to protect themselves they would tend to hold more reserves. We may thus hypothesise that the reserve ratio is positively related to this rate.

It follows, therefore, that equation 5.6 could be rewritten as

$$M3 = \left[\frac{1 + c(RS)}{c(RS) + r(RS,BR)}\right](BA) \qquad (5.7)$$

or, in an implicit form, as

$$(M3)^s = S\,(RS,\ BR,\ BA) \qquad (5.8)$$

where the partial derivatives with respect to RS and BA are positive, while with respect to BR they are negative.

The implication of this formulation is that money supply is jointly determined by the behaviour of members of the public as they affect the currency ratio, the behaviour of the banks through the reserve ratio, and that of the monetary authorities since BR and BA could be assumed to be under their control - but see below. The monetarists, however, would argue that the behaviour of the monetary authorities dominates the behaviour of the public and that of the banks, so that the money supply is still exogenous. Keynesians, on the other hand, would insist that it is the behaviour of the public and that of banks that dominates movements in the money supply, so that the latter cannot be considered as an autonomous variable that can easily be controlled by monetary policy-makers - it is, instead, an endogenous item, which is mainly determined by the joint economic behaviour of banks and other private economic agents (Tobin, 1963). To the extent that this analysis is correct, it obviously becomes increasingly more difficult for the monetary authorities to control the money supply. This argument is reinforced by what has come to be known as the 'Goodhart law', that 'any observed statistical regularity will tend to collapse once pressure is placed upon it for control purposes' (Goodhart, 1981, p. 116). This argument has become very relevant since the time the monetary authorities in the United Kingdom decided to go for monetary 'targetry'.

Equation 5.8 is, in fact, the formulation that we have adopted for the supply of money. This approach to modelling the UK money supply entails one particular weakness which needs spelling out. The monetary base defined for the purposes of the above analysis needs to be modified for application to the United Kingdom. It should be amended to include 'money at call', Treasury Bills, company tax reserve certificates, local authority bills and commercial bills of exchange. In other words, the monetary base should include all reserve assets sold to the banking sector, as well as currency. Such an approach, however, would require careful specification of the demands and supplies of all the reserve assets, and for the three sectors - private, banking and authorities - which entails severe problems in terms of proper specification of these equations (Parkin, 1973), and would dramatically increase the number of equations in the model. Clearly an expansion of this part of the model would increase the empirical knowledge on this particular sector of the economy. This is nevertheless one of the costs of our preference for employing a small model.

Finally, the interaction of the demand for and supply of money with the equilibrium condition

$$(M3)^d = (M3)^s = (M3)$$

would determine both the money stock (M) and the short-term rate of interest.

THE REST OF THE MONETARY SECTOR

We begin this section by rewriting the equations we have derived so far in this chapter in a linear form:

$$M3_t^d = d_0 + d_1(RS)_t + d_2(GDPN)_t + d_3(ROB)_t + d_4(M3)_{t-1} \tag{5.9}$$

$$M3_t^s = m_0 + m_1(RS)_t + m_2(BA)_t + m_3(BR)_t + m_4(M3)_{t-1} \tag{5.10}$$

$$M3_t^d = (M3)_t^s = (M3)_t \tag{5.11}$$

where in addition to the variables postulated above the term $(M3)_{t-1}$ is also included. In the demand for money equation, the justification is that it is assumed that the adjustment of money holders' portfolios to equilibrium does not occur in any year but only a fraction of the desired difference is in fact adjusted. This hypothesis implies that the $(M3)_{t-1}$ variable ought to appear as an explanatory variable in this equation. The inclusion of the same variable in the money supply equation is, again, the result of a partial-adjustment hypothesis. It can be argued that changes in money stock cause a discrepancy between desired and actual balance-sheet positions of the banks and other economic units. An injection, say of base money, changes the composition of financial assets available to banks and other economic units, and absorption of the new base money requires appropriate changes in asset yields. The banks and the public are thus induced to reshuffle their balance-sheets to adjust their desired and actual balance-sheet position; this adjustment is not instantaneous, it being assumed that only a fraction is adjusted in each period (Anderson and Burger, 1969).

Equations 5.9-5.11 determine, therefore, the money stock and the short-term rate of interest. The latter is assumed to influence the long-term rate (RL) - the 2½% Consol rate - via a simple term structure of interest rates. The level of nominal income is another determinant of the long-term rate; as the level of economic activity is stimulated and the demand for loans increases one would expect an increase in the long-term rate. We also assume a partial-adjustment hypothesis for this variable, too, which may be interpreted as reflecting a failure by bondholders to adjust fully within the period (Artis and Lewis, 1976). The determination of RL is therefore summarised in the following expression:

$$(RL)_t = r_0 + r_1(RS)_t + r_2(GDPN)_t + r_3(RL)_{t-1} \qquad (5.12)$$

The above relationships are, next, integrated with the government budget constraint in an attempt to account for the injection of new money and interest-bearing assets by the government into the economy.

THE GOVERNMENT BUDGET CONSTRAINT (GBC)

This constraint requires that in each period total government expenditure must be equal to the total flow of financing from all sources. It is in this sense that it accounts for the injection of new money and bonds - both short and long - into the economy as a result of fiscal actions. It may therefore be considered as a link between the government - and the monetary authorities - and the rest of the economy. This means that such a constraint restricts the government's freedom to assign arbitrary values to such policy variables as expenditures, taxes, borrowing from the public and issues of new money. In other words, given its policy instruments, the government can choose arbitrary values for the n - 1 of them, letting the remaining one be determined residually in a way that satisfies the constraint (Christ, 1968, p. 53).

A budget deficit or surplus involves the stock/flow changes in net claims held by the central bank and the private sector on the government. The GBC can therefore be written as:

$$G - T = \Delta(BF)_C + [\Delta(BF)_B + \Delta(BF)_P] \qquad (5.13)$$

where G = government expenditure on goods and services and transfer payments, T = tax revenues, $(BF)_B$ = banks' net holdings of government bonds, $(BF)_P$ = public's net holdings of government bonds, and $(BF)_C$ = central bank's claims on the government.

Since changes in the central bank's net claims on the government equal changes in base money, i.e.

$$\Delta(BF)_C = \Delta C_p + \Delta R \qquad (5.13a)$$

where C_p = currency held by the public, R = reserves of the commercial banks *minus* rediscounts and advances by the central bank, equation 5.13 can be expressed as

$$G - T = \Delta C_p + \Delta R + [\Delta(BF)_B + \Delta(BF)_P] \quad (5.13b)$$

The importance of equation 5.13b can be highlighted by assuming an increase in G and tracing through its impact. The increase in G, and the subsequent rise in income, does not necessarily lead to a rise in T by an equivalent amount. Ensuing changes in the budget deficit, represented by the left-hand side of equation 5.13b, must be matched by corresponding changes on the right-hand side of the same equation. Changes in base money and/or government bonds held by the public therefore ensue which affect interest rates and the stock of money. For the purpose of empirical investigation we write the GBC as follows:

$$(\Delta FR)_t + G_t = T_t + (\Delta GS)_t + (\Delta BA)_t \quad (5.13c)$$

This equation simply stipulates that the sources and uses of government funds must balance. The uses are current purchases of foreign exchange $(\Delta FR)_t$ and the various forms of government expenditures G_t. The sources are current tax revenues T_t, changes in the total stock of government debt held by the private and banking sectors $(\Delta GS)_t$ - long-term plus short-term debt - and changes in base money $(\Delta BA)_t$.

Equation 5.13c can be rewritten as

$$(\Delta BA)_t = (PSBR)_t + (\Delta FR)_t - (\Delta GS)_t \quad (5.14)$$

where $(PSBR)_t = G_t - T_t - (OGREV)$[5] is the 'Public Sector Borrowing Requirement'.

Equation 5.14, along with the PSBR identity, highlight the endogeneity of the monetary base (Goodhart, 1973b) and thus the difficulties of controlling the money supply via the monetary base (Foot, Goodhart and Hotson, 1979; Savage, 1980). The process by which the monetary base is affected by the elements on the right-hand side of equation 5.14 is straightforward: any excess of government expenditures over revenues - including sales of debt to the private and overseas sectors - increases the monetary base automatically through the increase in banks' deposits at the Bank of England, which is an element of the monetary base. Thus fluctuations in government-debt sales, errors in forecasting government expenditures and revenues and changes in foreign exchange reserves would so affect the monetary base as to render regulation of it practically impossible. We therefore utilise equation 5.14 to determine changes in the monetary base, and the level of this variable could then be determined via the following identity:

$$(BA)_t = (\Delta BA)_t + (BA)_{t-1} \quad (5.15)$$

The other elements of the GBC, except G_t and T_t, which will be discussed in Chapter 6, are determined as follows:

$$\Delta FR = CB + \Delta KM \quad (5.16)$$

where CB = current balance of the balance of payments, defined as

$$(CB)_t = [(XR)_t\ (PXD)_t] - [(QR)_t\ (PQD)_t] + OCB \tag{5.17}$$

and all the symbols have the same meaning as in Chapter 4. ΔKM stands for changes in capital movements, a variable which is treated as exogenous essentially because of the nature of our data, which are annual. It is very well known that capital movements is a very erratic variable which can only be explained satisfactorily when the time period used is as short as possible. Within a year time span all kinds of changes can, and do, take place which make it impossible to capture them in a proper manner. We have in fact experimented with such variables as changes in interest-rate differentials - difference between UK and US rates - changes in the current balance, and so on, with the resulting estimated equations proving to be extremely volatile and making very little economic or econometric sense. In particular there seem to be severe simultaneity problems in the estimation of this relationship, as well as problems concerned with the question of how to proxy 'confidence' (Latter, 1979) and 'speculation' (Cripps and Fetherston, 1979), which cause large and erratic errors in the estimated form of the equation. Latter (1979, p. 35) is quite explicit on these problems: 'External capital flows are somewhat poorly modelled against a background of considerable problems of simultaneity in the estimation and difficulties in proxying confidence.' For the same reasons the variable ΔGS is also treated as exogenous in this model.

EMPIRICAL EVIDENCE

The best estimates of the behavioural equations 5.9, 5.10 and 5.12 appear in Table 5.2. We note that all the variables have been transformed into logarithms. This transformation has been undertaken for two reasons: the results proved to be more satisfactory this way, and also the interpretation of the results is more convenient with this transformation because the elasticities are readily available. It must also be stressed that in all three equations the χ^2s and the F-test are all insignificant.

We begin our discussion on the empirical results of this section with the demand for money. Initially equation 5.9 was estimated by splitting nominal income (GDPN) into real income (GDPR) and a price variable $(PD)_t$. Two variables performed particularly badly: $(PD)_t$ and $(ROB)_t$.[6] The explanation of the bad performance of the 'own' rate could very well be due to multicollinearity. The partial correlation coefficient between ROB and RS is 0.99, clearly higher than the R^2 for this equation, which vindicates the multicollinearity argument. When changes in ROB were used, with the partial correlation coefficient between this variable and $(RS)_t$ being 0.33, and the price elasticity of the demand for money was constrained to unity by employing the ratio $\ell n(M3/PD)$, the results were quite acceptable, as is shown in the first equation in Table 5.2.

We have also tried other variables in an attempt to test further hypotheses concerning the demand for money. We have included the

Table 5.2

$$\ell n(M3/PD)^d_t = \underset{(2.21)}{-\,0.870} \; \underset{(2.09)}{-\,0.211}\; \ell n(RS)_t \; \underset{(2.79)}{+\,0.439}\; \ell n(GDPR)_t$$

$$\underset{(3.16)}{+\,0.182}\; \ell n\left[\frac{(ROB)_t}{(ROB)_{t-1}}\right] \underset{(4.14)}{+\,0.885}\; \ell n(M3/PD)_{t-1}$$

D-W = 1.87, S = 0.048, S/ME = 0.017, $\chi^2_2(5)$ = 8.15, $\chi^2_3(1)$ = 0.91,

F(1,15) = 0.67

$$\ell n(M3)^s_t = \underset{(1.94)}{0.645} \; \underset{(1.59)}{+\,0.070}\; \ell n\left[\frac{(RS)_t}{(RS)_{t-1}}\right] \underset{(2.68)}{+\,0.531}\; \ell n(BA)_t$$

$$\underset{(2.27)}{-\,0.170}\; \ell n(BR)_t \; \underset{(3.59)}{+\,0.636}\; \ell n(M3)_{t-1}$$

$\rho = \underset{(3.22)}{0.798}$, S = 0.039, S/ME = 0.013, $\chi^2_2(4)$ = 7.36, $\chi^2_3(1)$ = 0.22,

F(1,14) = 0.09

$$\ell n(RL)_t = \underset{(2.10)}{-\,1.125} \; \underset{(5.62)}{+\,0.340}\; \ell n(RS)_t \; \underset{(2.16)}{+\,0.442}\; \ell n(GDPR)_t$$

$$\underset{(2.15)}{+\,0.894}\; \ell n\left[\frac{(PD)_t}{(PD)_{t-1}}\right] \underset{(3.89)}{+\,0.418}\; \ell n(RL)_{t-1}$$

D-W = 2.00, S = 0.046, S/ME = 0.022, $\chi^2_2(6)$ = 2.99, $\chi^2_3(1)$ = 0.19,

F(1,15) = 0.15

rate of inflation $(RPD)_t$ to capture the degree of substitutability between money and real assets (Boughton, 1979, p. 38); in none of our tests was the inflation-rate coefficient significantly different from zero. Furthermore, we have attempted to determine the degree of substitution between domestic money and foreign assets by including in the set of regressors the short-term US Treasury Bill rate, as well as the Euro-dollar rate (Hamburger, 1977, pp. 30, 33); in none of these cases were we able to find any significant degree of substitution. This finding is important in that it shows that, contrary to Hamburger's (1977) results, which are based on the M1 definition of money, domestic short-term rates are, perhaps, preferable to foreign rates as a measure of the opportunity cost of holding money (see also Coghlan, 1980, pp. 134-5).

Clearly the demand for money is of vital importance in macroeconomic analysis in terms of the formulation and transmission of monetary policy. It has been demonstrated above that the transmission mechanism of monetary policy crucially depends on the way in which banks and the non-bank public react to policy actions. This response, in turn, depends on the degree of substitutability between alternative financial assets and money, on its own and in relation to the degree of substitutability between money and real assets (Goodhart and Crockett, 1970, p. 165). The higher the degree of substitution between alternative financial assets and money, the greater the variation of interest rates on financial assets, caused by policy-induced changes in the quantity of money. Any impact, therefore, on economic activity is restricted to the effect which is exerted by the corresponding changes in interest rates. The higher the degree of substitution between money and real assets in relation to the degree of substitution between money and financial assets, the smaller the impact on interest rates but the greater the variation of expenditures on goods and services caused by policy-induced changes in the money stock. In this way changes in the stock of money can exert a direct impact on aggregate demand and thus on economic activity.

The substitution relationship between money and alternative financial assets is usually described, and measured, by the interest elasticity of demand for money. This elasticity shows the percentage change in the money stock associated with a given percentage change in interest rates on alternative assets. A high interest elasticity implies that a small percentage change in interest rates on alternative financial assets is accompanied by a large percentage fall in the demand for money balances. A high interest elasticity therefore suggests a high degree of substitution. In Table 5.3 we report some estimates for the interest elasticity of the demand for money based on the empirical results of this book as well as those of other studies. It is clear from this table that the elasticity estimates, as suggested above - see the section on the transmission mechanism of monetary policy - are neither high enough to suggest a high degree of substitution between money and financial assets, nor low enough to imply that variations in the money stock would only have a direct impact on aggregate demand. As a tentative conclusion, therefore, one might argue that there are interest-rate effects as well as direct impacts of money stock changes on the level of economic activity in the United Kingdom.

The supply of money, as can be seen from Table 5.2 above, performs satisfactorily, with the exception of the coefficient on the changes in the rate of interest variable, which is insignificant. This is probably not a surprising result given that this rate, as one of the determinants of the money supply, makes more sense for the period since 1971 because the new system of monetary controls introduced then implied greater variability in interest rates than before. This may suggest that, although the sign is positive as expected, it would appear insignificant due to the small number of observations since 1971. The Bank Rate coefficient, as well as the rest, has the right sign and is statistically significant. Nevertheless. the significance of the Bank Rate coefficient must be treated with some caution, because the monetary authorities have not attempted in principle to control the money supply via the discount rate during the period under examination.

The way of modelling the supply of money differs from other [illegible]s studies inasmuch as it is a highly aggregated relationship. The more sophisticated models of the UK economy (see, for example, Ormerod, 1979a), such as the National Institute model, disaggregate the money stock into its constituent components, so comparisons are (strictly) not possible. There are, however, two studies by Crouch (1967, 1968) where models of the type M = mB, where m = the money multiplier - treated as constant - and B = monetary base, were tested. In both studies the results suggested a money supply relationship which was perfectly inelastic with respect to interest rates.

One very interesting aspect of the money supply theory, from an empirical point of view, is the interest elasticity of the money supply relationship. Any policy action of the monetary authorities to achieve a desired growth in the money stock affects both reserve aggregates and interest rates. Changes in interest rates, in turn, influence the portfolio decisions of banks and of the public, which in its turn can be a complicating factor in the achievement of a desired money stock. Thus the higher the numerical value of the interest elasticity of the money supply function, the more difficult it may be to implement monetary control through the control of reserve aggregates; and the lower the interest elasticity of the money supply function, then the easier it becomes for such a control. For example, suppose that the Bank of England via open-market operations attempts to reduce the volume of reserves available to the banking system. In that case, the Bank will have to sell government securities, thus causing interest rates to go up. If the amount of reserve assets held by the banking sector is very sensitive to changes in interest rates, then the increase in interest rates will induce the banking sector to hold a greater amount of interest-bearing reserve assets. This portfolio shift will therefore inevitably frustrate the policy of the authorities to decrease the amount of reserve assets going to the banking sector, and thus the money supply. However, this does not mean that monetary control is absolutely impossible. The stronger the interest-rate feedback, the larger the necessary magnitude of the open-market operation required to achieve a given change in the money stock and the larger the associated variance in interest rates. The monetary authorities, on the other hand, may not be prepared to allow these required changes, as has been the case in the United Kingdom for most of the postwar period. The empirical evidence provided in this study clearly indicates the importance of this factor, but at the same time it indicates that the interest sensitivity of this relationship appears to be rather low.

The interaction of the money demand and money supply determines

Table 5.3 Demand for money studies in the United Kingdom - summary of results

Author	Data	Money	Interest rate	Interest elasticity[c]	Income variable	Income elasticity[c]	Price
Kavanagh and	Annual: 1880-1961,	Broad	Long	-0.31(-0.22)[a]	GNP	1.149	-
Walters (1966)	1926-61	Broad	Long	-0.50(-0.25)[a]	GNP		-
Crouch (1967)	Quarterly:	London clearing					
	1954-65	banks	Long	-0.50	GNP	1.08	-
		Deposits (total)					
Fisher (1968)	Quarterly: 1955(I)	Narrow	Short	-0.11	PDI	0.686	-
	-67(II)	Broad	Short	-	PDI	0.742	-
		Narrow	Long	-0.30	PDI	0.686	-
		Broad	Long	-	PDI	0.742	-
Goodhart	Quarterly:						
and	1955(III)-	Narrow	Short	-1.05	GDP	1.25	-
Crockett	69(III)/1963(II)-	Narrow	Long	-0.80	GDP	1.09	-
1970	69(III)[b]	Broad	Short	-0.09/-0.21[b]	GDP	0.77/1.50[b]	-
		Broad	Long	-0.35/-0.51[b]	GDP	1.09/1.89[b]	-
Laidler and	Quarterly:1955(III)	Broad	Short	-0.008	GDP	0.68	1*
Parkin (1970)	-67(IV)				(perm.)		
Laidler (1971)	Annual: 1900-65	Broad	Long	-0.570	GDP	0.795	1*
	1900-13	Broad	Long	-0.268	GDP	1.241	1*
	1920-38	Broad	Long	-0.448	GDP	0.793	1*
	1946-65	Broad	Long	-0.739	GDP	0.684	1*
Price (1972)	Quarterly: 1964(I)-	Broad	Short	-			
	70(IV)(*persons*)	Broad	Long	-0.30	GDP	2.29	0.90
	Quarterly: 1964(I)-	Broad	Short	-0.36			
	70(IV)(*companies*)	Broad	Long	-	GDP	2.77	0.41
Hacche (1974)	Quarterly:	Narrow	Short	-0.081	TFE	0.391	1*
	1963(IV)-71(III)		Long	-0.184			
		Broad	Short	-0.091	TFE	0.450	1*
			Long	-			

	Persons	Broad	Short	-	PDI	0.927	1*
			Long	-0.069			
	Companies	Broad	Short	-0.067	TFE	0.511	1*
			Long	-0.197			
	Quarterly: 1963(IV)-72(IV)	Narrow	Short	-0.062	TFE	0.697	1*
			Long	-0.206			
		Broad	Short	-	TFE		1*
			Long	-			
	Persons	Broad	Short	-	PDI	1.081	1*
			Long	-0.110			
	Companies	Broad	Short	-0.044	TFE	2.206	1*
			Long	-0.696			
	Quarterly: 1963(IV)-72(IV)	Broad	Short	-0.248	TFE	0.995	1*
			Long	-			
			Own rate	0.537			
	Companies	Broad	Short	-	TFE	1.003	1*
			Long	-0.345			
			Own rate	0.568			
Artis and Lewis (1976)	Quarterly						
	1963(II)-70(IV)	Narrow	Long	-0.26	GDP	0.77	-
	1963(II)-71(IV)	Narrow	Long	-0.39	GDP	0.95	-
	1963(II)-73(I)	Narrow	Long	-0.66	GDP	1.24	-
	1963(II)-70(IV)	Broad	Long	-0.47	GDP	1.42	-
	1963(II)-71(IV)	Broad	Long	-0.52	GDP	1.48	-
	1963(II)-73(I)	Broad	Long	-3.00	GDP	4.27	-
Hamburger (1977)	Quarterly: 1963(II)-71(I)	Narrow	Short[e]	-1.20[f]	GDP	0.672	-
			Long[e]	-0.07[f]			
Coghlan[g] (1978)	Quarterly: 1964(I)-76(IV)	Narrow	Short	-0.300	TFE	1.008	0.709
This study	Annual: 1975-8	Broad	Short	-1.828	GDP	3.810	1*

Notes to Table 5.3

GNP = Gross National Product.
GDP = Gross Domestic Product.
PDI = Personal Disposable Income.
TFE = Total Final Expenditure.

a From the same equation estimated in first differences.
b Results for money on a broad definition for both M2 and M3 respectively.
c These are the long-run elasticities.
d Here only the results of the standard approach are summarised, and not the attempts to provide an improved specification.
e In this case the short rate is the three-month euro-dollar rate and the long rate is the dividend-price ratio on ordinary shares.
f These are not the interest elasticities, but the elasticity times one plus the rate of interest divided by the rate of interest.
g This is only one result from the tables presented, but given the evidence of stability discovered it does adequately summarise the results obtained.

*Price elasticity of unity imposed.

Source: Coghlan (1980).

the short-term rate of interest. In its turn the latter influences the long-term rate, via equation 5.12. It is obvious from Table 5.2 that this equation is well determined, with all the arguments on the right-hand side possessing highly significant coefficients. This particular result is very important, for it provides one of the links between the monetary and real sectors of our model - the other being via the liquid-assets variable - since changes in this rate affect expenditure decisions. The estimated form of this relationship does not differ substantially from similar equations embodied in the various models of the UK economy referred to above.

6

The Government Sector

General government expenditures, as given by the Central Statistical Office, are built up from the current and capital accounts of central government and local authorities. Expenditures by public corporations are given separately and do not constitute part of the expenditure made by general government.[1]

One of the most useful distinctions between types of government expenditure is the division between resource-using expenditure and transfer payments. The former consists of general government's final consumption and investment, both of which constitute part of GNP. But a substantial and increasing share of government expenditure takes the form of current grants, subsidies and capital transfers, all of which mostly entail a redistribution (transfer) of purchasing power from one group of people in society to another. Finally, of rather less importance are (debt) interest payments and net lending by general government. It is important that this type of heterogeneity of government expenditure should be borne in mind when total government expenditure is expressed as a proportion of GNP. It must be clear from the above that such a share is conceptually very different from the share of consumers' expenditure or investment in GNP. Unlike the latter the ratio of government expenditure to GNP can be equal to or even exceed unity without this meaning that the government absorbs the whole of national product.

Although the importance of government expenditure in a modern economy is undeniable, the study of it, in comparison with the study of other economic aggregates, has been grossly inadequate. This is especially so when it is considered that evidence shows conclusively that the evolution of capitalist economies is accompanied by a tendency of states' economic activities to expand. In the case of the UK economy, for example, the long-run upward trend of total government expenditure as a percentage of GNP is illustrated by the following historical figures: 1900, 14.4; 1930, 26.1; 1960, 34.6; 1977, 44.0. The relative neglect by economists of states' economic activities in a modern economy can be partly attributed to the fact that in orthodox economics, and more specifically in public finance studies, the main preoccupation has been the examination of the extent to which specific government activities hinder or promote the economic welfare of society. The latter is defined in the context of orthodox general competitive analysis based on individual choice and utility maximisation. This is a different pursuit from the study of the determinants of government economic activity. In what follows we provide a brief review of the various hypotheses on the behaviour of the modern state and more specifically on the tendency of the relative importance of government expenditure to increase.

EXPANDING STATE ACTIVITY - THEORETICAL FOUNDATIONS

The first major hypothesis which is referred to in almost every study of state expenditure is the work of Wagner, who writing in the second half of the nineteenth century formulated a 'law of expanding state expenditure'. According to Wagner's 'law' the public sectors of industrialising nations with rising *per capita* incomes tend to expand more rapidly than the rest of the economy. The empirical basis of the 'law' was provided by an examination of the industrialisation process in various countries - Britain, the USA, Germany, Japan and France. In Wagner's (1890, p. 16) own words:

> That law is the result of empirical observation in progressive countries, at least in our western European civilisation; its explanation, justification and cause is the pressure of social progress and the resulting changes in the relative spheres of private and public economy.

The growth in the relative importance of the public sector was attributed to a number of developments in an industrialising society, of which the following are the most important: (i) the increasing complexity of legal relationships and communications, which arises with the greater division of labour during industrialisation, as well as the rise in population density and urbanisation - both necessitate an expansion of the protective and administrative functions of the state; (ii) an expansion of cultural and welfare expenditure under the pressure of social progress; and (iii) technological progress and the accompanied increase in the scale of production which make public corporations preferable to private monopolies in the interest of economic efficiency.

Although it is emphasised that the conditions under which the 'law' is expected to operate are more likely to be present during industrialisation, research on its empirical validity in the last twenty years has been extended to include countries which have passed the stage of industrialisation. Most of the empirical work[2] seems to confirm the general proposition of expanding state activity. But the factors to which, according to Wagner, the unequal development of the two sectors of the economy should be attributed have often been questioned. It has been argued, for example, that although these factors constitute convincing arguments that the absolute level of public expenditures of a growing economy would increase with time, they fail to explain why any type of public expenditure would become an increasing fraction of national income. It has been remarked, however, that Wagner probably considered that the bulk of goods and services provided by the state are likely to be superior goods with an income elasticity of demand greater than unity. It was also observed that Wagner failed to reduce the complex factors involved in changing social and economic relationships into tractable functional relationships. Finally, it was pointed out that Wagner's 'law' depends on the validity of the organic theory of the state upon which it relies (Peacock and Wiseman, 1961, pp. 16-20).

A different and less grandiose hypothesis than Wagner's 'law', but one which had a considerable impact on subsequent research, was suggested by Peacock and Wiseman (1961) in explaining the growth of state expenditure in the United Kingdom in the period 1890-1955. The basic initial assumption is that the rates of growth of state expenditure are determined by the rates of growth of revenues from taxation. It is then claimed that 'when societies are not being subjected to unusual pressures, people's ideas about tolerable burdens of taxation, translated into ideas of reasonable tax rates, tend also to be fairly stable' (Peacock and Wiseman, 1961, p. xxiv). As a result it is expected that during such periods the share of state expenditures in GNP should remain roughly constant. But during large-scale disturbances people are likely to tolerate higher tax burdens so that there is a displacement effect, shifting state revenues and expenditures to new levels. With the return to normality 'new ideas of tolerable tax levels emerge, and a new plateau of expenditure may be reached, with public expenditures again taking a broadly constant share of gross national product though a different share from the former one' (Peacock and Wiseman, 1961, p. xxiv). The authors employ the idea of the displacement effect to explain the growth of state expenditures in the United Kingdom in the period 1890-1955. It is shown that the two world wars caused significant displacement effects in state expenditures.

Although the significance of the particular displacement effect in explaining the growth of state expenditure in the United Kingdom and other countries during the first half of the twentieth century cannot be denied, it must be emphasised that this is only a partial explanation. This is especially so when the period since 1955 is considered. In this period the share of state expenditure in GNP has risen from 33.3 per cent in 1955 to over 49 per cent in 1975. Also during the same period, which was free from any major social upheavals, the basic income-tax rate has fluctuated between 45 and 30 per cent, a fact which may cast doubt on the hypothesis of a stable tolerance of taxation burden in the absence of social disturbances. The best that can be said about the Peacock and Wiseman hypothesis is that it offers a plausible explanation of the unusually big shifts in state expenditure share; as Peacock and Wiseman (1979) subsequently explained, the displacement effect is a theory of structural breaks. It does not in any way offer a general theory of the growth and composition of state expenditure and does not adequately explain the causes of structural breaks. As Peacock and Wiseman (1961, p. xxiii) put it:

> the hypothesis we offer about this time pattern may be of some value for the explanation of the behaviour of public expenditures... we do not base our discussion upon any all-embracing theory of the state; our sole 'political' propositions are that governments like to spend more money, that citizens do not like to pay more taxes, and that governments need to pay some attention to the wishes of their citizens.

The rapid growth of state expenditures in the postwar period can be at least partly attributed to changing attitudes towards government expenditure under the influence of Keynesian ideas. It has often been argued, for example, that the postwar state's commitment to full employment, and generally the adoption of fiscal stabilisation policies, accounts for the expansion of the public sector. It must be pointed out, however, that the practice of demand stabilisation through fiscal policy does not by itself imply a permanently higher percentage of state expenditure to GNP. Peacock and Wiseman, after examining the relationship between state expenditures and unemployment for the period 1890-1955, concluded that although there seemed to be a short-term effect of fluctuations in unemployment on the percentage of government expenditures to GNP, there was no evidence of a permanent change in the level of expenditures following upon periods of high unemployment; this conclusion should be considered with caution, however, since it is only based on a simple comparison of the two time series - for a more reliable result multiple regression should be employed. But more recently it has been argued that, given the nature of the political setting, the undermining of the virtue of the balanced-budget rule by Keynesian ideas led to an asymmetrical application of fiscal policies: deficits tend to be created frequently, but surpluses are allowed to materialise rarely (Buchanan *et al.*, 1978, pp. 13-27). According to this view, political decisions are taken not by a small group of wise and enlightened persons who act without much regard to their political fortunes, as thought by Keynes, but by politicians whose main objective is to pursue such policies which will secure them the support of a majority of the electorate. Deficits are more beneficial to them than surpluses because they allow them to spend without raising taxes or charges. As a result, it is claimed that in a representative democracy there is a tendency towards deficit finance and uncontrolled growth of government expenditure.

The latter view on the behaviour of politicians is developed within the context of a rather recently developed area of orthodox economics known as 'public choice'. Public choice is nothing more than an application and extension of neoclassical economic theory to the realm of political or governmental choices. What is directly relevant for a study of the expansion of government expenditure is the strand of 'public choice' economics which develops a theory of bureaucratic behaviour. It is argued that bureaucrats, as constrained utility-maximising individuals, seek to expand the size of their bureaux since their career prospects, earnings and influence are directly related to the sizes of the budgets they administer and control. The consequence of this is that the public sector tends to expand beyond the level justified by genuine demands for public goods and services.[3]

Another development, set in the same conceptual framework, has been the idea that governments, in their effort to maintain power, time their policies according to a pattern which has been given the name of a 'political business cycle'. Assuming that the number of votes received is an increasing function of the level of employment and the degree of stability of prices, governments are supposed to increase unemployment right after an election and then allow it to decrease gradually to the lowest level just before the next election (Nordhaus, 1975; Frey, 1978). It is argued that inflation will also be low just before the election because (assuming an augmented Phillips curve) inflation expectations under the influence of recently decreasing actual inflation will be depressed. The model suggests a clearly specified fluctuation of the unemployment rate between elections and (to the extent that government employment is one of the policy variables) a similar fluctuation for the ratio of total employment to public-sector employment. The implications for government expenditure are obvious.

In a recent study Frey and Schneider (1978) developed a model of politico-economic interaction in the United Kingdom and produced evidence to support the hypothesis that changes in the various components of government expenditure are explained in terms of the state of popularity of the government as measured by Gallup Polls Ltd, ideological factors as expressed by the two-party system of this period, and economic constraints such as the balance of payments. In a subsequent study Chrystal and Alt (1979c) challenged the empirical basis of these results and suggested that a 'combination of the Wagner's law approach and some aspects of [government] reaction functions' is a superior approach.

Some rise in government expenditure as a percentage of total domestic expenditure or GNP should be expected because of the different productivity rates by which output in the two sectors of the economy, public and private, expands. Following the seminal work by Baumol (1967) it is conventional to identify the less technologically 'progressive' sector with the public sector and the more 'progressive' sector with the private sector (see also Baumol and Oates, 1975, ch. 17). It is assumed that productivity in the public sector lags behind productivity in the private sector, with the result that for the ratio of government expenditure to total domestic expenditure to remain constant over time, when both variables are measured in real terms, a rising proportion of national resources must be devoted to the public sector. At the same time, and for the same reason when the two variables are measured in nominal terms, the same ratio will be expected to rise through time.

In addition to the above, since most of public-sector output is non-marketed, and therefore no pricing takes place, measurement of it in real terms is based on the assumption that it tends to change in proportion to input changes. It is clear that such an assumption implies an aggregate production function for the public sector which is characterised by constant returns to scale and a zero productivity rate. Since a positive rate of productivity is more likely to occur this assumption results in an underestimation of the volume of output of the public sector, and an excessive increase in its implied 'price'. The importance of this factor, which is generally known as the 'relative price effect', in explaining the rise of the government expenditure ratio in the last twenty years is illustrated by the observation that while the deflator for total domestic expenditure rose from 100 in 1955 to 435 in 1977 the corresponding deflator for resource-using government expenditure, for the same period, has risen from 100 to 595.[4] Baumol and Oates (1975, p. 238) introduce a discussion of this important factor as follows:

> Many observers attribute rapidly increasing public expenditures to corruption or inefficiency in the public sector. Although there is, no doubt, some truth to these contentions, we will argue that the technological characteristics of many public services (even in a perfectly efficient and virtuous government sector) imply that their costs will rise more rapidly than the general level of prices.

Peacock and Wiseman (1979, p. 11) suggest that Baumol's theory of unbalanced growth can be thought of as 'the modern counterpart of Wagner's famous Law of Increasing State Activity'. Although an important consideration in explaining expanding state activity, the relative price effect does not by itself explain the behaviour of either the state or the consumers of the state's services. One would like an explanation of the response of these economic agents to the trend of the relative cost of public policies.

Finally, Baran and Sweezy (1966) in their analysis of 'monopoly capitalism' suggest that the expanding activity of the capitalist state is the result of the system's inability to generate sufficient 'effective demand' to ensure full utilisation of either labour or productive facilities; hence governments are expected to intervene and create additional effective demand by absorbing part of the continually mounting volume of surplus which could not be absorbed through private channels. In their own words: 'Given the inability of monopoly capitalism to provide private uses for the surplus which it can easily generate, there can be no doubt that it is to the interest of all classes - though not of all elements within them - that government should steadily increase its spending and its taxing' (Baran and Sweezy, 1966, p. 153). In the same tradition O'Connor (1973), in his development of the thesis of a 'fiscal crisis' of the state, suggests that in addition to the widening gap between aggregate effective demand and productive capacity, which leads to an expansion of social and defence expenses by the state, the expansion of the state sector is also necessary due to the growing socialisation of production which necessitates greater state intervention, in the form of provision of social capital to the monopoly sector, to ensure private accumulation and sufficient profitability.

The 'crisis of profitability', as an alternative to the under-consumption thesis, is a recurrent theme in Marxist explanations of growing state expenditure. As it is obvious from this short reference to a vast literature on this subject, a common element of the Marxist views on the economic activity of the state is their close association with Marxist theories of economic crises. Furthermore, in the Marxist and radical traditions the immediate causes of the growth of public expenditure is considered as a secondary problem, usually studied as a by-product of theoretical explanations of the state and its role in contemporary society (Gough, 1979, p. 84).

SIZE AND COMPOSITION OF GOVERNMENT EXPENDITURE, 1955-77

In what follows we examine the size and composition of government expenditure for the period 1955-77. This will provide useful background information to be used when regression analysis is employed to study the determinants of government expenditure.

When measured at current prices the ratio of total general government expenditure to total domestic expenditure increased from 33.1 per cent in 1955 to 44.7 per cent in 1977, with an over-all average rate of change of 1.4 per cent. But considering individual years it is observed that this increase was far from being evenly spread over the sample period. There was a considerable variation in annual rates of change, with a maximum increase of 10.2 per cent in 1974 and a maximum decrease of 5.1 in 1977. The over-all variation is clearly much greater than the corresponding variability of other national accounting aggregates when expressed as percentages of national income or domestic expenditure.

An examination of the pattern of change that emerges suggests that there is a different attitude towards government expenditure by the two major political parties (see Figures 6.1 and 6.2). In contrast, for example, to a relatively slow rate of growth during the Conservative rule in 1955-64, when the ratio rose by only 7.5 per cent, the subsequent six years of Labour rule led to a rise of over 15 per cent. Also, while the 1970-4 Conservative government maintained a relatively stable ratio, the same ratio increased exceptionally rapidly immediately after the Labour takeover in 1974, with a rise of 18.7 per cent in a little less than two years. The period of the first postwar Labour government, i.e. that of 1945-51, was rather exceptional in that the ratio decreased from the very high level at which it stood during the war. But the series of total government expenditure as a percentage of GNP produced by Peacock and Wiseman (1961, p. 166) show that in a peacetime period the first Labour government (1929-31) under Ramsay MacDonald led to a rise in this percentage from 24 in 1929 to 29 in 1931. This increase was fully reversed by subsequent non-Labour governments for the rest

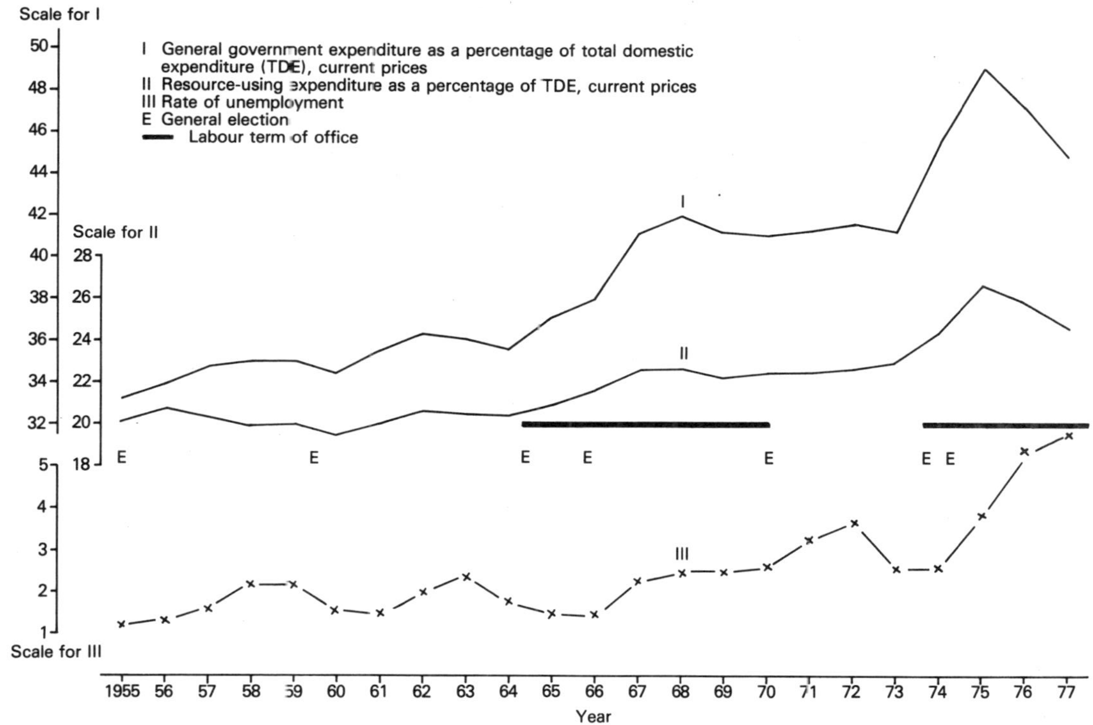
Scale for I
50
48
46
44
42
40
38
36
34
32
Scale for II
28
26
24
22
20
18
5
4
3
2
1
Scale for III
I General government expenditure as a percentage of total domestic expenditure (TDE), current prices
II Resource-using expenditure as a percentage of TDE, current prices
III Rate of unemployment
E General election
Labour term of office
I
II
III
E
1955
56
57
58
59
60
61
62
63
64
65
66
67
68
69
70
71
72
73
74
75
76
77
Year

Figure 6.1

As Figure 6.1, but variables measured at constant (1970) prices

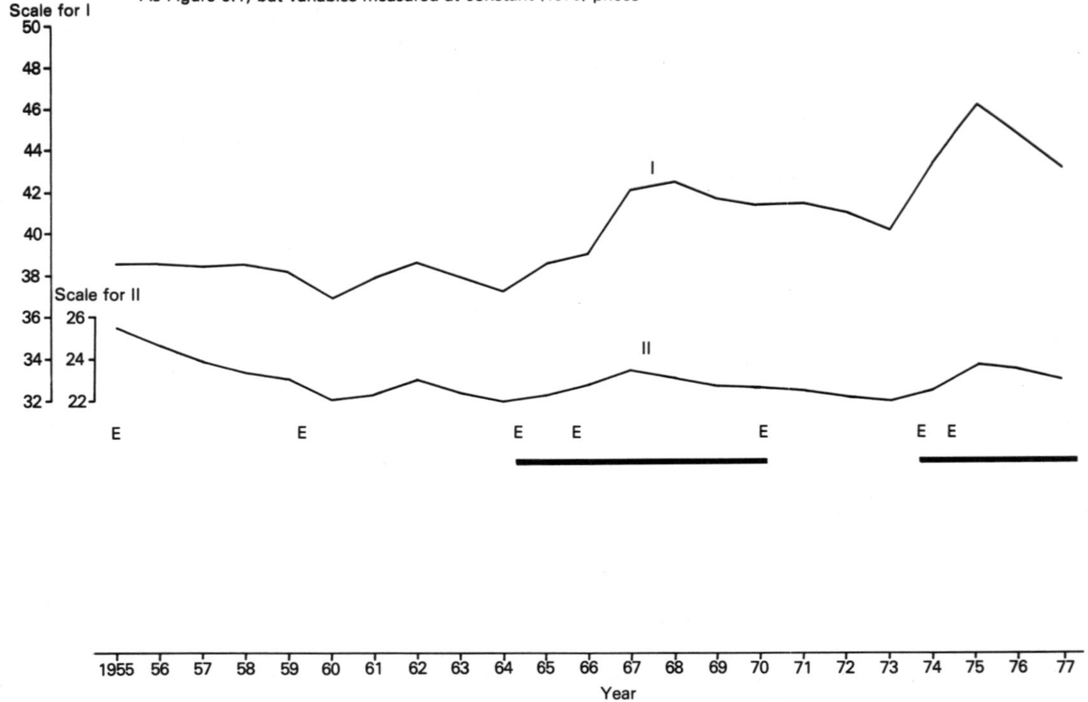

Figure 6.2

of the mid-war period. A further observation is that the bulk of the rise in government expenditure during a Labour administration tends to occur immediately after the resumption of office. It can be argued, for example, that the increasing radicalism which usually characterises the Labour Party when in opposition is injected in new policies after the electoral victory but gradually gives way in the face of intensifying economic problems, especially a balance-of-payments deficit. According to an economic adviser to the Labour government of 1964-7:

> Active Labour supporters, for example, who work for the return of a Labour government so that it may change society, argue that the first year or two is the time when it fights to put its principles into practice, and the latter period is when it surrenders to the forces of reaction, worn down and outmanoeuvred by the civil service. This view is not without some validity, particularly where it is a question of Labour's egalitarian policies for income distribution and the social services (Stewart, 1977, p. 245).

It is also argued that, in general, incoming governments, whether Labour or Conservative, in their first year or two tend to abolish or modify drastically the measures enacted by the previous government and repudiated by them when in opposition. In the wilderness of opposition a party turns into an irresponsible Mr Hyde who gives way to the virtuous Dr Jekyll only after the first year or two of resumption of power (Stewart, 1977, p. 4). The same ideas are expressed succinctly by Shanks (1977, pp. 91-2):

> Since Britain's basic problem is perceived as being economic weakness, the parliamentary opposition is always under pressure to distance itself from the government's economic policy and develop its own alternative strategy which can be put to the voters. Thus every new government brings in new policies, which usually have to be altered after two years (Labour in 1966 and again in 1975, the Conservatives in 1972), when they are seen to be irrelevant to the problems facing the country; problems of which no opposition party can hope to be fully informed. The situation is worsened by the fact that our two main political parties tend to identify, in opposition especially, with capital and labour respectively; thus not only their ideas but their values tend to differ.

This suggested pattern of behaviour seems to be consistent with the timing of significant changes in government expenditure as illustrated in Figures 6.1 and 6.2. Looking at the over-all pattern it can be argued that here we can see a political displacement effect - a structural break caused by the swing of the political pendulum. People are aware that the extent of government intervention in the economy is likely to be considerably greater with a Labour rather than with a Conservative government. When they therefore vote for a Labour government they take into account this prospect and it is in the light of this anticipation that they are likely to tolerate higher tax burdens. This is an extension, and not a rejection, of Peacock and Wiseman's analysis which has been applied to observed structural breaks caused by wars and other 'large-scale disturbances'. It seems that displacement effects caused by changes in government are more important in explaining the postwar experience.

Looking at the composition of general government expenditure it can be seen that the resource-using component, i.e. consumption plus investment, as a percentage of the total declined from 60.6 in 1955 to 55 in 1977. Up to 1974 this was exclusively due to the steady relative decline in consumption, while investment's relative importance increased, especially in the period 1964-70. However, after 1974 this pattern was reversed. It is, for example, noteworthy that the two periods 1965-7 and 1974-5, over which government expenditure rises more than in any other postwar period, were so dissimilar when the composition of such expenditure is considered. In 1965-7 it is investment and capital grants that rise the most, with consumption experiencing a relative decline. In contrast, in 1974-5 exactly the opposite happened. This difference is of course partly due to the introduction of the capital-grants scheme by the 1966 Labour government and the huge increases of public employees' salaries in 1974-5. But for the whole of the sample period both individually and jointly consumption and investment increased in relation to total domestic expenditure (TDE) from 20.1 per cent in 1955 to 24.6 per cent in 1977. (As expected, in comparison with the over-all ratio, this ratio was characterised by a smaller variability.) But the most rapidly rising component was capital transfers, with nearly the whole of this increase occurring in 1967-9, followed by current grants and subsidies. Thus over the whole period the composition of government expenditure changed in favour of transfer payments and against direct uses of resources by the state.

When TDE and government expenditure (GEX) are now measured at constant (1970) prices the picture that emerges is considerably different (Figure 6.2). First, over the same period the ratio of GEX to TDE rises from 38.6 to 43.0 per cent, which is a significantly smaller rise than in the case of current-prices valuation. Second, resource-using expenditure as a ratio of TDE declines from 25.6 per cent in 1955 to 23 per cent by 1959, around which point it remains for the rest of the period. Thus the rise in the over-all expenditure ratio is entirely attributed to the rise in non-resource-using expenditure, especially transfer payments, which went up from 13 per cent in 1955 to 20.1 per cent in 1977.

Turning now to a functional analysis of GEX we observe that the major changes are, first, the spectacular decline in the percentage of total expenditure devoted to defence, and second, the tremendous expansion of spending on social services, especially education, the personal social services and social security benefits. Of the rest, expenditure on housing and environmental services has tended to increase by more than the over-all average rate since 1972, while expenditure on employment services is characterised by very rapid rises after 1965.

Considering the above observations, which are partly illustrated in Figures 6.1 and 6.2, the following conclusions can be drawn: (i) the increase in the ratio of resource-using expenditure to TDE is entirely due to the relative price effect - when constant-prices valuation is used the ratio after an early decline in 1955-9 remains relatively constant; (ii) the increase in GEX in relation to TDE at constant prices is entirely due to a rapid increase in transfer payments; (iii) the rise in the relative importance of GEX occurs mainly during the first two years of each of the Labour governments which came into power in 1964, 1966 and 1974 - the 1970-4 Conservative government, despite its promises, failed to reverse this process; (iv) the major changes in the composition of GEX consist of a rapid and continuous fall in the relative importance of spending on defence and a significant increase in expenditure on social services; (v) the evidence does not suggest the presence of a political cycle *à la* Nordhaus - a preliminary examination of fluctuations in the share of government expenditure indicates that neither unemployment nor government expenditure exhibits changes which comply with the scenario implied by the political business cycle. This is confirmed in the studies by Chrystal and Alt (1979a, 1979b), in which, after an exhaustive search, the authors conclude that the evidence does not support the presence of a political business cycle in the UK economy. The lack of statistical significance of a pre-election dummy variable in our regression results - discussed later in this chapter - points to the same conclusion. This does not of course mean that governments do not prefer to fight elections at times when both unemployment and inflation are low. It means, though, that for various reasons they do not always manage to do so. Occasionally, for example, governments were forced to have the election before the end of the electoral calendar, according to the Constitution. It may also be that parties attribute to voters a much more sophisticated behaviour than the one hypothesised by exponents of the political cycle.

DETERMINANTS OF GOVERNMENT EXPENDITURE

Having discussed the various hypotheses on the development of government expenditure we can now, using regression analysis, attempt to provide a formal explanation of changes in the major expenditure components for the period under examination. We begin by splitting total government expenditure as follows:

$$(GEX)_t = (GCI)_t + (GT)_t + (NLG)_t \tag{6.1}$$

where GCI = general government consumption plus investment, GT = general government transfers, and NLG = general government lending.

We attempt to estimate GCI and GT as ratios of gross domestic product at market prices (GDPM), which we label as follows:

$$(RGCIM)_t = \left(\frac{GCI}{GDPM}\right)_t$$

and

$$(\text{RGTM})_t = \left(\frac{\text{GT}}{\text{GDPM}}\right)_t$$

with NLG being treated as completely exogenous. The following explanatory variables will be considered:

(1) *The relative price effect.* As explained above there is a tendency of the cost of many public services to increase more rapidly than the general price level. In addition to the basic factor, i.e. relatively low productivity, it should be added that the ratio of public consumption and investment (CGI) to gross domestic product at market prices (GDPM) - denoted RGCIM - will tend to rise whenever the price of inputs to the various public-sector programmes tends to rise more than the general price level. An example of this kind of effect was the very high rise in the cost of housing in the early 1970s. Expenditure on housing in the public sector is relatively greater than final expenditure on housing in the economy as a whole. The result of this, *ceteris paribus*, is to inflate RGCIM. We measure the total relative price effect in terms of the ratio of two deflators - the GCI deflator (GCID) and the GDPM deflator (PMD). The ratio of the former to the latter rose by 21.6 per cent over the period 1955-77. (As indicated in the preceding section this is the result of the assumption of relatively low productivity in the public sector, but also of the difficulty in observing and measuring such productivity.) It should be noted, however, that this is a technological variable and does not in any way account for the behaviour of the economic agents under study.

(2) *Unemployment.* An increase in unemployment is expected to inflate RGCIM and RGTM, through higher unemployment and unemployment-related benefits. Also for the period in question governments were expected to be less reluctant to increase public expenditure during periods of low economic activity and high unemployment rates. (It should be remembered that unemployment was characterised by an upward trend during 1955-77.) This is a rather weak assumption which does not depend on any specific stand on whether governments were committed to a policy of full employment or whether government policies were destabilising.

(3) *Political parties' attitudes towards government expenditure.* It is a fact of British politics that the attitude of the two major political parties towards government expenditure is different. This is of course not incidental. Despite repeated and consolidated compromises to the practice of a mixed economy Conservatives tend to believe that the free-enterprise competitive system, with as little government interference as possible, is the best way of optimising people's welfare. On the other hand, members of the Labour movement believe that systematic and manifold intervention by the state is necessary in order to ameliorate the effects of the defects and excesses of the capitalist system. Although there has been a considerable convergence towards the centre, it is still true that Conservatives in general are much closer to the principle of '*laissez-faire, laissez-passer*' than Labourites. Many of the latter

aspire to a fully fledged democratic socialist society. These differences are reflected in their pronouncements and policy record on government expenditure. To account for the political break a shift dummy variable is used - for some evidence on the relationship between the growth of the public sector and the political ideology of the party in government see Tufte (1978, pp. 96-100). This dummy (DV) takes the value of 1.0 for years of Labour administration and zero otherwise.

(4) *A demographic variable.* The expansion of the public sector in 1955-75 can be at least partly attributed to the rise in the percentage of the population who are relatively more dependent on the state. In this period total population increased by 9.4 per cent, while the numbers of persons under 15 and over 64 years of age increased by 11.8 and 35.8 per cent respectively. These two categories of persons constituted 34.1 per cent of the population in 1955 and 37.3 per cent in 1975. Also, only in the decade 1964-74, the number of full-time pupils on register increased by 26.1 per cent and the total number of students by 27 per cent. We thus employ a demographic variable (DEMO) which registers the number of persons under 15 and over 64 as a percentage of the total population. In the case of RGCIM we find that the demographic variable (DEM) is preferable inasmuch as it works more satisfactorily in terms of the sign of its coefficient and its statistical significance. DEM is defined as $0.5\,[(\mathrm{DEMO})_t + (\mathrm{DEMO})_{t-1}]$. (For a study which employs a series of demographic variables, see Kelley, 1976.)

(5) *The rate of inflation.* It can be argued that the presence of a fiscal drag, i.e. the tendency for the total yield of taxes to grow at a faster rate than money incomes when the income-tax system is progressive, combined with the permanent pressure on the authorities to expand the size and range of public programmes, could result, during a period of high rates of inflation and therefore a high rise in money incomes, in a more than proportional increase of public expenditures. Furthermore, while there are reasons to believe that expenditure of the personal sector is depressed as inflation rises, the procedure by which government expenditures are planned provides for a full coverage of rising costs due to inflation (Stewart, 1977, pp. 223-4). Finally, it has been established that inflation has a depressing effect on private spending (Davidson *et al.*, 1978; Hendry and Ungern-Sternberg, 1980). It should therefore be expected that the ratio of government spending to total spending will tend to rise with inflation. In this context it is assumed that the causal direction is from inflation to government expenditure. It has been argued (Peacock and Ricketts, 1978) that there is more than one way by which an opposite 'causation' can be supported. There is of course no *a priori* reason for which a double-directional action should be rejected. It has been suggested, for example, that an increase in government expenditure accompanied by a rise in taxation leads to a rise in wages and, therefore, prices as workers attempt to maintain the level of their take-home earnings. Furthermore, increases in expenditure financed through the printing of more money would,

according to monetarism, lead to a direct increase in the general price level.

(6) *Government expenditure rigidity.* In the early empirical work on government expenditure the standard procedure was to regress the ratio GEX to TDE on gross domestic product. A significant positive relationship was interpreted as a confirmation of Wagner's prediction. Furthermore, the same finding was occasionally taken as an indication that the income elasticity of demand for public goods and services was greater than unity. This of course was a very simplistic approach towards an explanation of expanding state activity because it abstracts from all other factors which influence the ratio GEX to TDE. In the context of the more sophisticated regression we use, the influence of GDPR on RGCIM and RGTM is not so straightforward. The most likely outcome is a negative coefficient, reflecting a cyclical behaviour for RGCIM according to which it tends to rise during the downswing of the cycle and to fall during the opposite phase of the cycle. This is so since planning of government expenditure is done over a number of years on the basis of an average predicted rate of growth of real gross domestic product (GDPR). As a result RGCIM will tend to decline when GDPR rises faster than average and increase when it rises slower than average. According to the regression results, in the case of government transfers no such cyclical behaviour should be expected to prevail, in which case the ratio RGTM would be positively related to changes in GDPR in conformity with the view of an income elasticity greater than unity (Kelley, 1976, also finds a negative income elasticity in a study which uses a set of demographic variables as regressors).

The equations to be estimated, then, take the following form:

$$(RGCIM)_t = r_0 + r_1(UNER)_t + r_2(GDPR)_t + r_3\left(\frac{GCID}{PMD}\right)_t + r_4(DV)_t + r_5(DEM)_t \qquad (6.2)$$

where UNER = unemployment rate and the rest of the variables are as defined above, with the following equation

$$(GCI)_t = (RGCIM)_t \times (GDPM)_t \qquad (6.3)$$

determining GCI. We also have

$$(RGTM)_t = s_0 + s_1(UNER)_t + s_2(GDPR)_t + s_3(RPD)_t + s_4(DV)_t + s_5(DEMO)_t \qquad (6.4)$$

where RPD = the rate of inflation, with

$$(GT)_t = (RGTM)_t \times (GDPM)_t \qquad (6.5)$$

defining GT. For completeness we also define GDPM:

$$(GDPM)_t = (GDPN)_t + (ITAX)_t - (SUB)_t \qquad (6.6)$$

where GDPN is the gross domestic product at current prices and factor cost, defined as

$$(GDPN)_t = (GDPR)_t \times (PD)_t \tag{6.7}$$

where PD is the GDP price deflator and ITAX and SUB are indirect taxes and subsidies respectively. Finally, GDPR is defined as follows:

$$(GDPR)_t = (CONR)_t + (IP)_t + (STB)_t + (IPC)_t + \left(\frac{GCI}{GCID}\right)_t + (XR)_t - (QR)_t - \left(\frac{ITAX}{PITD}\right)_t + \left(\frac{SUB}{PSUBD}\right)_t \tag{6.8}$$

where CONR, IP, STB, IPC, XR, QR are, respectively, real consumption, private fixed investment, stockbuilding, investment by public corporations, exports and imports, with PITD as an implicit deflator for indirect taxes, PSUBD as an implicit deflator for subsidies, and GCID as an implicit deflator for government consumption plus investment.

DETERMINANTS OF GOVERNMENT REVENUE

Government expenditure is one side of the budget constraint as used in our model. Government revenue is the main expenditure counterpart. It therefore seems wise to provide some analysis of government revenue, which (like government expenditure) is treated as endogenous. The following is an attempt to relate government revenue to relevant changes in the rest of the economy. Its rudimentary nature reflects the paucity of the treatment of this aspect of government activity in the rest of the UK models. In our model the following relationships determine the absolute values of direct and indirect tax revenue, while the corresponding tax rates are treated as exogenous variables. Total government taxes (TAX) is defined as

$$(TAX)_t = (ITAX)_t + (DTAXP)_t + (ODTAX)_t \tag{6.9}$$

where ITAX is indirect taxes, DTAXP is direct taxes of the personal sector, and ODTAX is other direct taxes, treated as exogenous.

Indirect taxes are hypothesised to depend on total domestic expenditure (TDE) and the dummy variable (DV) as defined above. So we have

$$(ITAX)_t = i_0 + i_1(TDE)_t + i_2(DV)_t \tag{6.10}$$

with

$$(TDE)_t = (GDPM)_t - [(XR)_t \times (PXD)_t] + [(QR)_t \times (PQD)_t] - (ITAX)_t + (SUB)_t \tag{6.11}$$

where XR is real exports, PXD is the implicit price deflator for exports, QR is real imports, and PQD is the implicit price deflator for imports.

Direct taxes of the personal sector are specified as

$$(DTAXP)_t = d_0 + d_1(CPY)_t + d_2(RPD)_t \tag{6.12}$$

where RPD is the rate of change of the GDP price deflator, and

$$(CPY)_t = (TAXR)_t \times (PY)_t \tag{6.13}$$

so that when personal income (PY) is multiplied by a weighted average of the basic income-tax rate (TAXR) the variable (CPY) is arrived at. In addition

$$(PY)_t = (EY)_t + (NIBG)_t \tag{6.14}$$

where EY stands for earned income and NIBG for national insurance benefits and other current grants from general government. The latter variable is treated as exogenous, while the former is endogenised as follows:

$$(EY)_t = e_0 + e_1(GDPN)_t + e_2(EMPL)_t \tag{6.15}$$

where EMPL stands for employment (as defined in Chapter 7).

Finally, disposable income (YD) is obtained according to the following identity:

$$(YD)_t = (PY)_t - (DTAXP)_t - (NIC)_t - (NTA)_t \tag{6.16}$$

with NIC being national insurance contributions, and NTA net transfers from abroad, both being treated as exogenous.

EMPIRICAL EVIDENCE

The estimated forms when employing the technique of instrumental variables appear in Table 6.1. Concentrating on this table we observe that all the variables appear to have a statistically significant influence on the dependent variables, with the coefficients possessing the expected signs. Another striking feature of all the estimated equations is the very low standard error of estimate as a percentage of the mean value of the dependent variables, as well as the low values of the χ^2-statistics and the F-statistic. All in all the over-all performance of the equations, when assessed using all the statistical criteria, seems to be remarkably good.

In the case of the government transfers ratio, GDP seems to be the most important explanatory factor in that it explains 50 per cent of its rise between 1958 and 1978; the next most important factor is unemployment, followed by the political dummy, with both inflation and the demographic variable having a very minor influence. In the case of resource-using expenditure, and for the same period, the relative price effect, GDP and the demographic variable seem to play prominent roles. It should be clear, however, that to the extent that the regressors exhibit considerable variability,

Table 6.1

$$(GEX)_t = (GCI)_t + (GT)_t + (NLG)_t$$

$$(RGCIM)_t = \underset{(3.02)}{-\ 0.299} + \underset{(2.58)}{0.006}\ [(UNER)_t - (UNER)_{t-1}] - \underset{(3.12)}{0.002}\ (GDPR)_t$$
$$+ \underset{(2.68)}{0.007}\ (DV)_t + \underset{(3.48)}{0.011}\ (DEM)_t + \underset{(5.65)}{0.207} \left(\frac{GCID}{PMD}\right)_t$$

$$D\text{-}W = 1.59,\ S = 0.005,\ S/ME = 0.021,\ \chi_2^2(5) = 5.47,$$
$$\chi_3^2(1) = 1.82,\ F(1,14) = 0.70$$

$$(GCI)_t = (RGCIM)_t \times (GDPM)_t$$

$$(RGTM)_t = \underset{(3.15)}{0.006}\ (UNER)_t + \underset{(1.93)}{0.001}\ (RPD)_t + \underset{(3.32)}{0.002}\ (GDPR)_t$$
$$+ \underset{(2.94)}{0.010}\ (DV)_t + \underset{(3.82)}{0.002}\ (DEMO)_t$$

$$D\text{-}W = 1.33,\ S = 0.006,\ S/ME = 0.042,\ \chi_2^2(8) = 7.62,$$
$$\chi_3^2(1) = 1.04,\ F(1,15) = 0.66$$

$$(GT)_t = (RGTM)_t \times (GDPM)_t$$

$$(GDPM)_t = (GDPN)_t + (ITAX)_t - (SUB)_t$$

$$(GDPN)_t = (GDPR)_t \times (PD)_t$$

$$(GDPR)_t = (CONR)_t + (IP)_t + (STB)_t + (IPC)_t + \left(\frac{GCI}{GCID}\right)_t + (XR)_t$$
$$- (QR)_t - \left(\frac{ITAX}{PITD}\right)_t + \left(\frac{SUB}{PSUBD}\right)_t$$

$$(TAX)_t = (ITAX)_t + (DTAXP)_t + (ODTAX)_t$$

$$(ITAX)_t = \underset{(8.30)}{-\ 0.534} + \underset{(8.27)}{0.065}\ (TDE)_{t-1} + \underset{(3.71)}{0.311}\ (DV)_t + \underset{(15.11)}{0.773}\ (ITAX)_{t-1}$$

$$\rho = \underset{(2.01)}{-\ 0.471},\ S = 0.218,\ S/ME = 0.026,\ \chi_1^2(2) = 5.51,$$

$$\chi_3^2(1) = 0.02,\ F(1,15) = 0.01$$

$$(TDE)_t = (GDPM)_t - [(XR)_t \times (PXD)_t] + [(QR)_t \times (PQD)_t] - (ITAX)_t + (SUB)_t$$

$$(DTAXP)_t = \underset{(5.99)}{0.284} [(CPY)_t - (CPY)_{t-1}] + \underset{(4.24)}{0.070} (RPD)_t + \underset{(2.78)}{0.034} [(RPD)_{t-1} - (RPD)_{t-2}] + \underset{(65.30)}{0.969} (DTAXP)_{t-1}$$

D-W = 1.78, S = 0.215, S/ME = 0.031, $\chi_2^2(4) = 4.77$, $\chi_3^2(1) = 0.002$, F(1,16) = 0.001

$$(CPY)_t = (TAXR)_t \times (PY)_t$$

$$(PY)_t = (EY)_t + (NIBG)_t$$

$$(EY)_t = -\underset{(1.72)}{16.832} + \underset{(16.46)}{1.296} (GDPN)_t - \underset{(4.94)}{0.463} (GDPN)_{t-1} + \underset{(1.74)}{0.766} (EMPL)_t$$

D-W = 2.28, S = 0.699, S/ME = 0.015, $\chi_2^2(8) = 13.63$, $\chi_3^2(1) = 1.37$, F(1,16) = 0.67

$$(YD)_t = (PY)_t - (DTAXP)_t - (NIC)_t - (NTA)_t$$

---

observations about their quantitative importance are critically dependent upon the beginning and the end of the period used for comparison.

In conclusion, then, it can be said that the substantial relative expansion of government expenditure in the postwar period can be attributed, first, to the tendency of the cost of public goods and services to rise more rapidly than the cost of private goods and services, and second, the tolerance of this development by both governments and the active promotion of a bigger public sector by Labour governments. The latter policy was (i) inspired by the Labour Party's lack of trust in the power of the 'invisible hand' to solve the problems of the UK economy (unemployment, unacceptable inequality in the distribution of income, regional differences), and (ii) accepted as a natural consequence of demographic developments (an increasing percentage of retired population) and a rising level of unemployment, especially in the 1970s. For the period in question Conservative governments failed to reverse the expansion of public expenditures which took place during the Labour terms of office.

The preceding analysis and supporting evidence suggest that the political ideology of the ruling political party, especially in the light of the UK political setting, constitutes a fundamental factor in understanding the development of public expenditures and revenues in the postwar period. Therefore, irrespective of the particular strand of economic analysis adopted, to neglect this political element would seem to be significantly costly in its consequences. At the same time, this element, in combination with a more broadly defined ideological element, as well as changing economic prescriptions, should be expected to render the government expenditures and revenues relationships more unstable than the rest of the model.

7

Inflation and Unemployment

Inflation may be conveniently defined as a sustained tendency for the general level of prices to rise. Perhaps this is the most obvious, but by no means the only, definition. In the 'quantity theory' tradition inflation is defined as an increase in the quantity of money at a faster rate than the increase in real national product; in the 'Keynesian' tradition inflation is often defined as an excess of aggregate demand over full-employment supply. These latter definitions, however, are weak in that they attempt to define inflation in terms of its possible causes without directly referring to the phenomenon to be explained.

Defining inflation as a sustained rise in prices implies that certain price increases may not be regarded as inflationary: a crop failure, for example, is normally accompanied by some price increases to 'clear' the market; similarly, an increase in import prices arising from a revaluation of the currency of a major UK-supplier country would constitute a once-for-all adjustment in the price level. In all these cases the rise in prices ought not to be viewed as inflationary since the chronic, self-sustaining character of inflation is completely absent.

A problem arises when one comes to considering what index numbers of prices should be utilised to indicate the existence of inflation. There is the retail price index as well as that of wholesale prices; there is also the implicit GDP deflator, which includes the prices of all 'final' goods and services entering gross domestic product. The problem is that each index may give a different measure of the rate of inflation; indeed, there exists the possibility of one of them rising while others show no change. Moreover, even if all indices moved exactly in step with one another, there may still be biases due to the way they are constructed. In particular, most price indices do not adequately take account of improvements in the quality of goods, nor do they incorporate satisfactorily the behaviour of prices of new goods. When new goods come on to the market they command higher prices than when they, at a later stage, become mass produced; price indices do not include the prices of new products until after they have become mass produced, which implies, of course, that the initial phase of falling prices is not reflected in whatever index is utilised. There is therefore the danger that price indices may indicate inflation where, in fact, it does not genuinely exist.

These problems may very well have been present during the period under examination. Assuming, however, that the introduced bias remains relatively constant, they do not constitute a real difficulty in the case where one is concerned with changes in the level of inflation. While it is true to say that up to 1959 inflation persisted at relatively low rates, and, indeed, appeared to be tailing off in 1959, it became obvious by 1966 that the inflation rate quickened, and after 1967 began to accelerate. By the early 1970s it had developed into a world-wide price explosion; and the situation has not much improved since. It is not at all surprising, then, that since the mid-1960s accelerating inflation has provoked a heated theoretical and empirical debate among economists encompassing all aspects of the phenomenon - its causes, consequences and possible cures.

The inflationary process of this period has been characterised by an important change in its nature: namely, that for the first time since 1939 rising inflation has been accompanied by increasing unemployment. Before 1914 an unemployment rate of 5 per cent was regarded as normal; in the interwar years the average rate of unemployment was approximately 10 per cent. Successive postwar governments have accepted a commitment to maintain full employment, which by the late 1940s was regarded as being about 3 per cent unemployment. Over the period 1948-74 an unemployment rate of over 3 per cent was unusual, and was only registered in two years, 1971 and 1972; however, since 1974 the unemployment rate has not fallen below 4 per cent. During the 1950s the average rate of unemployment was lower than 1.5 per cent and this experience of a protracted period of high and stable level of employment gave rise to the notion that a 1.5 per cent unemployment figure was almost the official 'norm' for full employment. As unemployment rose above 2 per cent, as it did in 1958-9 and in 1962-3, political pressures were applied to raise aggregate demand to reduce the 'unacceptably' high level of unemployment. During the 1960s the desire to mitigate inflation, particularly from the viewpoint of securing an appropriate external balance, led to the popularisation of the results of the Phillips-curve analysis. This purported to show a trade-off of the rate of unemployment against the rate of inflation, and raised the unofficial norm for 'acceptable' unemployment to about 2.25 per cent. The higher levels of inflation and of unemployment experienced in the 1970s have cast doubt on the possibility of trading off less inflation for more unemployment. It has also created a situation where even a 3 per cent level of unemployment may be regarded as too low for a full-employment 'norm' if there is to be a stable price level.

It should be observed that, not unlike inflation, measurements of unemployment are subject to error. The official statistics, for example, are based on registered unemployment, and hence the degree of reliability of published rates of unemployment depends on whether the rate of registration is close to unity and relatively stable. Evidence so far suggests that the registration rate of female unemployment is markedly unstable. In addition, part-time employment, especially in the case of the female population, has undergone substantial changes in the 1960s and 1970s. Given that these developments are not satisfactorily reflected in changes in the registration of unemployment, the over-all rates of official unemployment are not fully reliable. Notwithstanding these and other reservations the official statistics are the best, consistent, long-run indicators of changes in over-all unemployment rates, however approximate.

THEORETICAL CONSIDERATIONS

It is only since the end of the Second World War that most governments have attempted to influence the level of aggregate demand in the economy with the specific aim of maintaining or restoring acceptable levels of employment and relatively low levels of inflation. Prior to the Second World War (and especially before the publication of Keynes's *General Theory* in 1936) the predominant view was that unemployment and inflation could only be temporary phenomena, since market forces would always ensure the return of the economy to non-inflationary full employment. The Keynesian revolution in economic theory, with its emphasis on aggregate effective demand as a determinant of output and employment, has provided the theoretical background to the possibility of the economy resting at an under-employment equilibrium position - with what one might call *demand-deficient* unemployment. This can arise because aggregate effective demand is not sufficient to ensure full utilisation of the whole labour force of the economy. Thus the policy prescription of the standard, simple, Keynesian macroeconomic model is that fiscal and monetary policies should be used extensively to stimulate aggregate demand to restore non-inflationary full employment.

In this model, however, there is a strict dichotomy between behaviour at full employment and behaviour at less than full employment (Lipsey, 1978, p. 49). At less than full employment the price level is assumed to be fixed, and disturbances to the system are allowed to affect real income and employment - whereas at full employment it is real variables which are assumed given, so that disturbances to the system affect the price level only. This dichotomy is removed through the incorporation of the famous 'Phillips-curve' relationship (Phillips, 1958; Lipsey, 1960),[1] which 'implies that lower unemployment can be purchased at the cost of higher inflation' (Tobin, 1972, p. 4). The policy implications of such a trade-off are clear enough. To the extent that there is such a trade-off between inflation and unemployment, and a social welfare function could be chosen, then a point on the Phillips curve could be established which would represent the optimal combination available to policy-makers.

The empirical evidence clearly suggests the existence of a *short-run* trade-off between wage inflation and unemployment; but the evidence on the existence of a *long-run* trade-off is inconclusive. Parkin *et al.* (1976) have demonstrated that the Phillips model only retains its predictive capacity after 1967 if a variable approximating expectations of price changes is included along with unemployment as one of the explanatory variables. But this contention casts serious doubts on the existence of a long-run trade-off relation, for the expectations hypothesis flatly denies the possibility of a non-vertical Phillips relationship in the long run.

THE EXPECTATIONS HYPOTHESIS AND THE NATURAL RATE OF UNEMPLOYMENT

This hypothesis has been expounded by economists working within a more strictly neoclassical or monetarist tradition (see, for example, Friedman, 1968, 1975, 1977; Phelps, 1968). They argue that if policy-makers attempt to sustain a level of unemployment which does not coincide with the natural rate of unemployment (U^*),[2] they will, inevitably, plunge the economy into accelerating inflation if the target rate of unemployment is less than the natural rate, or into accelerating deflation if the target rate is greater than the natural rate. The argument may be clarified by referring to Figure 7.1, where $\dot{W}$ = rate of change of wages, $\dot{P}^e$ = expected rate of change of prices, and U = unemployment rate.

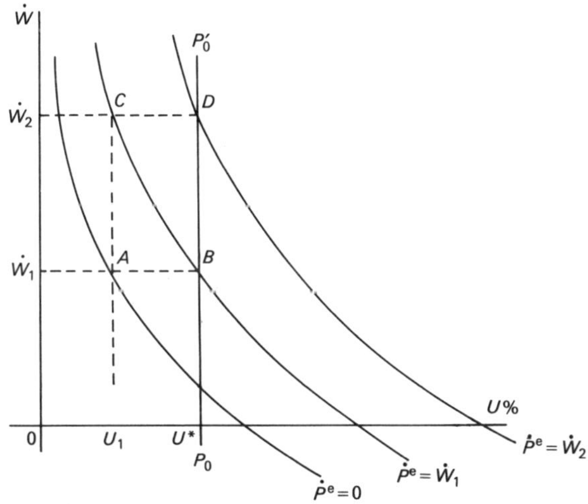

Figure 7.1

When anticipated or expected rates of inflation are taken into consideration, there is not one unique macro Phillips curve but instead a whole family of such curves with one curve for each expected rate of inflation. In Figure 7.1 three different trade-offs correspond to three different expected rates of inflation: $\dot{P}^e = 0$ when no price expectations prevail, $\dot{P}^e = \dot{W}_1$ and $\dot{P}^e = \dot{W}_2$ when $\dot{W}_1$ and

W_2 inflation rates are anticipated, respectively.

At the natural rate of unemployment U^* there is no inflation. If, now, the authorities reduced unemployment to U_1 by monetary expansion, then according to the Phillips-curve analysis a movement along the curve $\dot{P}^e = 0$ would produce $\dot{W}_1$ rate of increase in money wages - there is therefore a clear trade-off between inflation and unemployment. As soon as inflation begins to become positive, however, individuals and firms would start to expect future price increases and would take price expectations into consideration when entering into new contracts. If a real rate of wage increase of $\dot{W}_1$ is required, money wages would have to rise at a rate of $\dot{W}_1$ plus the expected rate of inflation and the short-run Phillips curve would shift upwards. To the extent that the actual rate of inflation is fully anticipated in wage bargains, money wage rates would have to increase to $\dot{W}_2 = 2\dot{W}_1$ to maintain the $\dot{W}_1$ real wages required to sustain an U_1 unemployment rate. If the authorities insist on maintaining the unemployment rate at U_1, through continuous monetary expansion, this process will continue, and the economy will eventually plunge into accelerating inflation (if U_1 were to the right of U^*, the result would of course be accelerating deflation). In contrast, if the authorities do not insist on maintaining U_1, the rising price level would reduce the real value of the money supply and unemployment would start rising towards its natural rate U^*. And when the rate of increase of the money supply is the same as the actual and expected rates of inflation unemployment would finally return to U^*. The economy would then arrive at point B on the new short-run Phillips curve $\dot{P}^e = \dot{W}_1$. Points like B and D trace the P_0P_0' relationship, which is the long-run Phillips curve; it is not a trade-off any more, rather it is vertical at U^*.

This theory can be expressed by the equation:

$$\dot{W} = f(U) + h\dot{P}^e \tag{7.1}$$

and for the 'natural-rate' hypothesis to hold the parameter h must be equal to unity. Thus the rate of money wage increase is determined by excess demand, proxied by the unemployment rate, plus the expected rate of inflation. When there is no excess demand the rate of increase of money wages would be equal to the expected rate of inflation; and when the latter is zero, wage inflation would also be zero. It follows that within the monetarist tradition inflation is caused by excess demand, which is mainly influenced by excessive monetary expansion and expected inflation rates.

The above analysis depends, of course, on inflation being fully anticipated, for if inflation is not fully anticipated, implying $h < 1$, the slope of the long-run Phillips curve would be steeper than that of the short-run curve, but it would be less than vertical. And in this case there would be a permanent trade-off between unemployment and inflation. The rationalisation here of h being less than 1.0 has been attributed to the original Keynesian idea of 'money illusion' prevailing in the supply of labour (Tobin, 1967).

Clearly the implications of the 'natural-rate' hypothesis for policy-makers are very strong indeed. First, inflationary policies which attempt to reduce unemployment below the equilibrium level (U^*) will eventually result in accelerating inflation and continuous disequilibrium. Second, no trade-off exists in the long run; but even in the short run 'Phillips curves result from misinformation and suboptimal adjustment to economic realities' (Santomero and Seater, 1978, p. 525). Acceptance, therefore, of this hypothesis implies that policy-makers are faced with a severe reduction in their policy options. A major implication of this analysis for mainstream economic theory has been the realisation of the lack of a rigorous microeconomic foundation of the theory of unemployment and inflation. This has led to the development of the so-called 'search theories' of unemployment, of which Phelps (1970) constitutes a representative approach. Most of these theories make the assumption that all unemployment is 'search unemployment', with the individual not being able to work and search simultaneously, so that when the individual embarks on search he is necessarily unemployed. With the further assumption that the individual attempts to maximise the present value of lifetime income, the individual's problem is to decide how long to search for, or equivalently to choose, an 'optimal reservation' (or 'acceptance') wage. If an offer is below the reservation wage, it is rejected, and search continues. If an offer is above the acceptance wage, it is accepted, employment begins, and search ends. The reservation wage is seen as that wage which equates the marginal costs and gains from search. If it is also assumed that the individual's perception of the rate of inflation lags behind the actual rate, then a Phillips-curve relationship emerges. An increase in the actual rate of inflation induces the individual to reduce his search and become employed, because he receives unexpectedly high wage offers, and as a result unemployment falls. Once, however, the individual's perceived rate of inflation equals the actual rate, the individual will have reverted to his original level of search and unemployment will have gone to its original rate. Thus an anticipated increase in the rate of inflation reduces unemployment temporarily, but ultimately leaves it unchanged. The short-run Phillips curve is negatively sloped and the long-run curve is vertical; there is no trade-off in the long run.

All these theories have come under severe attack. Perhaps the most important criticism derives from the inconsistency between search theory's implications and empirical observations. As Tobin (1972) has pointed out, in search-theoretic explanations of the Phillips curve all unemployment is assumed to be voluntary, with the important phenomenon of layoffs completely ignored. Furthermore, they are based on the background acceptance of 'clearing markets' and the tendency of the economy naturally to settle down at a full-employment equilibrium. This ignores any consideration of the institutional nature of the business sector, the segmentation of markets and the code of conduct of firms, i.e. ideas propounded by post-Keynesian or Marxist economists (for a guide see Eichner, 1979; also Akerlof, 1979). At a more empirical level there is the problem of the numerical value of h, where the evidence is rather inconclusive, ranging from the results provided by Solow (1969), who obtained an estimate for h of roughly 0.4, to the results of Saunders and Nobay (1972) and Parkin *et al.* (1976), who reported values for h which were close to 1.0. Cross and Laidler (1975) using data for twenty individual countries, found no evidence of a long-run trade-off for any country. However, according to Laidler and Parkin (1975), 'about half of the recent studies that have used this expectations hypothesis have generated a coefficient [on $\dot{P}^e$] significantly different from unity'. In addition, there is the undisputed observation that 'Although inflationary expectations have undoubtedly adjusted to the more rapid rates of inflation in the seventies, even the most casual observation of the economy shows that we are a very long way from a fully anticipated inflation' (Lipsey, 1978, p. 66). Furthermore, the natural-rate theories cannot yet explain why the postwar economy has experienced long periods for which the actual rate of unemployment has been greater than the natural rate without accelerating deflations at the same time, as such theorists would have us believe. Parkin *et al.* (1976) have produced estimates for the United Kingdom of approximately 2 per cent for the natural rate - in the US case the estimates are 5 and 6 per cent (Tobin, 1972). If this is a correct estimate, it then becomes very awkward to explain how the recent inflation has come about when the economy has been running below the natural rate, with the actual rate of unemployment rising to well over 2 per cent! In addition, it can be seen that although in the period 1950-65, when unemployment was very low, there were substantial positive rates of inflation, there were no signs of accelerating inflation.

Whereas these theories accept the possibility of a short-run Phillips curve, but not a long-run one, there exists a more 'radical' monetarist group, the so-called 'rational expectations' school,[3] that flatly denies the existence of both a short-run and a long-run Phillips curve. Quite briefly, the 'rational expectations' school argues that economic agents are rational and, as such, they are in a position to discern for themselves the 'correct theory' of what determines changes in the price level. All the determinants of inflation are known to, and understood by, the rational economic agents, who are supposed to possess all available information, including information about the likely course of economic policy. Prediction errors could of course arise when the economy is subject to random shocks, or indeed because economic agents possess incomplete or limited information about the inflationary mechanism. This situation, however, is unlikely to persist for long, for, since economic agents are rational, they are capable of quickly incorporating new experiences and information into their expectations, which implies that prediction errors are swiftly perceived and systematically eradicated. As a result economic agents form their expectations as accurately as possible, in that their price expectations are the same as those implied by the actual inflation-generating mechanism. Price expectations are therefore unbiased and the economy will always rapidly return to its long-run steady-state equilibrium, which must imply that no short-run or long-run Phillips curve exists.

The policy implications of 'rational expectations' are obvious. Rational economic agents can and do utilise their 'correct theory' to anticipate the impact of economic policies, so that when stabilisation actions by the authorities do occur they have no impact at all on real variables, since economic agents by making adjustments to nominal wages and prices will have neutralised in advance the effects of such actions. The only way policies can have even a short-run impact on real variables is for policy-makers to act in an unpredictable random fashion, in such a way that cannot be anticipated by the rational economic agents. We may refer to an example to clarify all these points. Suppose that the policy-makers announce their intention to increase the money stock, that economic agents are convinced that this increase will come about, and that the money stock does change eventually, as announced. Economic agents are supposed to react by increasing their price and wage expectations, in a way consistent with the price increases that are likely to come about from the monetary stimulus. Being rational, economic agents would actually correctly predict the price and wage changes induced by this policy and the result would be that real wages would not change, with neither employment nor output affected. The increase in the money supply would only cause inflation. If, however, policy-makers act in an unpredictable manner, they could cause changes in the real variables. But in this case they could very well induce economic agents to overestimate the inflationary impact of the policy action, so that producers may in the short run believe that the relative price of their product has fallen, and workers perceive a decline in their real wage. As a result employment and production might actually decline. But this result would not be in the intended direction and, in any case, it would be short-lived, since rational economic agents adjust their expectations in the proper direction as new information is gathered. To summarise, when rational expectations prevail, stabilisation policies are impotent, and even when they do affect real economic magnitudes not only is the impact of a short-run nature but it may not be in the intended direction.

Finally, despite the impact that this theory has had on the economics profession, it suffers none the less from some severe problems: one can argue that expectations are basically non-rational; that no costless procedure of gathering new information exists; that the private sector does not really acquire the same information as the authorities regarding the inflationary process; and that people do not really know enough about the operation of the economy and its structure, which, after all, is itself subject to unpredictable alterations (Friedman, 1979). But more important, the assumption that prices and the rate of inflation respond fully and immediately to anticipated policy changes implies complete denial of the possibility of prices being rigid and costly to adjust (Buiter, 1980). It also implies that workers always succeed in imposing on employers their perceived adjustments of wages irrespective of market structures.

KEYNESIAN UNEMPLOYMENT RECONSIDERED

A different reappraisal of unemployment theory has resulted from an attempt by a number of economists to rehabilitate Keynesian macroeconomics (Clower, 1965; Leijonhufvud, 1968; Barro and Grossman, 1976).

Consider the augmented Keynesian model (Blaug, 1973, p. 636) shown in Figure 7.2. In this model the 'notional' demand for labour, N^D, is a downward-sloping function of the real wage under the assumption of profit maximisation; the 'notional' supply of labour, N^S, is an upward-sloping function of the real wage under the assumption of utility maximisation. In the short run - the period in which labour is the only variable factor of production - labour requirements are related to output via the production function, $Y = Y(N)$. The LM and IS relationships determine the equilibrium level of output Y_1, which requires employment of N_1. In general equilibrium this level of employment corresponds to equilibrium in the labour market. In Figure 7.2 the 'notional' demand for labour is equal to the notional supply of labour at the real wage rate $(W/P)_1$. In the absence of general equilibrium, however, the 'effective' supply and demand curves - those that are relevant for actual trading in the economy -

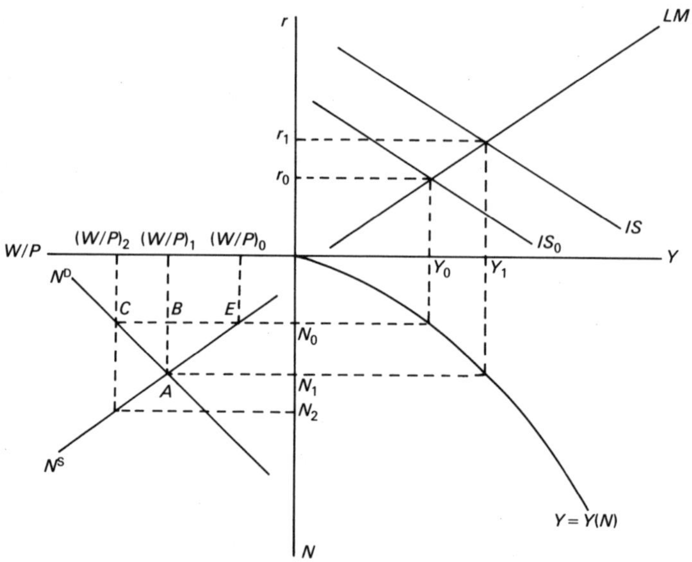

Figure 7.2

may be quite different from their 'notional' counterparts. We attempt to examine what happens in this case by assuming that the IS curve shifts to IS_0 - following an autonomous reduction in investment. The standard explanation of what would then happen is that, in the absence of any assumptions about wage rigidity, the whole process will rapidly be reversed by a fall in the average price level - operating through the well-known Pigou effect - and the labour market would never move away from equilibrium.

The real world, however, does not seem to work quite like this. When firms are faced with an unexpected reduction in demand, their reaction is first to build up inventories and second to reduce output and employment. Prices are not usually cut immediately. Moreover, since demand tends to fluctuate unpredictably, entrepreneurs are never sure whether a reduction in demand is of a permanent or a temporary nature. They are therefore expected to make quantity adjustments rather than price adjustments in view of this uncertainty. The shift, therefore, of the IS curve to IS_0 implies that output is, in fact, reduced to Y_0, and via the production function required employment falls from N_1 to N_0. Firms will employ N_0 units of labour only for all real wage rates below $(W/P)_2$. Thus the effective demand for labour is the line N^DCBE and is totally inelastic for all real wage rates below $(W/P)_2$. Firms are only interested in producing Y_0 and employing N_0 units of labour; it is just not profitable for firms to employ workers to produce goods which they cannot sell regardless of the wage rate. With the real wage now unchanged, the supply of labour is still at N_1, and involuntary unemployment of the magnitude N_1-N_0 thus emerges, despite the fact that the general equilibrium real wage $(W/P)_1$ still holds (there are also deflationary pressures in the goods market because of the income constraint due to the appearance of unemployment). The economy will therefore eventually rest at a new equilibrium, with both output and unemployment being well below their general equilibrium levels. The inevitable conclusion is that unemployment in the labour market is the direct result of a deflationary shock in the goods market; in other words, unemployment emerges because the excess supply in the labour market is not matched by effective excess demand in the goods market. This type of disequilibrium is, according to this analysis, precisely what Keynes was really attempting to put forward, rather than the comparative static type of analysis as it was thought to be in Hicks's (1937) contribution.

The policy implications of this analysis are quite straightforward: what is needed to eliminate what is called 'Keynesian unemployment' is government intervention to reflate the economy and restore the IS curve to its original position without causing any inflationary pressure. The expansion in effective aggregate demand would only tend to eliminate the downward pressure on prices - due to the excess supply in the goods market - thus keeping the price level to its original position.

This analysis, unfortunately, does not explain the observed fact that nowadays powerful trade unions can secure wage increases when excess demand in the economy does not exist. Neither does it consider the possibility of supply shocks emanating from increases in prices of imported inputs. These factors are, however, central to the analysis that has come to be known as neo-Keynesianism, which nevertheless retains the main elements of the analysis just put forward. Consider Figure 7.2 and assume that the economy is initially at equilibrium with income and employment at Y_1 and N_1 respectively; the real wage is $(W/P)_1$. Next, suppose that there is an autonomous rise in the cost of imported inputs and that trade unions respond to the consequent increase in output prices by forcing a rise in money wages to prevent any reduction in real wages - indeed, they may attempt to secure higher real wages in view of expected higher prices. The real wage is still at $(W/P)_1$ and excess demand is zero; however, the rise in prices, and money wages, has further implications. If the nominal money supply is not increased, both the LM and the IS curves shift to the left as the real quantity of money falls, intersecting each other to the left of Y_1, and aggregate demand is no longer sufficient to absorb the full-employment output. As demand falls, and in line with the assumption of quantity adjustments rather than price adjustments (see above), firms begin to decrease output and involuntary unemployment thus emerges. The higher unemployment implies higher marginal productivity of labour and firms will be willing to pay higher real wages than before. When real wages have reached the level aimed at by the unions, no further wage claims will occur and prices will cease to rise. The economy will come to rest at a new equilibrium with output and employment below their general equilibrium levels and with the cost inflation converging on a new equilibrium. Unemployment and inflation have thus moved together.

The above analysis implies that if policy-makers expand the money supply or government expenditure (or reduce taxes), or some combination of both, the LM and IS curves would revert back to their original positions, or at any rate to positions which re-establish the Y_1 level of output. In this case, however, prices and wages will continue to rise indefinitely and a rise in unemployment can only be prevented if the authorities continuously stimulate aggregate demand so that output is maintained at Y_1. To the extent that the real money supply and real government expenditure are not set at a level to provide the Y_1 level of output, inflation and unemployment may rise simultaneously. The policy recommendations then follow: demand management is required to reduce unemployment, while incomes policy should ensure that the prices of factors of production are kept from rising at rates which are incompatible with price stability. To quote Hicks (1975, p. 13):

> One is therefore led to be more charitable to the 'social contract' and to the '£6 limit' ... they are not all nice; they may not work ... yet, one after another, they may help us to get round this exceedingly difficult corner.

INFLATION-UNEMPLOYMENT AND THE EMPIRICAL EVIDENCE

A common feature of the studies which attempt to model the inflationary process is a two-equation system of wage and price inflation. In a general way such a system may be written as follows:

$$RPD = f\ (RW, X) \tag{7.2}$$

$$RW = g\ (RPD^e, Z) \tag{7.3}$$

where RPD = percentage rate of change of prices, RW = percentage rate of change of wages, RPD^e = expected RPD, and X,Z = vectors of additional variables.

We begin our discussion with the RPD equation. According to Solow (1969, p. 9), 'In general, one expects the rate of change of the price level to depend on current and recent changes in unit costs, and on the supply-demand balance in the current period and the recent past.' However, most studies utilising UK data have followed Neild's (1963, p. 51) proposition 'that manufacturers' prices are set by reference to costs when operating at some normal level of capacity and that they are not sensitive to moderate fluctuations in demand'. We utilise two cost elements: the wage rate and import prices - a subset of vector X. The importance of import prices arises from the relatively high average propensity to import, and we employ the rate of change of import prices (RPQD) for this purpose. Also included in the X vector is the growth of output per man (GOM), which can be thought of as a proxy for productivity; the sign of the coefficient of this variable is expected to be negative.

Turning to the wage equation, one important conclusion of the above analysis for the Phillips-curve relationship is that the wage equation ought to include a 'price-expectations' variable; without such a variable the RW equation does not perform satisfactorily. In other words, anticipated or expected changes in prices lead to changes in wages, and this effect should be included in any empirical investigation of this particular relationship. In common, therefore, with previous studies we attempt to model the anticipated rate of change of prices in this equation. The problem that arises when one undertakes this kind of estimation is, of course, the absence of direct observations on price expectations, and one is forced to make assumptions about the formation of expectations. The following alternative assumptions are usually adopted.

First,

$$(RPD)^e_t = (RPD)_t \tag{7.4}$$

This is the simplest assumption; it simply states that expectations of price changes are approximated by the current inflation rate (see, for example, Parkin and Sumner, 1972). These 'static expectations', when substituted in equation 7.3, and the latter is linearised, yield the following equation:

$$(RW)_t = a_0 + a_1(RPD)_t + a_2Z_t \tag{7.5}$$

where now all the variables are observable. This equation can easily be estimated.

Second,

$$(RPD)^e_t = (RPD)_t + \beta[(RPD)_t - (RPD)_{t-1}] \qquad (7.6)$$

This is the extrapolative hypothesis (Hicks, 1939), which asserts that expectations of future inflation are approximated by the current rate of inflation, together with a correction mechanism, i.e. $\beta(RPD_t - RPD_{t-1})$, which depends crucially on the value which the coefficient β assumes. If $\beta = 0$, then we have, as a special case, the hypothesis of 'static expectations', as in 7.4 above. If $\beta < 0$, it implies that economic units expect past inflation rates to reverse themselves (in the literature these expectations are called 'regressive' expectations). Finally, if $\beta > 0$, past inflation rates are expected to continue in the future. When hypothesis 7.6 is incorporated in the linearised form of 7.3, then equation 7.7 is obtained:

$$(RW)_t = b_0 + b_1(RPD)_t + b_1'[(RPD)_t - (RPD)_{t-1}] + b_2 Z_t \qquad (7.7)$$

where $b_0 = a_0$, $b_1 = a_1$, $b_1' = a_1\beta$, $b_2 = a_2$. Again all the variables are observable.

Third,

$$(RPD)^e_t = (RPD)^e_{t-1} + \gamma[(RPD)_{t-1} - (RPD)^e_{t-1}]$$

or

$$(RPD)^e_t = \gamma(RPD)_{t-1} + (1 - \gamma)\ (RPD)^e_{t-1} \quad \text{with } 0 < \gamma < 1 \qquad (7.8)$$

This is the 'adaptive' expectations hypothesis (Cagan, 1956; Solow, 1969). It states that expectations of future inflation rates are revised in each period by a constant fraction (γ) of the discrepancy between last period's actual rate of inflation and the rate expected to prevail in that period. For example, when the actual rate of inflation exceeds the expected rate of inflation, a higher expected inflation rate will be generated in the subsequent period, finally leading to a higher actual rate of inflation in this period. We may, next, substitute this assumption in the linearised form of equation 7.3 to get

$$(RW)_t = a_0 + a_1\ [\gamma(RPD)_{t-1} + (1 - \gamma)\ (RPD)^e_{t-1}] + a_2 Z_t \qquad (7.9)$$

Applying a Koyck transformation to this equation yields

$$(RW)_t = c_0 + c_1\ (RPD)_{t-1} + c_2 Z_t + c_3 Z_{t-1} + c_4\ (RW)_{t-1} \qquad (7.10)$$

where $c_0 = a_0\gamma$, $c_1 = a_1\gamma$, $c_2 = a_2$, $c_3 = -a_2(1 - \gamma)$, $c_4 = (1 - \gamma)$, and also

$$c_2\ c_4 + c_3 = 0$$

In other words, the coefficient of the Z variable multiplied by the coefficient of the lagged RW term plus the coefficient on Z_{t-1} must be equal to zero. This feature is quite interesting as well as necessary, because, to the extent that this condition is not satisfied, it would then constitute a rejection of this hypothesis, for equation 7.10 would then be the result of a different scheme (see Turnovsky, 1972, pp. 5-6, for such an example).

Fourth,

$$(RPD)^e_t = \sum_{i=0}^{n} \delta_i \, (RPD)_{t-i} \tag{7.11}$$

where

$$\sum_{i=0}^{n} \delta_i = 1$$

This hypothesis can be thought of as a generalisation of hypotheses 7.6 and 7.8. It implies that expectations of future inflation rates are generated by a general distributed lag of past price changes in such a way that the more distant inflation rates are less important; this is achieved by assigning goemetrically decreasing weights (δ_i) which sum to unity. As before, substitution of 7.11 into our linearised equation 7.3 results in the following relationship which can be easily estimated:

$$(RW)_t = a_0 + a_1 \sum_{i=0}^{n} \delta_i \, (RPD)_{t-i} + a_2 Z_t \tag{7.12}$$

When estimating the RW equation we have tried all these schemes concerning price expectations, with the best results reported below.

The Phillips-curve analysis suggests that one important variable that ought to be included in the Z vector is excess demand for labour, as proxied by the unemployment rate (UNER). This analysis, however, ignores one important consideration, namely the effect on the RW variable of an important 'cost-push' element in the form of changes in the strength of trade unions. The most influential attempt to establish this proposition has been the study by Hines (1964), who postulated that union strength is a source of wage inflation and that it can be appropriately proxied by the change in the percentage of the labour force unionised (NA). He also suggested that when unions become more aggressive, they both push harder on money wages and also raise the rate at which they recruit new members, so that the rate of increase of the percentage of the labour force unionised (GN) can be taken as an index of aggressiveness. Using a sample period from 1893 to 1961, not only did he find that the equations with the level of and change in unionisation performed satisfactorily but also that his hypothesis was superior to that of Phillips.

In addition to the basic equations 7.2 and 7.3, we also account for the unemployment-rate variable which appears in the $(RW)_t$ equation. To do this we begin with the following identity:

$$(EMPL)_t = (LS)_t - (UNE)_t \tag{7.13}$$

where EMPL = employees in employment, LS = total labour supply, assumed to be exogenously determined, and UNE = level of unemployment, with the unemployment rate defined as

$$(UNER)_t = \left(\frac{UNE}{LS}\right)_t \times 100 \qquad (7.14)$$

from which UNE can be determined by solving for $(UNE)_t$:

$$(UNE)_t = \frac{(UNER)_t \ (LS)_t}{100} \qquad (7.15)$$

with the further assumption that $(UNER)_t$ is endogenously determined. This is the procedure we have, in fact, adopted.

In a general way the specification of the UNER variable can take one of the following two forms:

$$UNER = U' \ (DEMV, \ TREND) \qquad (7.16)$$

$$UNER = U \ (DEMV, \ RW, \ TREND) \qquad (7.17)$$

where in the first function the unemployment rate is assumed (i) to depend negatively on demand variables (DEMV), and (ii) positively on a time trend reflecting productivity growth generated by capital accumulation and technical progress. In the second function one additional variable appears, the wage rate; the latter variable reflects the cost of labour and its coefficient should possess a positive sign. These two specifications correspond to the views taken on the causes of unemployment, where the first specification would be consistent with the neo-Keynesian argument that unemployment is mainly due to deficient aggregate demand, whereas the second specification would tend to support what we have already called 'search theorists', who argue that the labour-market mechanism as such is the prime influence of UNER through the wage rate. Our own empirical investigation clearly supports the demand-deficient specification. In none of the specifications we attempted, where we used a nominal or real RW with different lag structures, was any meaningful results produced. We have thus opted for the first specification where two variables were finally chosen to proxy 'demand variables': these were capacity utilisation (CU) and an index of industrial production (IPR).

We may now summarise the equations to be estimated:

$$(RPD)_t = r_0 + r_1 \ (RW)_{t-w} + r_2 \ (RPQD)_{t-q} + r_3 \ (GOM)_{t-m} + r_4 \ (DVO)_t + r_5 \ (DVO1)_t \qquad (7.18)$$

$$(RW)_t = w_0 + w_1 \ (UNER)_{t-u} + w_2 \ (RPD)_{t-r} + w_3 \ (NA)_t + w_4 \ (GN)_t + w_5 \ (DV1)_t + w_6 \ (DV2)_t + w_7 \ (DV3)_t \qquad (7.19)$$

$$(UNER)_t = u_0 + u_1 \ (CU)_{t-c} + u_2 \ (IPR)_{t-i} + u_3 \ (TREND)_t \qquad (7.20)$$

where w, q, m, u, r, c and i are specific lags to be determined empirically. In addition to the variables justified above there are some extra ones which are all dummies, as follows:

(a) DVO. This takes the value of 1.0 in 1969 and zero elsewhere to provide for the relatively large negative residual in this period. The large residual suggests that the unusually large import price increases in 1968, following the 1967 devaluation, were not passed on to consumers through increases in domestic prices, due to the highly deflationary policies of the government in 1968-9 aiming to ensure that devaluation was effective.
(b) DVO1. This takes the value of 1.0 in 1970, 1971 and 1972 and zero elsewhere to correct for relatively large positive residuals, which were probably due, initially, to a set of new policies by the Heath government. These had a direct impact on prices (a switch from direct to indirect taxation, abolition of subsidies, and rises in the prices of the nationalised sector's output) and were followed by a markedly laxed monetary policy in 1971-2.
(c) DV1. This takes the value of 1.0 in 1962, -1.0 in 1963 and 1964 and zero elsewhere, to allow for the effect of a pay pause in 1961-2 and the possible after-effects of the pause.
(d) DV2. This takes the value of 1.0 in 1965 and 1966 and -1.0 in 1967, with zero elsewhere, to provide for the tight incomes policy in 1965-6, including a pay freeze in 1966 supported by the TUC, and for the end of the freeze in 1967.
(e) DV3. This takes the value of 1.0 in 1968 and zero elsewhere to allow for a catch-up effect after the 1966-7 pay freeze.

In Table 7.1 we provide the estimates of the instrumental-variables technique. The over-all fit in all estimated equations is satisfactory. In all cases the coefficients are highly significant, with the exception of GOM in the RPD equation. The R^2 is over 98 per cent, and with all χ_2^2s being insignificant, independence of the chosen instruments with the error term in each equation is assured. In the case of the unemployment rate this was only possible with the inclusion of a two-year lag structure for the dependent variable; this is the reason for the appearance in this equation of two additional terms, $(UNER)_{t-1}$ and $(UNER)_{t-2}$, to the ones mentioned earlier. The Chow test is insignificant in all cases but the same is not true for the χ_3^2s, which are all significant, a result that clearly suggests unsatisfactory post-sample parameter stability. This last, unfortunate outcome is a problem not just in our case but in all those studies that attempt to model these particular relationships. However, all three equations possess a relatively small S/ME ratio, with, perhaps, the exception of the RPD equation. This latter relationship, however, bears a remarkable similarity to published work on the subject (Solow, 1969, for example), and seems to confirm the early findings of Dicks-Mireaux (1961).

An interesting finding emerges from the estimated form of the UNER equation. Sargent (1973), when testing the natural rate of

Table 7.1

$$(RPD)_t = \underset{(3.75)}{1.822} + \underset{(7.27)}{0.381}(RW)_t + \underset{(8.96)}{0.326}(RPQD)_{t-1} - \underset{(1.55)}{0.195}(GOM)_t$$

$$- \underset{(4.01)}{3.446}(DVO)_t + \underset{(3.80)}{2.147}(DVO1)_t$$

$DW = 1.99$, $S = 0.787$, $S/ME = 0.107$, $\chi_2^2(9) = 10.66$, $\chi_3^2(1) = 5.06$,

$F(1,14) = 4.50$

$$(RW)_t = - \underset{(13.82)}{71.455} - \underset{(10.91)}{2.627}(UNER)_t + \underset{(16.54)}{0.593}(RPD)_t$$

$$+ \underset{(17.34)}{0.503}\ [(RPD)_{t-1} - (RPD)_{t-2}] + \underset{(14.02)}{196.823}(NA)_t$$

$$+ \underset{(5.82)}{41.548}(GN)_t - \underset{(4.01)}{1.168}(DV1)_t - \underset{(6.98)}{2.151}(DV2)_t + \underset{(6.41)}{3.399}(DV3)_t$$

$DW = 2.20$, $S = 0.495$, $S/ME = 0.055$, $\chi_2^2(8) = 9.82$, $\chi_3^2(1) = 8.59$,

$F(1,11) = 5.18$

$$(EMPL)_t = (LS)_t - (UNE)_t$$

$$(UNE)_t = \frac{(UNER)_t\ (LS)_t}{100}$$

$$(UNER)_t = \underset{(4.41)}{5.265} - \underset{(2.19)}{0.046}\ [(CU)_t - (CU)_{t-1}] - \underset{(4.47)}{0.080}(IPR)_t$$

$$+ \underset{(9.44)}{0.976}(UNER)_{t-1} - \underset{(4.27)}{0.433}(UNER)_{t-2} + \underset{(4.99)}{0.242}(TREND)_t$$

$DW = 1.94$, $S = 0.200$, $S/ME = 0.071$, $\chi_2^2(5) = 5.96$, $\chi_3^2(1) = 8.93$,

$F(1,14) = 3.79$

unemployment hypothesis, under the assumption of 'rational expectations', argued that one major implication of this theory was that 'there is no better way to predict subsequent rates of unemployment than fitting and extrapolating a mixed autoregressive, moving average process of the unemployment rate itself' (p. 451). Our reported equation clearly shows that the UNER variable which includes lagged values of itself - of up to two years - and with two additional variables utilised as proxies for demand variables, together with a trend variable, performs much better than those equations we have tried that included only lagged values of the unemployment rate (which we have not reported here). This finding offers some tentative evidence which tends to reject Sargent's proposition,[4] mentioned above, and confirms our reservations expressed earlier on the validity of the natural rate of unemployment approach as well as the 'rational expectations' hypothesis.

This last conclusion is also supported by the evidence on the wage-rate equation. Clearly there is a trade-off between unemployment and wages, though expectations are important. The different hypotheses advanced about the formation of expectations (see above) have been tried and the only one that produced satisfactory results is the one reported in Table 7.1. This scheme supports the extrapolative hypothesis; and with $\beta = 0.847$, it follows that economic agents expect past inflation rates to continue in the future. Moreover, the long-run Phillips curve is simply non-vertical because the coefficient on the $(RPD)_t$ variable is well below unity.

The hypothesis advanced by Hines (1964) is also supported. Both the NA and GN variables are highly significant with the correct signs. At the same time, however, the UNER variable is also significant and correctly signed, whereas in Hines's study this particular variable loses its significance when NA and GN are included in this equation (a result that led him to the conclusion that his hypothesis was superior to that of Phillips). Our results therefore suggest that, if anything, the two hypothesis are both relevant in terms of explaining movements in wages over the period covered in this study.

This last finding is of some interest, given the importance that has been attached to the wage equation in the literature. It would thus seem useful to compare our results with a sample of previous work in this area. In Table 7.2 we reproduce a sample of estimated wage equations. First of all we note that most of the variables differ in each case. The dependent variable used is the weekly wage rate of manual workers in both the Johnston and Timbrell (1973), and Parkin *et al.* (1976) studies, while the Nordhaus (1972) study employs hourly earnings. The independent variables also differ. The price-expectations variable ($\dot{p}^e$) in the Nordhaus study is represented by an imposed distributed-lag scheme, and in the Johnston and Timbrell study by a lagged average of the previous twelve months' change in the retail price index. In the Parkin *et al.* study disaggregated price-expectations variables are used: employers' estimates of export ($\dot{p}^e_F$) and home output ($\dot{p}^e_E$) prices, and employees' estimates of domestic prices ($\dot{p}^e_C$). None of the coefficients of the above variables is statistically significant, with the exception of the coefficient on employers' estimates of home output prices in the case of the Parkin *et al.* study. Furthermore, in the Johnston and Timbrell study the variable n/N is used, which is the proportion of workers receiving increases, while Parkin *et al.* employ incomes-policy dummies (ℓ_1: 1961.III-1962.II and ℓ_2: 1966.III-1967.II), and tax variables - a combined coefficient is shown in Table 7.2. Again, none of these variables appears to be significant. Clearly

Table 7.2 Augmented Phillips equations: some sample results

Equation key	Constant	Regression coefficients						Estimation period and frequency of observations
		b_1 or b_1'	b_2	b_3	b_4	b_5	$\bar{R}^2$	
		(1/U)	$(\dot{P}^e)$					
Nordhaus	0.0543	-0.151 (0.389)	0.608 (0.890)				n.a.	Annual: 1955-71
		(U)	$(\dot{P}^e)$	(n/N)				
Johnston and Timbrell	-3.19	2.699 (1.96)	0.60 (1.39)	1.71 (0.41)			0.684	Annual: 1959-71
		(U)	$(\dot{p}^e_F \dot{P}_E+\dot{P}_C)$	$(T_1+T_2+T_3)$	(ℓ_1)	(ℓ_2)		
Parkin, Sumner and Ward	3.98	-0.644 (0.70)	0.854 (not sign?)	-0.296 (not sign)	0.152 (0.10)	-1.050 (0.70)	0.475	Quarterly: 1956:II-1971:IV

Key: Regression coefficients b_1 or b_1' refer to U or 1/U respectively; b_2 to price-expectations variables; b_3, b_4 and b_5 vary between studies (see text). Figures in parentheses are t-ratios, except in the case of Nordhaus, who gives standard errors. The dependent variable is a version of the rate of change of wages, on various definitions. The variable T_i is defined as $T_i = \Delta(1 + t_i)/(1 + t_i)$, where t_1 = employers' national insurance contributions as percentage of average wage; t_2 = employees' national insurance contributions as proportion of average wage; t_3 = rate of income tax.
Source: Artis (1981).

the coefficients on the unemployment-rate variable are insignificant or appear to have the 'wrong' sign.

Comparing the results of Table 7.2 with our results of Table 7.1, it is obvious that in our case the hypothesis of 'extrapolative' expectations, along with the Hines hypothesis, seem to perform satisfactorily - not forgetting, of course, the significant dummy variables.

Finally, there is another hypothesis, much discussed in the literature, the so-called 'real wage resistance', according to which (in logarithms):

$$\Delta(RW)_t = g[((RW/RPD)_t\lambda)^* - ((RW)_{t-1}/(RPD)_t)\lambda] \qquad (7.21)$$

where $(RW/RPD)^*$ = the desired or target real wage, $[(RW)_{t-1}/(RPD)_t]$ = actual real wages, and λ = the retention ratio, i.e. the net-of-tax wage. This hypothesis makes changes in the nominal wage rate to adjust according to the gap between a desired after-tax real wage and the actual real wage. The speed of this adjustment is influenced by the state of unemployment and of incomes policy, or

$$g = h\ (UNER,\ DV_i) \qquad (7.22)$$

where DV_i would be dummies for incomes policies.

Desired or target real wage is determined by the scheme:

$$(RW/RPD)^*_t = f(\lambda^e,\ (RPD)^e,\ T) \qquad (7.23)$$

namely, by expected future λ and RPD, and T = time trend (for further details on this hypothesis see, for example, Artis, 1981, pp. 73-6). When equations 7.21 - 7.23 are linearised, different testable equations can arise depending on the assumptions one cares to make on the variables involved, especially λ^e and $(RPD)^e$ (see Artis, 1981, for an example). In our case we have tried a number of specifications, but none provided any meaningful results; so our preferred equation remains the one reported in Table 7.1.

8

The Full Annual Model in Summary Form

The aim of this chapter is to summarise the model we have estimated, and to bring out some of its important features. The estimates presented below are the instrumental-variables estimates; in the case of this particular estimation technique, the 'GIVE' programme treats all the exogenous and predetermined variables appearing in the equation - including the constant - plus the lagged regressand as well as the lagged regressors as legitimate instrumental variables. In addition to these, additional instruments have been used, as we indicate in the following equations. The summary of the model appears immediately below; this is followed by a list of the definitions and sources of the variables utilised for the estimation of the model. Finally, we discuss some of the important features of the annual model and attempt briefly to compare them with the ones of some of the major models referred to in the Introduction.

SUMMARY OF INSTRUMENTAL-VARIABLES TECHNIQUE FOR THE ANNUAL MODEL

$$(1) \quad (APC)_t = \underset{(3.94)}{0.47302} - \underset{(3.13)}{0.00413}\,[(RL)_t - (RPD)_t] - \underset{(3.71)}{0.00468}(RPD)_t + \underset{(2.95)}{0.21430}\left(\frac{LA}{YD}\right)_t + \underset{(3.54)}{0.32313}\left(\frac{TYDR}{YDR}\right)_t - \underset{(2.19)}{0.00082}\,(RPD)_{t-2}$$

$$\rho = \underset{(5.90)}{0.81326},\ S = 0.006,\ S/ME = 0.007,\ \chi_2^2(9) = 13.98,$$

$$\chi_3^2(1) = 1{\cdot}44,\ F(1,13) = 0.48$$

Additional instruments: $(YD)_{t-3}$, $(PCD)_{t-1}$, $(PCD)_{t-2}$, $(UNER)_{t-1}$, $[(GDPR)_{t-1} - (GDPR)_{t-2}]$, $(GDPR_{t-2} - GDPR_{t-3})$, $(IPR)_{t-1}$, $(BR)_{t-1}$

$$(2)\quad (CON)_t = (APC)_t \times (YD)_t$$

$$(3)\quad (CONR)_t = \left(\frac{CON}{PCD}\right)_t$$

$$(4)\quad (PCD)_t = \underset{(70.86)}{0.93788}\,(PD)_t$$

$$\rho = \underset{(6.14)}{0.81517}$$

$$(5)\quad (LA)_t = \underset{(1.95)}{6.48887} + \underset{(15.64)}{1.15330}\left(\frac{(M3)_t + (M3)_{t-1}}{2}\right) + \underset{(1.77)}{0.34546}\left(\frac{\Delta(GS)_t + \Delta(GS)_{t-1}}{2}\right)$$

$$\rho = \underset{(6.30)}{0.85355}$$

$$(6)\quad (TYDR)_t = [(YDR)_t + (YDR)_{t-1} + (YDR)_{t-2} + (YDR)_{t-3} + (YDR)_{t-4}]/5$$

$$(7)\quad (YDR)_t = \left(\frac{YD}{PCD}\right)_t$$

$$(8)\quad (IP)_t = -\underset{(3.58)}{2.96890} + \underset{(2.49)}{0.02228}\,(CU)_t + \underset{(11.65)}{0.41996}\,(IF)_t + \underset{(4.28)}{1.56472}\,(CC)_t + \underset{(2.39)}{0.08468}\,[(GDPR)_{t-1} - (GDPR)_{t-2}]$$
$$-\underset{(3.50)}{0.03077}\left[(RL)_{t-2} - \left(\frac{(RPD)_{t-1} + (RPD)_{t-2} + (RPD)_{t-3}}{3}\right)\right] + \underset{(3.21)}{0.41088}\,(IP)_{t-1}$$

$$\rho = -\underset{(1.92)}{0.55405},\ S = 0.103,\ S/ME = 0.021,\ \chi^2_2(6) = 8.22,$$

$$\chi^2_3(1) = 11.77,\ F(1,12) = 6.90$$

Additional instruments: $(IPR)_{t-1}$, $[(CONR)_{t-1} - (CONR)_{t-2}]$

$$(9)\quad (CU)_t = \underset{(5.53)}{64.10057} + \underset{(6.35)}{84.57442}\left(\frac{(IPR)_{t-1} - (IPR)_{t-2}}{(IPR)_{t-2}}\right) + \underset{(2.43)}{0.29894}\,(CU)_{t-1}$$

$$\rho = -\underset{(2.87)}{0.58592}, \; S = 2.361, \; S/ME = 0.025, \; \chi_1^2(1) = 0.09,$$

$$\chi_3^2(1) = 0.17, \; F(1,16) = 0.13$$

(10) $$(IPR)_t = \underset{(3.80)}{2.58870}\,[(GDPR)_t - (GDPR)_{t-1}] + \underset{(120.30)}{0.99274}\,(IPR)_{t-1}$$

$$D\text{-}W = 1.84, \; S = 1.595, \; S/ME = 0.017, \; \chi_2^2(3) = 3.01,$$

$$\chi_3^2(1) = 0.19, \; F(1,18) = 0.17$$

Additional instruments: $(IP)_{t-1}$, $(SA)_{t-1}$

(11) $$(STB)_t = \underset{(7.06)}{0.08964}\,[(IPR)_t - (IPR)_{t-1}] + \underset{(3.64)}{0.06031}\,[(IPR)_{t-1} - (IPR)_t$$

$$- \underset{(2.25)}{0.04035}\left((RL)_{t-1}\left[\frac{(RPD)_t + (RPD)_{t-1} + (RPD)_{t-2}}{3}\right]\right)$$

$$+ \underset{(3.08)}{0.06812}\,(GSAI)_t$$

$$D\text{-}W = 2.24, \; S = 0.172, \; S/ME = 0.459, \; \chi_2^2(6) = 3.04,$$

$$\chi_3^2(1) = 0.93, \; F(1,16) = 0.43$$

Additional instruments: $(CU)_{t-1}$, $(SA)_{t-1}$,

$[(GDPR)_{t-1} - (GDPR)_{t-2}]$

(12) $$(XR)_t = \underset{(6.80)}{5.95105} + \underset{(34.18)}{0.03703}\,(WD)_t + \underset{(1.77)}{0.00870}\,(WPA)_t$$

$$+ \underset{(3.44)}{0.02444}\,(WPA)_{t-1} - \underset{(2.50)}{2.79870}\,(PXFD)_{t-1}$$

$$- \underset{(2.99)}{4.68520}\,(PXFD)_{t-2}$$

$$D\text{-}W = 2.35, \; S = 0.142, \; S/ME = 0.013, \; \chi_1^2(3) = 2.12,$$

$$\chi_3^2(1) = 0.72, \; F(1,14) = 0.24$$

(13) $$(PXFD)_t = \underset{(19.53)}{0.57300} + \underset{(6.59)}{1.08282}\,(PD)_t - \underset{(2.56)}{1.24513}\,(PD)_{t-1}$$

$$+ \underset{(2.42)}{0.56588}\,(PD)_{t-2}$$

$$D\text{-}W = 1.85, \; S = 0.038, \; S/ME = 0.035, \; \chi_2^2(3) = 2.17,$$

$$\chi_3^2(1) = 1.65, \; F(1,16) = 0.62$$

Additional instruments: $(PQD)_{t-1}$, $(CU)_{t-1}$

(14) $$(PXD)_t = \left(\frac{PXFD}{ER}\right)_t$$

(15) $$(QR)_t = -\underset{(1.75)}{4.11760} + \underset{(2.30)}{0.23107}\,(GDPR)_t + \underset{(2.33)}{3.64649}\,(PD)_{t-1}$$

$$- \underset{(2.68)}{2.69460}\,(PQD)_{t-1} + \underset{(2.60)}{0.41579}\,(QR)_{t-1}$$

$$= \underset{(3.02)}{0.65895},\ S = 0.257,\ S/ME = 0.025,\ \chi_2^2(9) = 15.61,$$

$$\chi_3^2(1) = 3.96,\ F(1,14) = 1.75$$

Additional instruments: $(CU)_{t-1}$, $(XR)_{t-1}$,

$$[(CONR)_{t-1} - (CONR)_{t-2}],\ \left(\frac{(WD)_t + (WD)_{t-1}}{2}\right),$$

$(GCI)_{t-1}$, $(IP)_{t-1}$

(16) $$(GEX)_t = (GCI)_t + (GT)_t + (NLG)_t$$

(17) $$(RGCIM)_t = \underset{(3.02)}{0.29946} + \underset{(2.58)}{0.00612}\,[(UNER)_t - (UNER)_{t-1}] - \underset{(3.12)}{0.00235}\,(GDPR)_t$$

$$+ \underset{(2.68)}{0.00749}\,(DV)_t + \underset{(3.48)}{0.01124}\,(DEM)_t + \underset{(5.65)}{0.20746}\left(\frac{GCID}{PMD}\right)_t$$

$$D\text{-}W = 1.59,\ S = 0.0047,\ S/ME = 0.021,\ \chi_2^2(5) = 5.47,$$

$$\chi_3^2(1) = 1.82,\ F(1,14) = 0.70$$

Additional instruments: $(DEMO)_t$, $(UNER)_{t-1}$, $(RPD)_{t-1}$

(18) $$(GCI) = (RGCIM)_t \times (GDPM)_t$$

(19) $$(RGTM)_t = \underset{(3.15)}{0.00578}\,(UNER)_t + \underset{(1.93)}{0.00063}\,(RPD)_t + \underset{(3.32)}{0.00166}\,(GDPR)_t$$

$$+ \underset{(2.94)}{0.01047}\,(DV)_t + \underset{(3.82)}{0.00170}\,(DEMO)_t$$

$$D\text{-}W = 1.33,\ S = 0.006,\ S/ME = 0.042,\ \chi_2^2(8) = 7.62,$$

$$\chi_3^2(1) = 1.04,\ F(1,15) = 0.66$$

Additional instruments: $(DEM)_t$. $(PQD)_{t-1}$, $(WR)_{t-1}$,

$$[(UNER)_{t-1} - (UNER)_{t-2}],\ \left(\frac{GCID}{PMD}\right)_{t-1}$$

(20) $$(GT)_t = (RGTM)_t \times (GDPM)_t$$

(21) $$(GDPM)_t = (GDPN)_t + (ITAX)_t - (SUB)_t$$

(22) $$(GDPN)_t = (GDPR)_t \times (PD)_t$$

(23) $$(TAX)_t = (ITAX)_t + (DTAXP)_t + (ODTAX)_t$$

(24) $$(ITAX)_t = -\underset{(8.30)}{0.53438} + \underset{(8.27)}{0.06483}\,(TDE)_{t-1} + \underset{(3.71)}{0.31060}\,(DV)_t$$

$$+ \underset{(15.11)}{0.77316}\,(ITAX)_{t-1}$$

$$= -\underset{(2.01)}{0.47085}, \; S = 0.218, \; S/ME = 0.026, \; \chi_1^2(2) = 5.51$$

$$\chi_3^2(1) = 0.02, \; F(1,15) = 0.01$$

(25) $$(TDE)_t = (GDPM)_t - [(XR)_t \times (PXD)_t] + [(QR)_t \times (PQD)_t]$$

$$- (ITAX)_t + (SUB)_t$$

(26) $$(DTAXP)_t = \underset{(5.99)}{0.28376}\,[(CPY)_t - (CPY)_{t-1}] + \underset{(4.24)}{0.07012}\,(RPD)_t$$

$$+ \underset{(2.78)}{0.03390}\,[(RPD)_{t-1} - (RPD)_{t-2}] + \underset{(65.31)}{0.96855}\,(DTAXP)_{t-1}$$

$$D\text{-}W = 1.78, \; S = 0.215, \; S/ME = 0.031, \; \chi_2^2(4) = 4.77,$$

$$\chi_3^2(1) = 0.002, \; F(1,16) = 0.01$$

Additional instruments: $[(RPD)_{t-3} - (RPD)_{t-4}], [(CPY)_{t-2} - (CPY)_{t-3}$

(27) $$(CPY)_t = (TAXR)_t \times (PY)_t$$

(28) $$(PY)_t = (EY)_t + (NIBG)_t$$

(29) $$(EY)_t = -\underset{(1.72)}{16.83237} + \underset{(16.46)}{1.29554}\,(GDPN)_t - \underset{(4.94)}{0.46271}\,(GDPN)_{t-1}$$

$$+ \underset{(1.74)}{0.76628}\,(EMPL)_t$$

$$D\text{-}W = 2.28, \; S = 0.699, \; S/ME = 0.015, \; \chi_2^2(8) = 13.63,$$

$$\chi_3^2(1) = 1.47, \; F(1,16) = 0.67$$

Additional instruments: $(GDPR)_{t-1}$, $(IPR)_{t-1}$, $(CU)_{t-1}$, $(IP)_{t-1}$, $(XR)_{t-1}$, $(EMPL)_{t-1}$, $(PD)_{t-1}$

(30) $(YD)_t = (PY)_t - (DTAXP)_t - (NIC)_t - (NTA)_t$

(31) $(GDPR)_t = (CONR)_t + (IP)_t + (STB)_t + (IPC)_t + \left(\frac{GCI}{GCID}\right)_t + (XR)_t - (QR)_t - \left(\frac{ITAX}{PITD}\right)_t + \left(\frac{SUB}{PSUBD}\right)_t$

(32) $(PD)_t = (PD)_{t-1} + [(PD)_{t-1} \times (RPD)_t \times 0.01000]$

(33) $\underset{}{(RPD)_t} = \underset{(3.75)}{1.82171} + \underset{(8.96)}{0.32583}\ (RPQD)_{t-1} + \underset{(7.27)}{0.38073}\ (WR)_t$

$- \underset{(1.55)}{0.19524}\ (GOM)_t - \underset{(4.01)}{3.44626}\ (DVO)_t + \underset{(3.80)}{2.14725}\ (DVO1)_t$

D-W = 1.99, S = 0.787, S/ME = 0.107, $\chi_2^2(9) = 10.66$,

$\chi_3^2(1) = 5.06$, F(1,14) = 4.50

Additional instruments: $(NA)_t$, $(GN)_t$, $(WP)_t$, $(WP)_{t-1}$

(34) $(WR)_t = - \underset{(13.82)}{71.45504} + \underset{(16.54)}{0.59307}\ (RPD)_t - \underset{(10.91)}{2.62649}\ (UNER)_t$

$+ \underset{(17.34)}{0.50246}\ [(RPD)_{t-1} - (RPD)_{t-2}]$

$+ \underset{(14.02)}{196.82315}\ (NA)_t + \underset{(5.82)}{41.54763}\ (GN)_t - \underset{(4.01)}{1.16786}\ (DV1)_t$

$- \underset{(6.98)}{2.15080}\ (DV2)_t + \underset{(6.41)}{3.39847}\ (DV3)_t$

D-W = 2.20, S = 0.495, S/ME = 0.065, $\chi_2^2(8) = 9.82$,

$\chi_3^2(1) = 8.59$, F(1,11) = 5.18

Additional instruments: $(CU)_{t-1}$, $(RPQD)_{t-1}$

(35) $(EMPL)_t = (LS)_t - (UNE)_t$

(36) $(UNE)_t = [(UNER)_t \times (LS)_t]/100$

(37) $(UNER)_t = \underset{(4.41)}{5.26507} - \underset{(2.19)}{0.04609}\ [(CU)_t - (CU)_{t-1}] - \underset{(4.47)}{0.07956}\ (IPR)_t$

$+ \underset{(9.44)}{0.97572}\ (UNER)_{t-1} - \underset{(4.27)}{0.43299}\ (UNER)_{t-2}$

$+ \underset{(4.99)}{0.24186}\ (TREND)_t$

$D\text{-}W = 1.94,\ S = 0.200,\ S/ME = 0.071,\ \chi^2_2(5) = 5.96,$

$\chi^2_3(1) = 8.93,\ F(1,14) = 3.79$

Additional instruments: $(GDPR)_{t-1}$, $(EMPL)_{t-1}$, $(IP)_{t-1}$, $(XR)_{t-1}$

(38) $$\ell n \left(\frac{M3}{PD}\right)^d_t = \underset{(2.21)}{-\ 0.86976} - \underset{(2.09)}{0.21060}\ell n\ (RS)_t + \underset{(2.79)}{0.43889}\ell n\ (GDPR)_t + \underset{(3.97)}{0.88479}\ell n \left(\frac{M3}{PD}\right)_{t-1} + \underset{(3.16)}{0.18210}\ell n \left(\frac{(ROB)_t}{(ROB)_{t-1}}\right)$$

$D\text{-}W = 1.87,\ S = 0.048,\ S/ME = 0.017,\ \chi^2_2(5) = 8.15,$

$\chi^2_3(1) = 0;91,\ F(1,15) = 0.67$

Additional instruments: $\ell n\ (BR)_t$, $\ell n\ (RL)_{t-1}$, $\ell n \left(\frac{(RS)_{t-1}}{(RS)_{t-2}}\right)$

(39) $$\ell n\ (M3)^s_t = \underset{(1.94)}{0.64528} + \underset{(1.59)}{0.07002}\ \ell n \left(\frac{(RS)_t}{(RS)_{t-1}}\right) + \underset{(2.68)}{0.53138}\ell n\ (BA)_t - \underset{(2.27)}{0.17000}\ell n\ (BR)_t + \underset{(3.59)}{0.63636}\ell n\ (M3)_{t-1}$$

$= \underset{(3.22)}{0.79802},\ S = 0.039,\ S/ME = 0.013,\ \chi^2_2(4) = 7.36,$

$\chi^2_3(1) = 0.22,\ F(1,14) = 0.09$

Additional instruments: $\ell n\ (RL)_{t-1}$, $\ell n\ (GDPR)_{t-1}$, $\ell n \left(\frac{(PD)_{t-1}}{(PS)_{t-2}}\right)$

(40) $$\ell n\ (M3)^d_t = \ell n\ (M3)^s_t = \ell n\ (M3)_t$$

(41) $$\ell n\ (RL)_t = \underset{(2.10)}{1.12459} + \underset{(5.62)}{0.33980}\ell n\ (RS)_t + \underset{(2.16)}{0.44146}\ell n\ (GDPR)_t + \underset{(2.15)}{0.89422}\ell n \left(\frac{(PD)_t}{(PD)_{t-1}}\right) + \underset{(3.89)}{0.41749}\ell n\ (RL)_{t-1}$$

$D\text{-}W = 2.00,\ S = 0.046,\ S/ME = 0.022,\ \chi^2_2(6) = 2.99,$

$\chi^2_3(1) = 0.19,\ F(1,15) = 0.15$

Additional instruments: $\ell n\ (M3)_{t-1}$, $\ell n\ (BR)_t$, $\ell n \left(\frac{(ROB)_t}{(ROB)_{t-1}}\right)$

$\ell n \left(\frac{(RS)_{t-1}}{(RS)_{t-2}}\right)$

(42) $$(BA)_t = \Delta(BA)_t + (BA)_{t-1}$$

(43) $$\Delta(BA)_t = (PSBR)_t + \Delta(FR)_t - \Delta(GS)_t$$

(44) $(PSBR)_t = (GEX)_t - (TAX)_t + (OGREV)_t$

(45) $\Delta(FR)_t = (CB)_t + (DKM)_t$

(46) $(CB)_t = [(PXD)_t \times (XR)_t] - [(PQD)_t \times (QR)_t] + (OCB)_t$

Please note that the ordinary least squares estimates are presented in an appendix at the end of the book. The reason we report these estimates is simply to examine whether substantial differences exist between the two sets of estimates (instrumental variables and ordinary least squares) which would indicate that simultaneity bias exists and to see whether the use of the instrumental-variables technique produces more reliable results. A cursory look shows that (as it turns out) in most cases the two sets of results do not differ significantly. One should also note that in the case of the OLS technique the χ^2_1-statistic is always insignificant, which means that dynamic specification of all the equations is satisfactory in terms of this particular test.

DEFINITION OF VARIABLES AND SOURCES
(£1,000m unless otherwise stated.)

Endogenous Variables

BA Monetary base, defined as currency held by the public plus reserves of the banking sector (*Bank of England Quarterly Bulletin - BEQB*)

ΔBA Changes in BA

CB Balance-of-payments current account (*ET*)

CON Consumers' expenditure, current prices (*Economic Trends - ET*)

CONR Consumers' expenditure, 1970 prices (*ET*)

CPY Personal income (PY) multiplied by a weighted average of the basic income-tax rate (TAXR)

CU Index of capacity utilisation (Mica, 1978)

DTAXP Direct taxes of the personal sector, current prices (*National Income and Expenditure - NIE*)

EMPL Employees in employment (*ET*)

EY Earned income of the personal sector, current prices (*ET*)

ΔFR Changes in foreign reserves (*NIE*)

GCI General government consumption plus investment, current prices (*ET*)

GDPM Gross domestic product (GDP) at market prices, current prices (*ET*)

GDPN GDP at factor cost, current prices (*ET*)

GDPR GDP at factor cost, 1970 prices (*ET*)

GEX General government expenditure, current prices (*ET*)

GT General government transfers, current prices (*ET*)

IP Gross domestic fixed capital formation of the private sector, 1970 prices (*ET*)

ITAX Total indirect taxes, current prices (*NIE*)

IPR Index of industrial production (*ET*)

LA Selected liquid assets of the personal sector: national savings, tax instruments, deposits with the banking sector and building societies, as well as with finance houses (*Financial Statistics* - *FS*)

LS Total labour supply: EMPL + UNE (level of unemployment) (*ET*)

M3 Money stock of M3 variety (*BEQB*)

PD GDP price deflator, 1970 = 1.0

PCD Consumers' expenditure implicit price deflator, 1970 = 1.0

RPD $[((PD)_t - (PD)_{t-1})/(PD)_{t-1}] \times 100$

PSBR Public Sector Borrowing Requirement (*NIE*)

PXD Implicit price deflator for exports, 1970 = 1.0

PXFD Price index of exports in foreign currency: PXD multiplied by the exchange rate (ER)

PY Income of the personal sector, current prices (*NIE*)

QR Imports, 1970 prices (*ET*)

RGCIM GCI/GDPM

RGTM GT/GDPM

RL Long-term rate of interest: 2½% Consol rate (*ET*)

RS Short-term rate of interest: local authority rate on temporary debt (*BEQB*)

STB Stockbuilding, 1970 prices (*ET*)

TAX Total taxes, current prices (*NIE*)

TDE Total domestic expenditure at factor cost, current prices (*ET*)

UNE Total unemployed, excluding school-leavers (*ET*)

UNER Rate of unemployment (*ET*)

WR Rate of change of basic weekly wage rates - manual workers: all industries and services (*ET*)

XR Exports, 1970 prices (*ET*)

YD Total personal disposable income, current prices (*ET*)

YDR Real total personal disposable income, 1970 prices (*ET*)

Exogenous Variables

BR Annual weighted average of Bank Rate/Minimum Lending Rate (*ET*)

CC Capital consumption at current replacement cost deflated by the implicit deflator for private investment (*NIE*)

DEM $[(DEMO)_t + (DEMO)_{t-1}]/2$

DEMO Demographic variable: number of persons under 16 and over 65 as a percentage of total population (*Annual Abstract of Statistics - AAS*)

DKM Capital movements (*ET*)

DV Dummy variable taking the value of 1.0 for years of Labour administration, and zero otherwise

DVO Dummy variable taking the value of 1.0 in 1969 and zero elsewhere

DVO1 Dummy variable taking the value of 1.0 in 1970, 1971 and 1972 and zero elsewhere

DV1 Dummy variable taking the value of 1.0 in 1962, -1.0 in 1963 and 1964 and zero elsewhere

DV2 Dummy variable taking the value of 1.0 in 1965 and 1966 and -1.0 in 1967 and zero elsewhere

DV3 Dummy variable taking the value of 1.0 in 1968 and zero elsewhere

ER Effective foreign exchange rate, 1970 = 1.0 (*ET*)

GCID GCI price deflator, 1970 = 1.0

GN $(N_t - N_{t-1})/N_{t-1}$, where N = percentage of labour force unionised - total membership of trade unions over total working population (*AAS*)

GOM Growth of output per person employed (*ET*)

ΔGS Changes in total government debt (*NIE*)

GSA1 $[(SA)_{t-1} - (SA)_{t-1}]/(SA)_{t-2}$, where SA = index of volume of retail sales (*ET*)

IF Internal funds of the corporate sector: undistributed income minus stock appreciation plus net capital transfers, deflated by the implicit deflator for private investment (*NIE*)

IPC Investment of public corporations, 1970 prices (*ET*)

NA $(N_{t-1} + N_{t-2})/2$, with N as in (GN) above

NIBG National insurance benefits and other current grants from general government, current prices (*NIE*)

NIC National insurance contributions, current prices (*NIE*)

NLG General government lending (*ET*)

NTA Net transfers from abroad (*NIE*)

OCB $CB_t - [(PXD)_t \times (XR)_t] - [(PQD)_t \times (QR)_t]$, i.e. other current balance

ODTAX TAX - ITAX - DTAXP, i.e. other direct taxes

OGREV PSBR - (GEX - TAX), i.e. other government revenue

PITD Implicit deflator for indirect taxes, 1970 = 1.0

PMD GDPM price deflator, 1970 = 1.0

PQD Implicit price deflator for imports, 1970 = 1.0

PSUBD Implicit deflator for subsidies, 1970 = 1.0

ROB Inter-bank rate since 1964; before 1964 Bank Rate (*BEQB*)

RPQD $[((PQ)_t - (PQ)_{t-1})/(PQ)_{t-1}] \times 100$

SUB Subsidies, current prices (*ET*)

TAXR Weighted average of the basic income-tax rate (*AAS*)

TYD Trend of personal disposable income, current prices

WD World demand - world trade exports, f.o.b., in real terms (*FS*)

WPA $[(WP_t + (WP)_{t-1}]/2$, where WP = price index of world exports (*FS*)

SOME IMPORTANT FEATURES OF THE MODEL

Our model broadly belongs to the mainstream Keynesian tradition of income-expenditure macroeconomic models, the main blocks of which are built around the main components of national final expenditure. In Figure 8.1 we produce a flow-chart which summarises in a very general and simple way the main elements and interrelationships of our model. In this chart exogenous variables are encased in double-line boxes; endogenous variables are determined by the variables, to which they are linked by inward-pointing arrows. Given the aggregate nature of the model the following broad categories of expenditures are explained: consumption, private fixed investment, stockbuilding, imports, exports and general government expenditure. The main direction of influence in determining the volume of each type of spending is the level, or changes in the level, of aggregate demand, with income featuring more prominently in expenditure-determining relationships than relative prices. But unlike most of the existing 'big' models of the UK economy,[1] we find that the rate of interest is always a statistically significant factor affecting the level of private spending - albeit, in accordance with the Treasury model, not a quantitatively very important one (Budd, 1979, p. 8; HM Treasury, 1979, p. 72). In line, however, with the reported latest versions of the other models a wealth effect - through inflation and the level of liquid assets of the personal sector - seems to be very important in the highly aggregate consumption function we use (the National Institute model is an exception - see Ormerod, 1979b, pp. 117-18). Finally, price effects play an important role in the determination of imports and exports, which is a pretty conventional result in an aggregate model.

The monetary sector of the model consists of the money demand and money supply, the interaction of which determines the short-term rate of interest, which in turn is used to estimate a long-term rate of interest on the basis of a hypothesis of a stable term structure of interest rates. Any attempt to incorporate a more sophisticated treatment of the monetary and financial sectors would have resulted in an undesirable increase of the size of the model (for a description of the problems confronting the financial modeller in the United Kingdom see HM Treasury, 1979, pp. 74-81). The price level is determined in terms of labour cost, import prices and changes in productivity, while the wage equation is a type of augmented Phillips curve expanded to allow for an independent effect of trade-union militancy. Finally, unemployment is determined by the level of aggregate demand without any reference to a production function or factor prices.

The lack of any direct link between money and prices in our model is not unique in UK modelling. It is only very recently, and again only in the case of the London Business School model, that an attempt is made for an explicit and formal establishment of a relation between money and prices - an approach related to the mainstream of thought in the international monetarist tradition (Dornbusch, 1976). Under a flexible exchange-rate regime, changes in the money supply affect prices via changes in the exchange rate as follows: 'For a given level of domestic real income and for given values of the external variables, an exogenous increase in the supply of money will lower the exchange rate which, in turn, will cause inflation and raise the level of domestic prices until the level of real balances is restored to the equilibrium level' (Ball, Burns and Warburton, 1979, p. 93).

In common with other models of the UK economy our model incorporates the government budget constraint and attempts to provide for the effect of financing the government deficit on the net wealth of the private sector and, therefore, on private spending - liquid assets of the personal sector, which significantly affect consumers' expenditure, are associated with changes in money stock and government debt. The model attempts to innovate in its treatment of the government sector, which is endogenised to a much greater degree than in other models. Clearly government revenues (although not tax rates) are mostly endogenised in all models. The same is not true, however, for the government-expenditure variable; in our case this important variable is in fact endogenised to a very large extent,

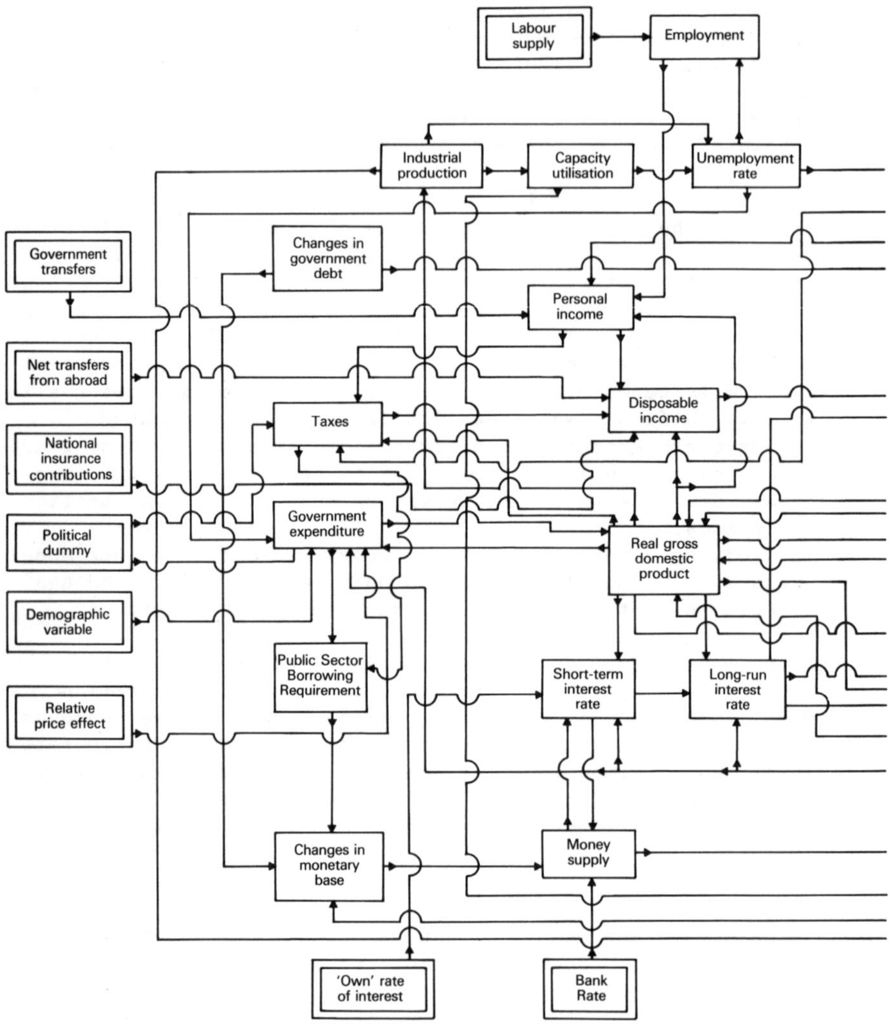

Figure 8.1 *Flow chart of annual model*

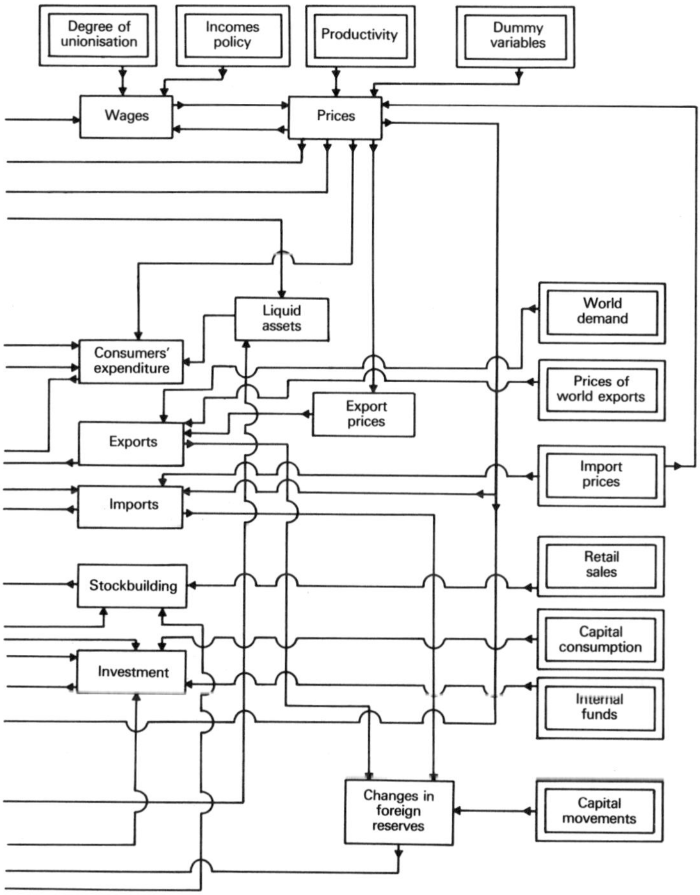

Figure 8.1 *cont.*

and incorporated in the model via appropriate government reaction functions for general government consumption and investment and government transfers. And although this procedure entails problems when we come to considering policy questions (see Chapter 9), nevertheless it is very important to adopt this procedure, since neglect of it implies a bias inasmuch as the interrelationships between government expenditures and the variables determining them would be completely absent from the model, as we have already demonstrated in Chapter 6 on the modelling of the government sector. Given the frequent change of governments, however, such reaction functions are unlikely to be stable relationships.

In the sense that income effects play a more important role than price effects our model appears to be close to the post-Keynesian tradition - although this is partly inevitable given the aggregate nature of the model. It should be clear, however, that a model reflecting post-Keynesian views should include the following further features which constitute some of the main tenets of this tradition: a careful examination of the problems of income distribution and economic growth, a detailed consideration and modelling of credit (rather than simply money), as well as a proper distinction between the factors affecting the secular growth of output and those influencing the cyclical movements around a trend; and they would also encapsulate the existence and growth of multinational companies and trade unions.[2] It is worth noting, however, that despite the expanding disaggregation of existing models the degree to which they manage to incorporate neoclassical views on the importance of relative prices is rather limited - none, for example, employs a fully fledged neoclassical investment function; on the contrary, the conventional accelerator principle seems to be the most dominant approach adopted.

The chosen size of the model has, of course, meant that we had to treat as exogenous variables which are definitely endogenous, such as the exchange rate, the government debt, the cash flow of the company sector, etc., or to ignore entirely other equally, or even more, significant factors such as changes in the distribution of income, industrial relations, productivity and competitiveness, capital consumption, the degree of monopoly, etc. It must be noted, however, that most of the latter variables are also ignored by the big forecasting models. It seems that at the present state of economic modelling formalised models are grossly elliptical, and partial pictures of the economy, with a very short-term perspective, intended only to be used in answering a very specific and rather limited set of questions.

It is true to say that the available models of the UK economy - with the probable exception of the Cambridge growth model (Barker, 1976) - are basically demand models. Thus even large disaggregated models are simply an elaboration of the standard macro model. Recently, however, there has been an attempt to emphasise the need to incorporate fully the supply side of the economy in modelling projects. Klein (1978, p. 2) suggests that Keynes's 'analysis dealing with supply has been largely played down by the profession at large - not by all students of macroeconomics'. He goes on:

> In terms of the history of economic thought the above [supply] approach means thinking in terms of the empirical implementation of the Walrasian system. Essentially, Tinbergen implemented the Keynesian system and Leontief implemented a part of the Walrasian system. By putting the two together, with due allowance to Kuznets for making the data bases of final demand and national income available, a complete synthesis of supply and demand in the economy as a whole can be put together. This gives the antecedents of what is meant by modelling supply, taking into account what is needed from demand models at the same time (Klein, 1978, p. 4).

It would therefore seem that incorporating the supply side of the economy in macroeconomic models does not present intractable problems; it would nevertheless raise fundamental theoretical questions concerning the workings of the present capitalist economies.

9

Dynamic Behaviour and Policy Characteristics of the Model

Any dynamic econometric model which purports to show the impact of macroeconomic policies must be able to track the historical data reasonably well. The process which enables us to examine this property of a model is called *simulation*. This way of evaluating and validating simultaneous-equation models, like the one presented in this book, is of paramount importance because, although each individual equation may have a very good statistical fit (as conventionally measured), the whole model may fail to reproduce the historical time series satisfactorily. Similarly, the individual equations of a model may perform poorly on standard statistical criteria, and yet the model as a whole may be capable of reproducing the historical data rather closely. This could easily happen 'since the behaviour of the model as a dynamic system may bear little relation to the way individual equations fit the historical data' (Pindyck and Rubinfeld, 1976, p. 317).

It is therefore very important to provide satisfactory evaluation criteria by which the simulation performance of a model can be judged. Only when this is done should policy evaluation exercises be undertaken. The aim of this chapter is to provide such criteria before the policy issues are discussed. In addition, the optimal control approach to policy evaluation, which attempts to overcome some of the problems of the simulation approach, is discussed in a subsequent section, where a number of control exercises are carried out to highlight the importance of this approach to policy-making.

THE MEANING OF SIMULATION

Assume the following linear, non-stochastic, dynamic system:

$$\sum_{j=1}^{n} a_{ij}Y_{jt} + \sum_{j=1}^{n} b_{ij}XY_{jt-1} + \ldots + \sum_{j=1}^{n} c_{ij}Y_{jt-p} + \sum_{k=1}^{m} d_{ik}X_{kt} = g_i$$

where $i = 1,2,3, \ldots, n$, a_{ij}, b_{ij}, c_{ij}, d_{ik} are (all four of them) coefficients on the variables Y_j and X_k, and g_i represent constants. For $a_{ij} = 1$ when $i = j$ this is equivalent to a system of n simultaneous equations with, in turn, each of $Y_1, Y_2, \ldots, Y_n$ as the dependent variable or regressand in the corresponding regression. To illustrate, let it be assumed that $n = m = p = 2$; we then have the following system of two simultaneous equations:

$$Y_{1t} + a_{12}Y_{2t} + b_{11}Y_{1t-1} + b_{12}Y_{2t-1} + c_{11}Y_{1t-2} + c_{12}Y_{2t-2}$$

$$+ d_{11}X_{1t} + d_{12}X_{2t} = g_1$$

$$a_{21}Y_{1t} + Y_{2t} + b_{21}Y_{1t-1} + b_{22}Y_{2t-1} + c_{21}Y_{1t-2} + c_{22}Y_{2t-2}$$

$$+ d_{21}X_{1t} + d_{22}X_{2t} = g_2$$

Coefficients on the variables Y and X as well as the constants g_i are either specified on *a priori* grounds, or they are least squares estimates. Thus the set of regressors in an equation may include contemporaneous endogenous variables, that is, any Y_{it}, lagged values of these, and exogenous variables indicated by X_k. For actual values of all regressors each equation provides series of estimated values of the dependent variable.

In this context simulation is defined as the solution of the n-equation system for values of the endogenous variables over the period t to t + r, that is

$$Y_{1t}, Y_{1t+1}, Y_{1t+2}, \ldots, Y_{1t+r}$$

using the values of the exogenous variables X_{kt} X_{kt+1} $X_{kt+2}, \ldots, X_{kt+r}$, and the predetermined values of the endogenous variables, that is, values for the endogenous variables determined prior to t, or

$$Y_{it-1}, Y_{it-2}, Y_{it-3}, \ldots, Y_{it-p}$$

The latter are taken as the starting-point of simulation and are called the initial conditions. Given these two sets of values, namely exogenous and predetermined variables, as well as the estimated parameters, simulated values of Y_i over $t, \ldots, t + r$ can be traced as follows. The first-period computed values, Y^s_{it}, are obtained from the system merely by using values of the exogenous variables for the first period and all the initial conditions. In the next period we use the computed values Y^s_{it}, the first p - 1 initial conditions and the given values of the exogenous variables in period t + 1 to compute the next series of simulated values Y^s_{it+1}; we continue in this manner until t + r is reached, so that the initial conditions are eventually phased out and any past values of endogenous variables used are simulated ones. A dynamic model therefore provides its own momentum for generating a constant stream of values for the endogenous variables without any reference, after a certain point, to their real values. It should by now be clear that these values are different from the estimated values since the latter are permanently based on actual values of all regressors.

The simulation process can be continued long enough to generate series of values for a post-sample period (usually called *ex post* forecasts). Furthermore, given forecasts, over a future period, of the exogenous variables, the same process produces *ex ante* forecasts of the endogenous variables. In this study we will confine ourselves to historical simulation, which entails generation of simulated series of values only over the sample period.

A simple example may be used to illustrate these points; consider the following macroeconomic model:

$$Y_t = C_t + I_t + G_t \tag{9.1}$$

$$C_t = b_0 + b_1 Y_{t-1} \tag{9.2}$$

$$I_t = i_0 + i_1 (Y_{t-1} - Y_{t-2}) \tag{9.3}$$

where Y = gross national product, C = consumption, I = investment, and G = government expenditure. In this simple model consumption is related to income, and investment to changes in income; it is thus the standard multiplier-accelerator model, with C, I and Y being the endogenous variables, and G the variable determined outside the model, i.e. treated as an exogenous variable.

This model can now be solved analytically using the following notation:

$$L^n Y_t = Y_{t-n}$$

where L = the lag operator. The above equations could be rewritten as

$$Y_t - C_t - I_t = G_t \tag{9.1a}$$

$$-b_1 LY_t + C_t + 0.I_t = b_0 \tag{9.2a}$$

$$-i_1 [L(1 - L)]Y_t + 0.C_t + I_t = i_0 \tag{9.3a}$$

Applying any technique of solving simultaneous equations, solutions for the endogenous variables can be arrived at. By rearrangement we then have:

$$Y_t - (b_1 + i_1) Y_{t-1} + i_1 Y_{t-2} = G_t + b_0 + i_0 \tag{9.4}$$

$$C_t - (b_1 + i_1) C_{t-1} + i_1 C_{t-2} = (b_0 + b_1 i_0) + b_1 G_{t-1} \tag{9.5}$$

$$I_t - (b_1 + i_1) I_{t-1} + i_1 I_{t-2} = (1 - b_1) i_0 + i_1 (G_{t-1} - G_{t-2}) \tag{9.6}$$

These are second-order difference equations.[1] Given the estimated values of the parameters (b_0, b_1, i_0 and i_1), initial values for the endogenous variables (i.e. 'base-year' values), and values for the exogenous variables covering the period of simulation (as well as lagged values of these as required), equations 9.4-9.6 will give us time paths for each of the endogenous variables Y, C and I. These paths will be the simulated values of the endogenous variables. This is essentially what is meant by 'simulation'. We may assign hypothetical values to the above as follows:

$b_0 = 1.0$, $b_1 = 0.75$, $Y_{t-1} = 25$, $G_t = 9$, $G_{t-2} = 9$

$i_0 = 0.5$, $i_1 = 0.15$, $Y_{t-2} = 20$, $G_{t-1} = 9$, $G_{t+i} = 9$

$I_{t-1} = 0$, $C_{t-1} = 16$

$I_{t-2} = 7.5$, $C_{t-2} = 18.5$

Successive substitutions in equations 9.4-9.6 will give us the simulated paths for each of the variables Y, C and I; these paths are given in Table 9.1 for thirty periods.

An interesting facet of these simulated paths is that they can reveal whether the system is dynamically stable, i.e. whether it converges to an equilibrium when an exogenous shock occurs, such as a change in G_t. In order to investigate this case let us begin by solving the second-order difference equations 9.4-9.6; it can be shown[2] that these solutions are:

$$Y_t = B_1\left[\frac{(b_1 + i_1) + ((b_1 + i_1)^2 - 4i_1)^{\frac{1}{2}}}{2}\right]^t + B_2\left[\frac{(b_1 + i_1) - ((b_1 + i_1)^2 - 4i_1)^{\frac{1}{2}}}{2}\right]^t + \left[\frac{G_t + i_0 + b_0}{1 - b_1}\right] \quad (9.7)$$

$$C_t = B_3\left[\frac{(b_1 + b_1 i_1) + ((b_1 + i_1)^2 - 4i_1)^{\frac{1}{2}}}{2}\right]^t + B_4\left[\frac{(b_1 + i_1) - ((b_1 + i_1)^2 - 4i_1)^{\frac{1}{2}}}{2}\right]^t + \left[\frac{(b_0 + b_1 i_0) + b_1 G_{t-1}}{1 - b_1}\right] \quad (9.8)$$

$$I_t = B_5\left[\frac{(b_1 + i_1) + ((b_1 + i_1)^2 - 4i_1)^{\frac{1}{2}}}{2}\right]^t + B_6\left[\frac{(b_1 + i_1) - ((b_1 + i_1)^2 - 4i_1)^{\frac{1}{2}}}{2}\right]^t + \left[\frac{(1 - b_1)i_0 + i_1\,(G_{t-1} - G_{t-2})}{1 - b_1}\right] \quad (9.9)$$

Table 9.1 Simulated values of simple model

Period	Y_t	C_t	I_t
1	30.000	19.750	1.250
2	33.750	23.500	1.250
3	36.375	26.313	1.063
4	38.175	28.281	0.894
5	39.401	29.631	0.770
6	40.235	30.551	0.684
7	40.801	31.176	0.625
8	41.186	31.601	0.585
9	41.447	31.889	0.558
10	41.625	32.085	0.539
11	41.745	32.218	0.527
12	41.827	32.309	0.518
13	41.882	32.370	0.512
14	41.920	32.412	0.508
15	41.946	32.440	0.506
16	41.963	32.459	0.504
17	41.975	32.472	0.503
18	41.983	32.481	0.502
19	41.989	32.487	0.501
20	41.992	32.491	0.501
21	41.995	32.494	0.501
22	41.996	32.496	0.500
23	41.998	32.497	0.500
24	41.998	32.498	0.500
25	41.999	32.499	0.500
26	41.999	32.499	0.500
27	42.000	32.499	0.500
28	42.000	32.500	0.500
29	42.000	32.500	0.500
30	42.000	32.500	0.500

where B_1, B_2, B_3, B_4, B_5 and B_6 are constants which depend on the initial values that variables Y_t, C_t and I_t happen to take. We also note that the expressions:

$$\left[\frac{G_t + i_0 + b_0}{1 - b_1}\right], \left[\frac{(b_0 + b_1 i_0) + b_1 G_{t-1}}{1 - b_1}\right]$$

$$\left[\frac{(1 - b_1)i_0 + i_1(G_{t-1} - G_{t-2})}{1 - b_1}\right]$$

are the equilibrium values for the variables Y_t, C_t and I_t

respectively. The system would be stable if any divergence between the actual values of the endogenous variables and their equilibrium values disappears through time; otherwise the system is unstable. The solutions 9.7-9.9 suggest that there are four possibilities.[3] (1) The system can be stable, with the endogenous variables converging to some equilbrium values without oscillations. This happens when the roots

$$\left[\frac{(b_1 + i_1) + [(b_1 + i_1)^2 - 4i_1]^{\frac{1}{2}}}{2}\right] \text{ and}$$

$$\left[\frac{(b_1 + i_1) - [(b_1 + i_1)^2 - 4i_1]^{\frac{1}{2}}}{2}\right]$$

are less than unity and have no imaginary component.[4] (2) The system can be stable but converging with oscillations. This comes about when the roots are absolutely less than unity with imaginary components. (3) The system can be unstable and non-oscillatory, when at least one root is absolutely greater than unity without imaginary components. (4) Finally, the system can be unstable and oscillatory; this occurs when at least one root is absolutely greater than unity with imaginary components. It is, however, obvious that the values of the roots depend critically on the parameters b_1 and i_1. In a general way one can say that to the extent that both b_1 and i_1 are less than unity, the solution will be stable, while if either is greater than unity the solution will be unstable. Furthermore, the roots will have an imaginary component if

$$4i_1 > (b_1 + i_1)^2$$

or

$$b_1 < (2(i_1)^{\frac{1}{2}} - i_1)$$

In Table 9.2 we present four cases for Y_t, C_t and I_t where we simulate the model with the same initial conditions as above. The only difference is that in the case of Table 9.2 we assume an exogenous shock whereby G_t increases to 10 throughout the period, and four values for i_1 are assumed: $i_1 = 0.15$, $i_1 = 0.80$, $i_1 = 1.50$ and $i_1 = 2.50$; b_1 remains the same as above, i.e. 0.75.

In case I the roots are 0.68 and 0.22 and the system is stable without oscillations. In case II, with the roots being 0.78 ± 0.45i, the system is stable but oscillatory. In case III the system is unstable - the roots are 1.13 ± 0.49i - and oscillatory. In case IV, with roots 4 and 1.25, the system is non-oscillatory and unstable.

This analysis is applicable when the model is linear; when the model is non-linear, as is the case with the annual model we have developed for the purposes of this book, this analysis is no longer applicable. What one can do in the case of a non-linear model is to, first, linearise the model about some nominal solution path and then examine its stability; this is as far as one can go (Pindyck and Rubinfeld, 1976, p. 345).

The values of the endogenous variables simulated in this way can be compared with their actual time paths, a process which enables one to form some judgement as to how well the model performs as an interdependent unit in tracking the movements of certain strategic economic variables. A number of criteria can be employed for this purpose.

The criterion mostly used is the *root-mean-square error* (RMSE), defined as

$$\text{RMSE} = \left[\frac{1}{T} \sum_{t=1}^{T} (Y_t^a - Y_t^s)^2 \right]^{\frac{1}{2}}$$

where Y_t^a = actual value of variable, Y_t^s = simulated value of variable, and T = the number of periods used for simulation. Sometimes the RMSE is expressed in proportional form as follows:

$$\text{RMSEP} = \left[\frac{1}{T} \sum_{t=1}^{T} \frac{(Y_t^a - Y_t^s)^2}{Y_t^a} \right]^{\frac{1}{2}}$$

The RMSE and the RMSEP measure the 'deviations' of the simulated variable from its actual time path.

Another criterion is the *mean simulation error* (MSE), defined as

$$\text{MSE} = \frac{1}{T} \sum_{t=1}^{T} (Y_t^a - Y_t^s)$$

or the same but expressed in proportional form:

$$\text{MSEP} = \frac{1}{T} \sum_{t=1}^{T} \left[\frac{Y_t^a - Y_t^s}{Y_t^a} \right]$$

The trouble with the MSE and the MSEP is that they may give a false picture of the accuracy of a simulation process inasmuch as they may be close to zero if large positive errors tend to outweigh large negative errors. By contrast, the RMSE measure, by its very construction, does not distinguish between negative and positive errors and penalises large errors more heavily than the MSE measure; it is for this reason that the RMSE measure is usually preferred.

Another important criterion is how well the model tracks down periods which correspond to turning-points in the endogenous variables. This criterion is probably of more relative importance than the criteria referred to above since it refers to the ability

Table 9.2 Simulated values of simple model

Period	Case I: $i_1 = 0.15$ Y_t	C_t	I_t	Case II: $i_1 = 0.80$ Y_t	C_t	I_t	Case III: $i_1 = 1.50$ Y_t	C_t	I_t	Case IV: $i_1 = 2.50$ Y_t	C_t	I_t
1	31.000	19.750	1.250	34.250	19.750	4.500	37.750	19.750	8.000	42.750	19.750	13.000
2	35.650	24.250	1.400	44.588	26.688	7.900	58.938	29.313	19.625	87.938	33.063	44.875
3	38.935	27.738	1.198	53.211	34.441	8.770	87.484	45.203	32.281	190.422	66.953	113.469
4	41.194	30.201	0.993	58.307	40.908	7.399	119.934	66.613	43.320	410.527	143.816	256.711
5	42.734	31.896	0.839	59.307	44.730	4.577	150.124	90.950	49.174	869.659	308.900	550.764
6	43.782	33.051	0.731	56.780	45.480	1.300	169.379	113.593	45.786	1811.574	653.244	1148.330
7	44.494	33.836	0.657	52.064	43.585	-1.521	167.416	128.034	29.382	3724.968	1359.681	2355.287
8	44.977	34.370	0.607	46.775	40.048	-3.273	134.118	126.562	-2.444	7588.709	2794.726	4783.984
9	45.305	34.733	0.573	42.350	36.081	-3.731	62.141	101.588	-49.447	15362.387	5692.532	9659.855
10	45.528	34.979	0.549	39.723	32.762	-3.040	-49.859	47.606	-107.465	30967.483	11522.790	19434.693
11	45.680	35.146	0.533	39.190	30.792	-1.602	-193.894	-36.394	-167.500	62249.854	23226.613	39013.242
12	45.782	35.260	0.523	40.467	30.393	0.074	-349.974	-144.421	-215.553	124904.818	46688.391	78206.427
13	45.852	35.337	0.515	42.871	31.350	1.521	-485.100	-261.481	-233.620	250327.522	93679.613	156637.909
14	45.900	35.389	0.510	45.577	33.153	2.424	-555.014	-362.825	-202.189	501313.903	187746.642	313557.261
15	45.932	35.425	0.507	47.847	35.183	2.665	-509.632	-415.261	-104.371			
16	45.954	35.449	0.505	49.202	36.886	2.316	-302.650	-381.224	68.574			
17	45.969	35.465	0.503	49.850	37.901	1.584	94.985	-225.988	310.972			
18	45.979	35.476	0.502	48.840	38.114	0.727	679.191	72.239	596.953			
19	45.986	35.484	0.502	47.614	37.630	-0.016	1397.203	510.393	876.809			
20	45.990	35.489	0.501	46.230	36.711	-0.481	2136.419	1048.902	1077.517			
21	45.993	35.493	0.501	45.065	35.673	-0.607	2722.640	1603.315	1109.325			
22	45.996	35.495	0.501	44.367	34.799	-0.432	2932.810	2042.980	879.830			
23	45.997	35.497	0.500	44.217	34.275	-0.059	2526.363	2200.608	315.756			
24	45.998	35.498	0.500	44.542	34.162	0.380	1296.602	1895.773	-609.170			
25	45.999	35.498	0.500	45.167	34.407	0.761	-860.690	973.452	-1844.142			
26	45.999	35.499	0.500	45.875	34.875	1.000	-3869.956	-644.518	-3235.438			
27	45.999	35.499	0.500	46.473	35.407	1.067	-7404.866	-2901.467	-4513.399			
28	46.000	35.500	0.500	46.833	35.855	0.978	-10844.514	-5552.649	-5301.865			
29	46.000	35.500	0.500	46.913	36.125	0.788	-13281.358	-8132.385	-5158.872			
30	46.000	35.500	0.500	46.748	36.185	0.564	-13604.784	-9960.018	-3654.766			

of a model to track down reasonably well sudden changes in the historical data. For two models, one of which has, for the same variable, a relatively high RMSE, say, but is able to capture turning-points, while the other has a relatively low RMSE, but fails on turning-points, most econometric investigators would probably pick the one which satisfactorily tracks turning-points.

Other criteria relate to the dynamic response of the model: that is, whether the model responds to changes in exogenous variables or strategic parameters in a way which is consistent with economic theory and well-established empirical findings. The sensitivity of a model to changes in the initial conditions, or small changes in the estimated coefficients or values of the exogenous variables, is another criterion which tests the simulation ability of a model, since these small changes should not significantly affect its performance.

The importance of all these criteria can be highlighted by repeating that it is very likely that in a multi-equation model where individual equations perform extremely well in terms of standard statistical criteria, the model as a whole could very well fail when the above criteria are applied to test its tracking performance.

SIMULATION RESULTS OF THE ANNUAL MODEL

We now turn our discussion to our annual model and its simulation performance. The simulated values for some important variables, along with their historical (actual) values, are provided in Tables 9.3(a)-9.3(d); in these tables we also provide the RMSEP. We also provide figures for most of these variables (Figures 9.1-9.11).

The over-all simulation performance of the model is satisfactory. The RMSEPs are quite low and Figures 9.1-9.11 reveal that most turning-points are tracked satisfactorily; it would therefore be fair to say that the simulated series seem to reproduce the general long-run behaviour of the actual series. However, it is also true to say that some RMSEPs are quite high, and there are short-run fluctuations in the actual series which are not reproduced properly, with some turning-points being missed altogether.

In particular, the variables which do not perform satisfactorily in terms of short-run fluctuations and turning-points are APC, GDPR, RL and UNER, while in terms of the RMSEP the variables are UNER, WR and (to a lesser extent) RPD. The bad tracking performance of the GDPR variable can be attributed, to a large extent, to the extremely bad performance of the STB variable (not reported here). Since GDPR influences APC through YDR, it is not surprising that the simulated values of APC do not appear to track down the historical values adequately. But APC is also influenced by the RL variable, which does not perform well either. The latter variable is heavily influenced by GDPR and also by RS. Moreover, the way that the short-term rate of interest is utilised for simulation purposes creates one important problem. Recall that the money supply and the money demand equations have the same dependent variable - the money stock. When simulating the model the demand for money equation is solved

Table 9.3(a) Actual and simulated values with RMSEP

	APC		CONR		GDPR		GEX	
Year	A	S	A	S	A	S	A	S
1965	0.912	0.914	28.754	29.024	38.491	38.130	13.309	13.505
1966	0.909	0.943	29.280	28.895	39.224	37.586	14.449	14.545
1967	0.915	0.915	29.891	30.621	40.262	39.792	16.672	16.323
1968	0.921	0.881	30.638	32.589	41.721	43.221	18.289	17.896
1969	0.919	0.892	30.839	32.644	42.408	43.997	18.984	18.934
1970	0.911	0.908	31.696	32.115	43.368	43.262	20.867	21.549
1971	0.915	0.895	32.675	32.971	44.402	44.122	23.445	24.127
1972	0.895	0.875	34.542	33.666	45.040	44.956	26.316	26.905
1973	0.883	0.880	36.062	34.317	48.745	46.243	30.503	29.336
1974	0.859	0.875	35.631	33.786	48.007	45.729	39.146	36.708
1975	0.847	0.818	35.257	34.606	47.190	47.783	51.642	49.923
1976	0.854	0.851	35.405	33.838	48.844	47.902	58.362	54.325
1977	0.856	0.812	35.116	36.195	49.606	51.484	61.738	61.102
1978	0.856	0.826	37.037	37.262	51.215	52.497	71.351	71.072
RMSEP	0.027		0.035		0.030		0.032	

Table 9.3(b) Actual and simulated values with RMSEP

	IP		M3		QR		RL	
Year	A	S	A	S	A	S	A	S
1965	4.405	4.402	13.427	13.372	8.644	8.985	6.42	7.07
1966	4.344	4.369	13.912	13.974	8.873	9.124	6.80	6.95
1967	4.488	4.110	15.293	15.001	9.502	9.727	6.69	6.78
1968	4.906	4.794	16.407	16.255	10.216	10.824	7.39	8.20
1969	5.211	5.522	16.919	16.892	10.559	11.335	8.88	9.49
1970	5.343	5.381	18.529	18.159	11.101	11.460	9.16	9.53
1971	5.584	5.428	20.944	19.543	11.635	11.824	9.05	9.87
1972	5.899	5.866	26.245	21.909	12.764	12.445	9.11	10.54
1973	6.154	6.023	33.466	25.948	14.212	13.318	10.85	10.56
1974	5.889	5.565	37.685	29.055	14.334	13.129	14.95	12.19
1975	5.660	5.456	40.571	33.424	13.281	12.683	14.66	14.88
1976	5.777	6.193	45.129	38.901	13.815	13.221	14.25	13.83
1977	6.182	6.318	49.566	46.141	13.916	13.964	12.32	12.03
1978	6.755	6.943	56.931	56.035	14.475	14.478	12.38	13.13
RMSEP	0.042		0.117		0.045		0.085	

Table 9.3(c) Actual and simulated values with RMSEP

	RPD		TAX		UNER		WR		XR	
Year	A	S	A	S	A	S	A	S	A	S
1965	5.3	4.1	9.270	9.497	1.5	1.5	4.3	4.0	8.395	8.450
1966	2.9	2.6	10.155	10.390	1.5	2.2	4.6	1.9	8.725	8.861
1967	2.7	2.8	11.419	11.654	2.3	2.9	3.9	3.0	8.864	9.247
1968	3.5	4.0	13.092	13.358	2.5	2.4	6.6	7.3	9.898	10.116
1969	3.6	4.4	14.896	14.685	2.5	1.9	5.3	7.4	10.862	10.777
1970	7.8	8.6	16.482	16.572	2.6	2.4	9.9	11.1	11.451	11.360
1971	10.9	10.7	16.454	16.989	3.3	3.3	12.9	13.4	12.290	11.872
1972	10.1	10.1	18.136	18.866	3.7	3.7	13.8	13.8	12.443	12.549
1973	7.6	5.9	20.273	19.933	2.6	3.8	13.7	9.7	13.968	13.840
1974	17.1	15.0	24.970	24.130	2.6	4.2	19.8	12.9	14.851	14.519
1975	27.7	26.3	31.674	30.127	3.9	4.5	29.5	26.9	14.444	14.347
1976	13.9	14.2	36.271	34.514	5.3	4.7	19.3	21.6	15.753	15.816
1977	11.6	13.0	41.474	40.440	5.7	4.5	6.6	12.0	16.906	16.778
1978	10.1	13.9	46.457	46.483	5.6	4.0	14.0	20.3	17.298	17.669
RMSEP	0.163		0.029		0.287		0.348		0.019	

Table 9.3(d) Actual and simulated values with RMSEP

	YDR	
Year	A	S
1965	31.539	31.760
1966	32.200	30.651
1967	32.677	33.483
1968	33.279	36.985
1969	33.554	36.614
1970	34.775	35.357
1971	35.717	36.837
1972	38.600	38.493
1973	40.866	39.007
1974	41.449	38.614
1975	41.615	42.300
1976	41.468	39.770
1977	41.014	44.566
1978	43.281	45.104
RMSEP	0.055	

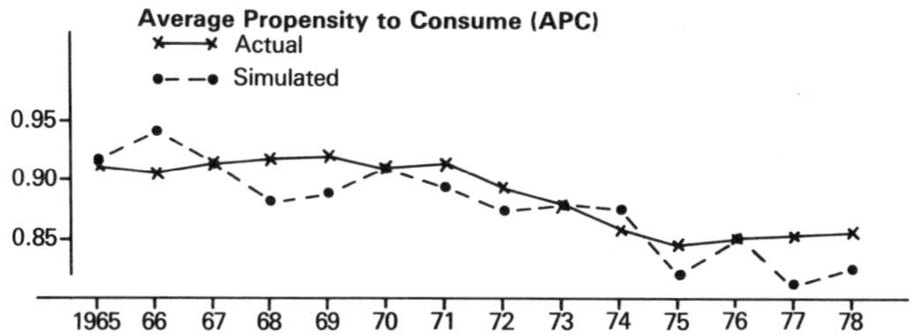

Figure 9.1

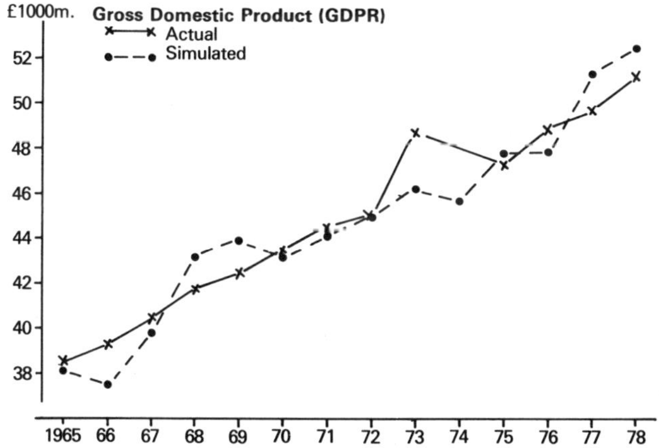

Figure 9.2

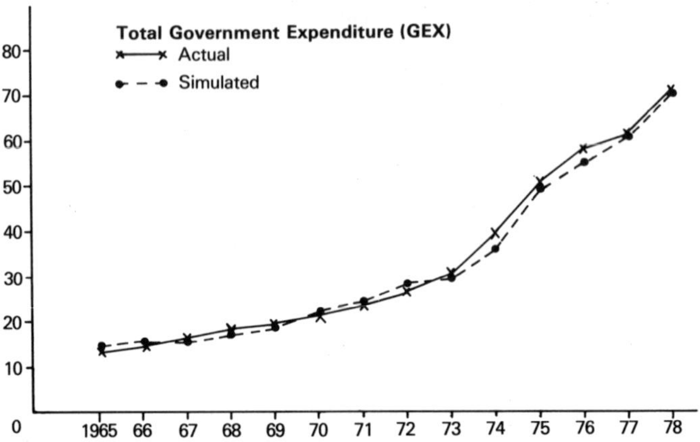

Figure 9.3

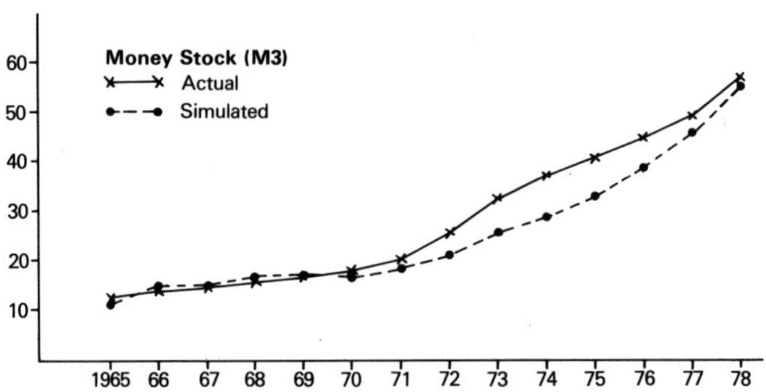

Figure 9.4

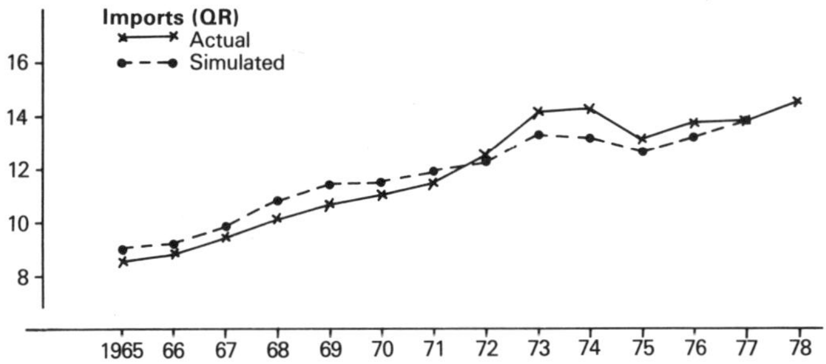

Figure 9.5

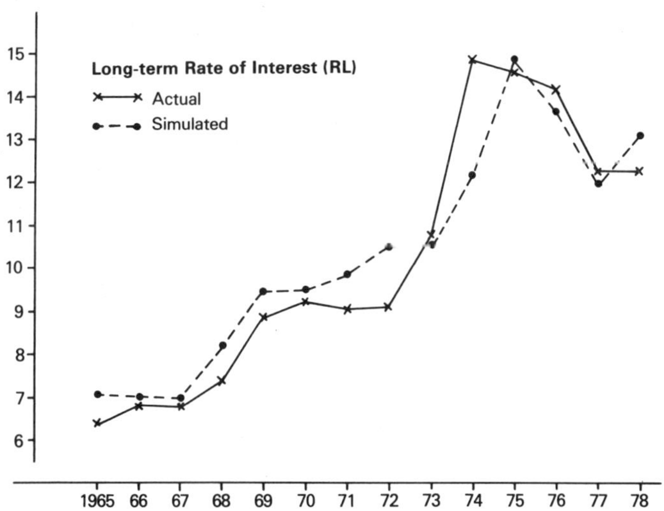

Figure 9.6

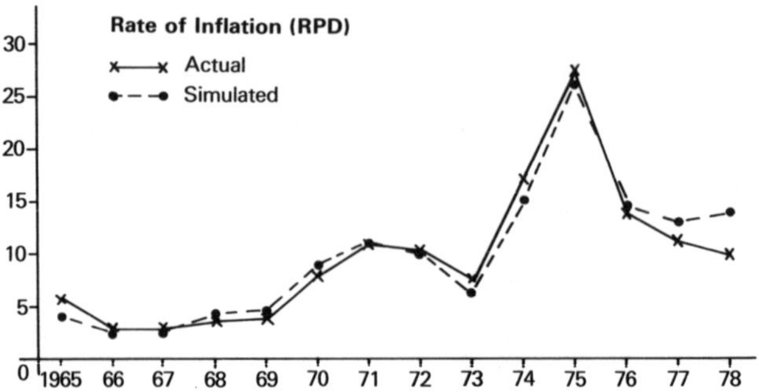

Figure 9.7

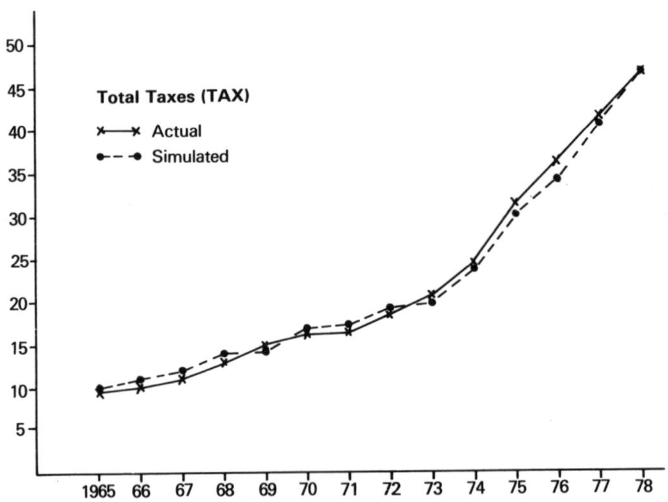

Figure 9.8

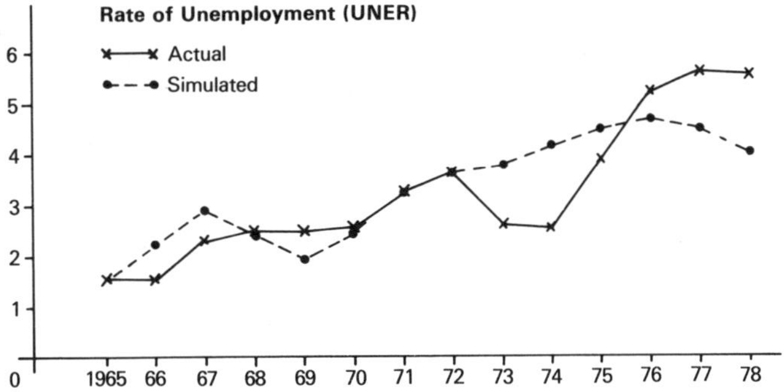

Figure 9.9

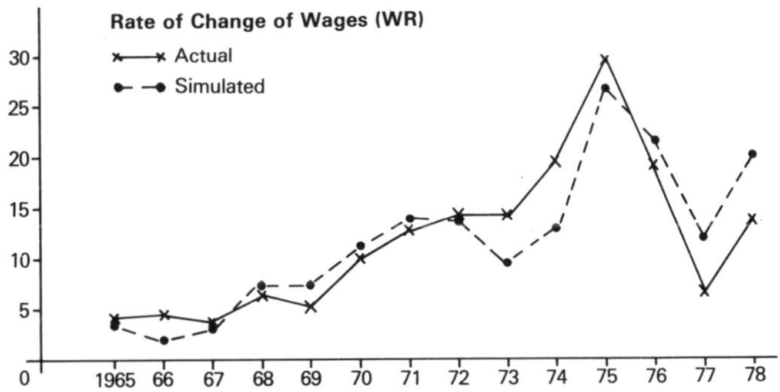

Figure 9.10

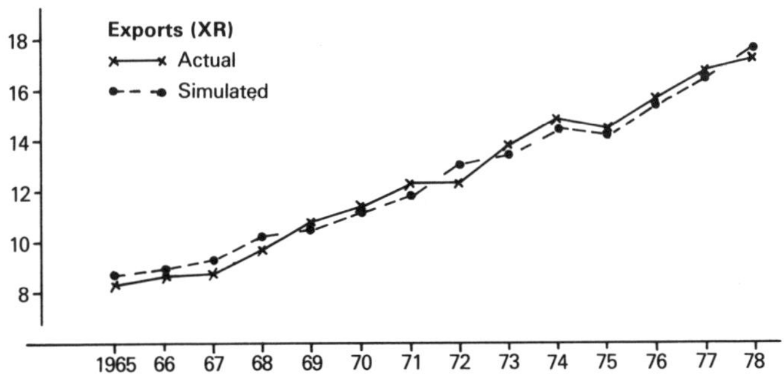

Figure 9.11

for RS, so that the short-term rate of interest becomes the dependent variable, as if that were the variable to be explained in the first place. Clearly this biases the simulation results, since the equation which actually explains the short-term rate of interest is expected to be different from the one derived from the estimated demand for money relationship. This bias is immediately transmitted to the long-term rate of interest - to the APC - and to the money stock. This last variable, then, influences the liquid assets component, which enters the APC relationship directly. Finally, since one of the important determinants of the unemployment rate is GDPR, through its impact on the IPR variable, not surprisingly UNER does have its problems as well.

In an attempt to examine the validity of the arguments just put forward, the STB variable is exogenised along with the WR variable, for which, according to a recent observation, 'there is no consensus among economists about what determines the course of money wages. Most econometric model-builders override the money-wage equation [if any] in their models when they are actually forecasting' (*Midland Bank Review*, 1980, p. 12); once this is done the whole model is simulated again. The results for the variables APC, GDPR, RL and UNER appear in Table 9.4 (see also Figures 9.12-9.15). The picture that emerges from these results is that there is an over-all improvement in the tracking ability of the variables referred to in this table. The RMSEP falls significantly in all four cases, and the turning-points are, now, captured more satisfactorily than before.

Table 9.4 Actual and simulated values with RMSEP

	APC		GDPR		RL		UNER	
Year	A	S	A	S	A	S	A	S
1965	0.912	0.912	38.491	38.215	6.42	7.11	1.5	1.5
1966	0.909	0.923	39.224	38.547	6.80	7.29	1.5	2.0
1967	0.915	0.924	40.262	39.486	6.69	6.99	2.3	2.7
1968	0.921	0.896	41.721	41.997	7.39	8.07	2.5	2.8
1969	0.919	0.891	42.408	43.734	8.88	9.19	2.5	2.3
1970	0.911	0.893	43.368	44.193	9.16	9.47	2.6	2.3
1971	0.915	0.900	44.402	43.914	9.05	9.77	3.3	3.0
1972	0.895	0.880	45.040	44.401	9.11	10.36	3.7	3.7
1973	0.883	0.852	48.745	47.841	10.85	11.15	2.6	3.7
1974	0.859	0.869	48.007	45.992	14.95	13.31	2.6	3.7
1975	0.847	0.844	47.190	45.191	14.66	15.13	3.9	4.9
1976	0.854	0.846	48.844	47.140	14.25	13.54	5.3	5.6
1977	0.856	0.830	49.606	49.833	12.32	11.12	5.7	5.2
1978	0.856	0.830	51.215	51.721	12.38	11.86	5.6	4.6
RMSEP	0.021		0.023		0.075		0.212	

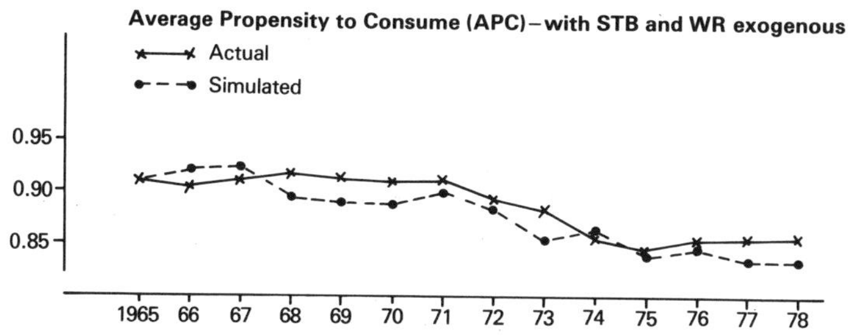

Figure 9.12

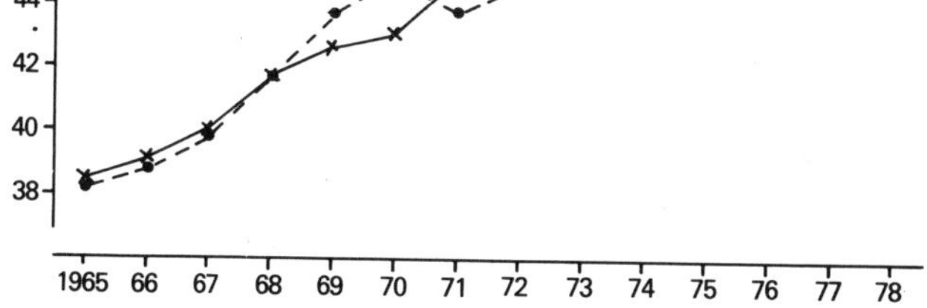

Figure 9.13

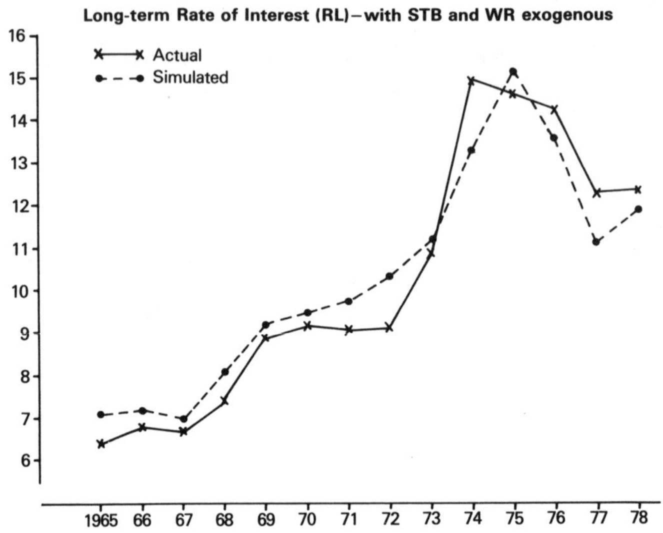

Figure 9.14

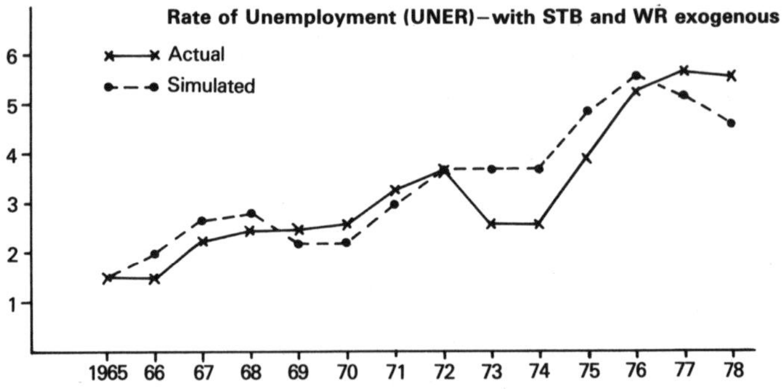

Figure 9.15

In addition to the above experiments we have also simulated the model by varying the initial conditions; whereas all the simulations reported in Tables 9.3 and 9.4 relate to the year 1965 as the starting period, these additional exercises refer to consecutive years in 1960-4 as starting periods. The results of these simulations do not differ significantly from the ones reported above; it follows, therefore, that our annual model is not sensitive to the initial conditions. The same applies to small changes in the parameters and exogenous variables of the model; exercises of this kind have in fact been undertaken and they confirm this conclusion.

The over-all conclusion that follows from this discussion is, then, that our model simulates satisfactorily the historical values of most of the important endogenous variables. The next step is to examine the dynamic response of the model to changes in exogenous variables and strategic parameters and consider whether their impact is in agreement with that of economic theory. This is taken up in the next section.

MODEL BEHAVIOUR AND DYNAMIC MULTIPLIERS

In this section we are interested to determine how changes in the exogenous variables (or parameter estimates) of a model are likely to influence the endogenous variables of the same model over time. We might wish, for example, to determine how changes in some exogenous policy variables, or exogenous variables such as world demand (WD), will affect future values of GDPR and its components, unemployment, prices, etc. We would wish, in other words, to utilise our model in this case to make statements about the dynamic behaviour, i.e. the response over time, of our model to changes in particular variables; one useful way of determining these dynamic responses of a model is to derive and examine the so-called 'dynamic multipliers'. In general these multipliers can be derived as follows. First, a control solution of the endogenous variables is established by the methods described above in the first section of this chapter using actual, i.e. historical, values of the exogenous variables. We then make a new simulation corresponding to 'disturbed', different, specific values of the exogenous variables (or parameter estimates) to see how much influence on the system, measured by departure from the control solution, they have. Finally, we compare the control solution,

$$y^s_{i,t_1}, \ldots, y^s_{i,t_1+1}, \ldots, y^s_{i,t_1+2}, \ldots, y^s_{i,t+s}$$

based on the actual values of the exogenous variables,

$$x_{i,t_1}, \ldots, x_{i,t_1+1}, \ldots, x_{i,t_1+2}, \ldots, x_{i,t_1+s}$$

with the 'disturbed' solution,

$$y^+_{i,t_1}, \ldots, y^+_{i,t_1+1}, \ldots, y^+_{i,t_1+2}, \ldots, y^+_{i,t_1+s}$$

corresponding to the new, different, values of the exogenous variables,

$$x^+_{i,t_1}, \; . \; . \; . \; , \; x^+_{i,t_1+1}, \; . \; . \; . \; , \; x^+_{i,t_1+2}, \; . \; . \; . \; , \; x^+_{i,t+s}$$

We use the ratio of the difference between the two solutions, 'disturbed' and control, i.e. y^+_{i,t_1+s} and y^s_{i,t_1+s}, on the one hand, and the difference between the two sets of exogenous variables, 'disturbed' and actual, i.e. x^+_{i,t_1+s} and x_{i,t_1+s}, on the other, to derive multiplier effects for a number of periods of dynamic simulations. These are, then, the 'dynamic multipliers' (see Klein, 1974, ch. 6, pp. 226-80, for a detailed exposition of all these). It must be stressed that implicit in this kind of exercise there is the assumption that the structure of the model is policy-invariant, i.e. it is not affected by policy changes; the same applies in the case of exogenous shocks.

Let us now return to the very simple model of equations 9.1-9.3 with the assumptions made there on the values of the parameters, exogenous variables and lagged variables. We may obtain the dynamic multipliers of the model when G_t is increased by 1.0 in the first period only, and, alternatively by 1.0 throughout the period. First, we establish the control solutions, as in Table 9.1, without the change in G. Next, we simulate the model once again to establish the 'disturbed' solution corresponding to G_t changing by 1.0 in the first period only, and also to G_t changing by 1.0 throughout the whole period. In the latter case, forming the ratio

$$\left[\frac{Y^+_t - Y^s_t}{G^+_t - G_t}\right]$$

(in the former case the difference $Y^+_t - Y^s_t$ suffices) for Y_t, and similarly for C_t and I_t, we derive the dynamic multipliers for these endogenous variables, which are shown in Tables 9.5 and 9.6 - Table 9.5 corresponds to G_t changing by 1.0 in the first period only, and Table 9.6 to G_t changing by 1.0 throughout the period. In both cases the impact multiplier is the initial first-period change, 1.0 in the case of Y_t and 0 in the case of C_t and I_t.

In the case of Table 9.5 the long-run multiplier is the sum of all the dynamic multipliers - 4 in the case of Y_t, 3 for C_t, and 0 in the case of I_t. Table 9.6 is essentially the same as Table 9.5 inasmuch as in the former table the dynamic multipliers converge to the long-run values of Table 9.5. This is not surprising since in the case of Table 9.6 the exogenous change in G_t is sustained throughout the period; each dynamic multiplier in Table 9.6 in each period is simply the sum of all dynamic multipliers of Table 9.5 of the previous periods.

In the case of the annual model we examine its dynamic behaviour by undertaking a number of experiments; the results of these experiments appear in Tables 9.7-9.13. The description of these

Table 9.5 Dynamic multipliers

Period	Y_t	C_t	I_t
1	1.0000	0.0000	0.0000
2	0.9000	0.7500	0.1500
3	0.6600	0.6750	-0.0150
4	0.4590	0.4950	-0.0360
5	0.3140	0.3440	-0.0300
6	0.2140	0.2360	-0.0220
7	0.1450	0.1600	-0.0150
8	0.0990	0.1090	-0.0100
9	0.0670	0.0740	-0.0070
10	0.0460	0.0500	-0.0050
11	0.0310	0.0340	-0.0030
12	0.0210	0.0230	-0.0020
13	0.0140	0.0160	-0.0015
14	0.0100	0.0110	-0.0010
15	0.0070	0.0070	-0.0007
16	0.0040	0.0050	-0.0005
17	0.0030	0.0030	-0.0004
18	0.0020	0.0022	-0.0003
19	0.0014	0.0015	-0.0002
20	0.0009	0.0014	-0.0001
21	0.0006	0.0010	-0.0001
22	0.0004	0.0008	-0.0001
23	0.0003	0.0005	-0.0001
24	0.0002	0.0003	0.0000
25	0.0001	0.0002	0.0000
26	0.0001	0.0001	0.0000
27	0.0000	0.0000	0.0000
28	0.0000	0.0000	0.0000
Sum	4.0000	3.0000	0.0000

experiments now follows:

(a) Table 9.7: government expenditure increased by £1000m and is financed through printing more money via changes in the monetary base.
(b) Table 9.8: government expenditure increased by £1000m and is financed through borrowing by the government - the variable Δ(GS) adjusts appropriately in this case.
(c) Table 9.9: government expenditure increased by £1000m and is financed through increases in taxes.
(d) Table 9.10: exogenous change in world demand - a 10 per cent increase in the variable WD is assumed.
(e) Table 9.11: some form of import controls is introduced; the constant of the import equation is changed from -4.11760 to -6.11760.

Table 9.6 Dynamic multipliers

Period	Y_t	C_t	I_t
1	1.0000	0.0000	0.0000
2	1.9000	0.7500	0.1500
3	2.5600	1.4250	0.1350
4	3.0190	1.9200	0.0990
5	3.3330	2.2640	0.0690
6	3.5470	2.5000	0.0470
7	3.6920	2.6600	0.0320
8	3.7910	2.7690	0.0220
9	3.8580	2.8430	0.0150
10	3.9040	2.8930	0.0100
11	3.9350	2.9270	0.0070
12	3.9560	2.9500	0.0050
13	3.9700	2.9660	0.0035
14	3.9800	2.9770	0.0025
15	3.9870	2.9840	0.0018
16	3.9910	2.9890	0.0013
17	3.9940	2.9920	0.0009
18	3.9960	2.9942	0.0006
19	3.9974	2.9957	0.0004
20	3.9983	2.9971	0.0003
21	3.9989	2.9981	0.0002
22	3.9993	2.9989	0.0001
23	3.9996	2.9994	0.0000
24	3.9998	2.9997	0.0000
25	3.9999	2.9999	0.0000
26	4.0000	3.0000	0.0000
27	4.0000	3.0000	0.0000
28	4.0000	3.0000	0.0000

(f) Table 9.12: an incomes policy is hypothesised for the years 1970-8 whereby the variable WR is held constant and equal to its 1970 value for the whole 1970-8 period.
(g) Table 9.13: this is a combination of Tables 9.11 and 9.12; import controls and incomes policy are introduced simultaneously.

We begin by discussing Tables 9.7-9.9 together. The experiments concerned with these three tables relate to the impact of changes in government expenditure on the economy. In terms of theoretical and empirical considerations this type of analysis has been referred to in the literature as the 'crowding-out' debate. In the simple Keynesian multiplier analysis a change in government expenditure induces multiple changes in total spending. This analysis, however, pays little attention to the way government budgets are financed. As a result, it has been severely challenged by a number of

Table 9.7 Changes in government expenditure financed through money

Year	CB	CONR	GDPR	IP	M3	QR	RL	RPD	STB	UNER	XR
1965	-0.833	3.251	4.923	0.000	1.620	1.137	-0.097	1.306	1.160	-1.013	0.000
1966	-0.788	1.794	2.917	0.708	3.112	1.183	-0.028	3.106	0.358	-2.155	-0.031
1967	-0.768	1.560	1.746	0.158	4.262	1.027	-0.042	2.274	-0.504	-1.415	-0.125
1968	-1.080	2.333	2.587	-0.039	5.207	1.231	0.046	0.872	0.092	-0.835	-0.186
1969	-1.045	2.278	2.382	0.133	5.735	1.305	0.185	0.748	0.127	-0.851	-0.167
1970	-0.760	1.148	0.818	0.068	6.079	1.013	0.117	0.713	-0.378	-0.574	-0.194
1971	-0.725	1.145	0.604	-0.159	6.526	0.891	-0.114	0.192	-0.281	-0.158	-0.263
1972	-0.660	1.007	0.388	-0.103	6.958	0.834	-0.145	-0.073	-0.070	-0.042	-0.305
1973	-0.596	0.441	-0.416	-0.069	7.300	0.659	-0.118	-0.212	-0.217	0.113	-0.321
1974	-0.450	0.037	-1.046	-0.139	7.234	0.454	-0.390	-0.573	-0.278	0.418	-0.333
1975	-0.637	0.340	-0.463	-0.160	7.511	0.538	-0.489	-0.698	0.036	0.473	-0.358
1976	-1.039	-0.083	-0.942	-0.001	7.695	0.541	-0.485	-0.501	-0.022	0.365	-0.448
1977	-1.264	-0.121	-0.980	-0.061	8.155	0.571	-0.479	-0.529	-0.085	0.447	-0.485
1978	-1.287	-0.180	-1.063	-0.033	8.887	0.594	-0.612	-0.638	-0.026	0.487	-0.459
Mean	-0.852	1.068	0.818	0.022	6.163	0.856	-0.189	0.428	-0.006	-0.339	-0.263

Table 9.8 Changes in government expenditure financed through borrowing

Year	CB	CONR	GDPR	IP	M3	QR	RL	RPD	STB	UNER	XR
1965	-0.672	2.349	3.975	0.000	0.180	0.918	0.884	1.053	0.936	-0.817	0.000
1966	-0.437	0.153	1.181	0.571	0.116	0.684	1.091	2.197	-0.026	-1.499	-0.025
1967	-0.301	-0.322	-0.054	-0.065	-0.017	0.368	0.720	0.904	-0.718	-0.482	-0.093
1968	-0.515	0.459	1.085	-0.215	-0.045	0.533	0.624	-0.323	0.080	0.008	-0.113
1969	-0.408	0.264	0.870	0.049	-0.039	0.544	0.577	-0.031	0.108	-0.215	-0.066
1970	-0.153	-0.596	-0.334	-0.013	-0.075	0.276	0.286	0.158	-0.341	-0.063	-0.080
1971	-0.223	-0.208	0.051	-0.184	-0.060	0.270	0.164	-0.143	-0.110	0.146	-0.124
1972	-0.240	-0.099	0.222	-0.049	-0.033	0.316	0.163	-0.088	0.092	0.010	-0.130
1973	-0.121	-0.558	-0.445	-0.002	-0.058	0.193	0.029	-0.029	-0.138	0.034	-0.128
1974	-0.053	-0.583	-0.643	-0.095	-0.084	0.104	-0.167	-0.311	-0.156	0.251	-0.141
1975	-0.235	-0.175	-0.114	-0.080	-0.037	0.200	-0.180	-0.376	0.091	0.238	-0.146
1976	-0.318	-0.405	-0.433	0.319	-0.036	0.192	-0.197	-0.192	0.005	0.136	-0.172
1977	-0.359	-0.444	-0.543	-0.026	-0.042	0.180	-0.213	-0.228	-0.077	0.211	-0.191
1978	-0.456	-0.366	-0.465	-0.028	-0.042	0.203	-0.262	-0.329	0.002	0.245	-0.184
Mean	-0.321	-0.038	0.311	-0.007	-0.019	0.356	0.251	0.161	-0.018	-0.128	-0.114

Table 9.9 Changes in government expenditure financed through taxation

Year	CB	CONR	GDPR	IP	M3	QR	RL	RPD	STB	UNER	XR
1965	-0.651	2.231	3.850	0.000	0.174	0.889	0.855	1.020	0.906	-0.792	0.000
1966	-0.400	-0.020	1.004	0.533	0.106	0.631	1.021	2.091	-0.058	-1.423	-0.024
1967	-0.276	-0.399	-0.093	-0.082	-0.021	0.332	0.659	0.797	-0.694	-0.415	-0.089
1968	-0.487	0.378	1.054	-0.205	-0.042	0.502	0.573	-0.345	0.103	0.024	-0.106
1969	-0.377	0.166	0.807	0.056	-0.036	0.508	0.533	-0.019	0.103	-0.208	-0.060
1970	-0.132	-0.662	-0.360	-0.013	-0.072	0.246	0.254	0.150	-0.336	-0.051	-0.075
1971	-0.211	-0.237	0.072	-0.178	-0.055	0.252	0.149	-0.147	-0.092	0.145	-0.117
1972	-0.224	-0.148	0.215	-0.039	-0.030	0.296	0.152	-0.081	0.093	0.004	-0.121
1973	-0.105	-0.590	-0.438	-0.001	-0.055	0.174	0.023	-0.026	-0.139	0.034	-0.119
1974	-0.044	-0.593	-0.607	-0.092	-0.080	0.092	-0.164	-0.304	-0.147	0.245	-0.131
1975	-0.220	-0.189	-0.093	-0.074	-0.033	0.186	-0.172	-0.359	0.092	0.225	-0.136
1976	-0.286	-0.415	-0.409	0.033	-0.033	0.176	-0.186	-0.177	0.004	0.126	-0.159
1977	-0.327	-0.442	-0.507	-0.025	-0.039	0.164	-0.200	-0.212	-0.074	0.199	-0.177
1978	-0.425	-0.359	-0.422	-0.026	-0.037	0.189	-0.243	-0.307	0.004	0.228	-0.170
Mean	-0.297	-0.091	0.291	-0.007	-0.018	0.331	0.232	0.149	-0.017	-0.118	-0.106

Table 9.10 A 10 per cent change in WD

Year	CB	CONR	GDPR	IP	M3	QR	RL	RPD	STB	UNER	XR
1965	0.167	1.000	1.717	0.000	0.079	0.396	0.378	0.455	0.404	-0.353	0.585
1966	0.263	0.157	0.735	0.247	0.061	0.347	0.510	1.008	0.042	-0.693	0.619
1967	0.333	-0.045	0.265	-0.0001	0.010	0.250	0.413	0.568	-0.258	-0.331	0.621
1968	0.358	0.336	0.876	-0.070	0.004	0.371	0.467	0.129	0.076	-0.178	0.693
1969	0.441	0.266	0.880	0.049	0.008	0.427	0.552	0.305	0.090	-0.323	0.783
1970	0.624	-0.004	0.561	0.022	0.001	0.390	0.527	0.455	-0.086	-0.317	0.839
1971	0.656	0.102	0.703	-0.038	0.004	0.429	0.550	0.388	-0.024	-0.272	0.872
1972	0.847	0.162	0.829	-0.006	0.013	0.501	0.627	0.401	0.044	-0.323	0.940
1973	1.012	0.089	0.819	0.011	0.019	0.557	0.668	0.469	0.006	-0.364	1.098
1974	1.179	-0.133	0.463	-0.003	-0.011	0.529	0.686	0.389	-0.097	-0.288	1.077
1975	1.449	-0.120	0.368	-0.055	-0.039	0.544	0.679	0.181	-0.093	-0.155	0.977
1976	1.395	0.018	0.573	-0.052	-0.023	0.670	0.605	0.137	0.014	-0.146	1.046
1977	1.872	-0.157	0.336	-0.011	-0.032	0.723	0.476	0.207	-0.041	-0.168	1.058
1978	2.313	-0.298	0.085	-0.049	-0.069	0.751	0.402	0.105	-0.110	-0.069	1.090
Mean	0.922	0.098	0.658	0.003	0.002	0.492	0.539	0.371	-0.002	-0.284	0.878

Table 9.11 Import controls

Year	CB	CONR	GDPR	IP	M3	QR	RL	RPD	STB	UNER	XR
1965	0.211	1.157	1.989	0.000	0.091	-0.223	0.438	0.524	0.468	-0.408	0.000
1966	0.543	1.361	2.880	0.286	0.168	-0.546	1.066	1.697	0.524	-1.217	-0.012
1967	0.922	0.952	2.605	0.284	0.156	-0.988	1.421	2.193	0.084	-1.475	-0.061
1968	1.303	0.760	2.546	0.106	0.097	-1.311	1.820	1.742	-0.046	-1.255	-0.124
1969	1.489	0.886	2.880	0.037	0.061	-1.434	2.131	1.347	0.059	-1.130	-0.158
1970	1.782	0.807	2.904	0.050	0.049	-1.510	2.179	1.431	0.024	-1.185	-0.186
1971	2.092	0.309	2.219	0.010	0.006	-1.682	2.105	1.429	-0.195	-1.092	-0.250
1972	2.302	0.101	1.830	-0.111	-0.037	-1.787	1.974	1.061	-0.236	-0.819	-0.339
1973	2.916	-0.143	1.438	-0.133	-0.084	-1.857	1.650	0.674	-0.195	-0.596	-0.408
1974	4.355	-0.209	1.294	-0.146	-0.097	-1.872	1.630	0.494	-0.137	-0.458	-0.446
1975	4.923	-0.113	1.497	-0.115	-0.064	-1.730	1.893	0.591	-0.021	-0.492	-0.529
1976	5.479	-0.544	0.628	-0.060	-0.110	-1.661	1.484	0.558	-0.227	-0.411	-0.749
1977	5.863	-0.638	0.318	-0.178	-0.172	-1.537	0.911	0.164	-0.251	-0.132	-0.901
1978	5.994	-0.859	-0.106	-0.159	-0.256	-1.432	0.703	-0.208	-0.180	0.086	-0.933
Mean	2.870	0.273	1.780	-0.009	-0.014	-1.398	1.535	0.978	-0.024	-0.756	-0.364

Table 9.12 Incomes policy

Year	CB	CONR	GDPR	IP	M3	QR	RL	RPD	STB	UNER	XR
1965	0.004	0.003	0.014	0.000	0.004	0.003	0.018	0.108	0.005	-0.003	0.000
1966	0.041	-0.010	0.098	0.003	0.038	0.027	0.172	0.986	0.036	-0.025	-0.003
1967	0.021	-0.368	-0.340	0.024	-0.002	-0.034	0.092	0.286	-0.076	0.037	-0.028
1968	0.015	-0.336	-0.350	-0.042	-0.033	-0.052	-0.044	-0.293	-0.060	0.176	-0.045
1969	-0.026	-0.113	-0.100	-0.017	-0.043	-0.009	-0.197	-0.799	0.049	0.136	-0.015
1970	0.017	-0.039	-0.041	0.019	-0.019	-0.003	-0.195	-0.410	0.041	0.028	0.002
1971	-0.075	-0.070	-0.213	0.009	-0.055	-0.054	-0.380	-1.232	-0.056	0.021	0.008
1972	-0.155	0.321	0.167	-0.037	-0.048	-0.033	-0.480	-1.390	0.036	-0.001	0.029
1973	-0.030	0.818	0.923	0.015	0.091	0.089	-0.065	0.171	0.220	-0.250	0.102
1974	-0.394	0.357	0.213	0.101	-0.018	-0.022	-0.240	-1.117	-0.077	-0.339	0.084
1975	-1.615	0.633	-0.113	-0.061	-0.435	-0.211	-1.793	-6.462	-0.277	-0.075	0.102
1976	-1.476	2.530	2.590	-0.143	-0.177	-0.054	-1.562	-4.437	0.486	-0.454	0.499
1977	-0.545	3.464	4.172	0.221	0.389	0.018	-0.249	-0.765	0.692	-1.561	0.888
1978	-2.937	2.573	2.644	0.248	-0.079	-0.479	-0.643	-3.923	-0.228	-1.814	0.787
Mean	-0.511	0.697	0.690	0.024	-0.028	-0.058	-0.398	-1.377	0.056	-0.295	0.172

Table 9.13 Import controls plus incomes policy

Year	CB	CONR	GDPR	IP	M3	QR	RL	RPD	STB	UNER	XR
1965	0.192	1.163	1.952	0.000	0.077	-0.231	0.368	0.108	0.454	-0.402	0.000
1966	0.510	1.484	2.922	0.277	0.145	-0.550	0.911	0.986	0.526	-1.217	-0.003
1967	0.821	1.244	2.669	0.281	0.090	-1.007	1.022	0.286	0.068	-1.505	-0.028
1968	1.150	1.565	3.040	0.082	0.040	-1.296	1.206	-0.293	0.013	-1.388	-0.045
1969	1.271	2.100	3.715	0.051	0.019	-1.396	1.371	-0.799	0.148	-1.463	-0.015
1970	1.526	2.232	3.871	0.063	0.033	-1.512	1.481	-0.410	0.056	-1.651	0.002
1971	1.650	2.125	3.535	0.001	-0.028	-1.707	1.319	-1.232	-0.158	-1.657	0.008
1972	1.724	2.573	3.941	-0.112	-0.037	-1.777	1.288	-1.390	-0.062	-1.613	0.028
1973	2.413	2.990	4.590	-0.072	0.080	-1.741	1.693	0.171	0.119	-1.817	0.102
1974	3.153	2.562	3.995	-0.013	-0.021	-1.879	1.765	-1.117	-0.148	-1.886	0.084
1975	2.465	2.786	3.713	-0.148	-0.440	-2.079	0.380	-6.462	-0.339	-1.683	0.102
1976	3.594	4.600	6.297	-0.240	-0.209	-1.959	0.379	-4.437	0.370	-2.052	0.499
1977	5.384	5.485	7.806	0.088	0.314	-1.924	1.462	-0.765	0.569	-3.086	0.888
1978	3.087	4.735	6.476	0.102	-0.128	-2.394	1.134	-3.923	-0.273	-3.319	0.787
Mean	2.067	2.689	4.180	0.026	-0.005	-1.532	1.127	-1.377	0.096	-1.767	0.172

economists - mainly monetarists - who argue that government spending financed by means other than money creation may reduce private spending to such an extent that there will be little, if any, net increase in total spending. This is the notorious 'crowding-out' thesis of private expenditure by fiscal actions (Friedman, 1972), known to Keynes (1931) as 'diversion'. It is thus asserted that government spending financed by either taxation or borrowing from the public is mainly a resource transfer from the private sector to the government, with little net effect on total spending. It can have a strong stimulative influence on the economy if, and only if, the increased government expenditure is financed by monetary expansion.

The current debate on the 'crowding-out' issue focuses on the impact of the method of financing government spending, and, in turn, has led to increased analysis of the so-called government budget constraint - discussed in Chapter 5. This constraint specifies that the total flow of government expenditure must equal the total flow of financing from all sources. The total flow of financing includes taxes, net government borrowing from the public, and the net amount of new money issued. Budget deficits or surpluses alter the size of public debt, and the method of financing such deficits or disposing of such surpluses affects the composition of private wealth. Hence, any discussion of the effects of fiscal policy actions should distinguish the different monetary repercussions that result from such alternative modes of financing budget deficits or disposing of budget surpluses. It is for this very reason that the experiments reported in Tables 9.7-9.9 have been undertaken in this way.

In a general way the impact of changes in government expenditure on the economy can be studied in terms of direct impacts and feedback responses to government expenditure changes.[5]

Direct impacts refer to the initial or first-round impact of the change in government expenditure and the associated changes due to the way the government expenditure is financed. One may distinguish three types of direct impacts: (i) the direct fiscal impact, which is the impact of a change in government expenditure on the level of income in view of the fact that government expenditure is a component of aggregate expenditure; (ii) the direct wealth impact, which is the change in consumption induced by changes in wealth associated with changes in the supply of government debt; and (iii) the direct portfolio impact, which is the change in consumption, investment, and stockbuilding associated with the direct impact of a change in the supply of government debt on the rate of interest.

Feedback responses arise as a result of the initial change in income. The following feedback responses are present in the annual model: a positive feedback response on consumption, investment, stockbuilding and imports; and a negative feedback response on consumption, investment and stockbuilding due to the income-induced rise in interest rates.[6] Furthermore, the income-induced changes in prices affect exports and imports, as well as consumption.

The impacts just described can be utilised now to explain the results in Tables 9.7-9.9. Before this is done it is important to note that because of the endogeneity of the government expenditure in our model, and in order to account for the exogenous changes in this variable, we introduce a variable in the GCI equation which takes the value of zero in the control solution, and whichever value one wishes to change government expenditure by, in the 'disturbed' solution. Returning to Tables 9.7-9.9, the first comment one can make is that no matter how increases in government expenditure are financed, the impact on the level of income and its components in the first two years is always positive and substantial. In the case, however, of a money-financed increase in government expenditure the impact is stronger. This can be explained by the fact that in this case there is a direct portfolio effect, in addition to the other effects, which is absent in the other cases; and also to the greater impact on the 'liquid assets' variable of a unit change in the money stock than of a similar change in total government debt. In the tax-financed case the impact is the weakest of the three due to the absence in this instance of both a direct wealth effect and a direct portfolio effect.

In the subsequent years, although the impact is still positive in some years, the negative feedback responses become so important so as to outweigh the positive ones, which results in negative over-all impacts in some years. In particular, in the money-financed case these negative effects become important after eight years, so that by the end of the simulation period the impact on GDPR as well as on its components is negative. However, the average impact over the whole period is positive, with the exception of stockbuilding. We may note in passing that the money stock increases significantly over the period; the increase is more than the required £1000m to finance the increase in government expenditure, which is, of course, due to the endogeneity of the money stock. And it is also responsible for the over-all decrease in interest rates - the average decrease being -0.189. The behaviour of the price level is also of some interest; it is not affected by movements in the money stock, but it follows the behaviour of GDPR as unemployment is more sensitive than RPD to GDPR movements.

In the other two cases the negative feedback effects become pronounced sooner than in the money-financed case, so that in terms of GDPR some negative values are encountered before 1973, but it is the components of GDPR that turn negative well before 1973. It would seem that the main reason for all these results is the absence of the direct portfolio impact in both the bond-financed and tax-financed cases, as well as the direct wealth impact, which is absent in the tax-financed case, while in the bond-financed case it is weaker than in the money-financed case. This also explains to a large extent the upward tendency of interest rates - compare Tables 9.8 and 9.9 with 9.7. The average impact over the entire period on the constituent parts of GDPR are all negative, while the average impact on GDPR is positive in both cases. The reason behind this result is that the government expenditure component of GDPR, not reported in the above tables, increases throughout the period more than the exogenous £1000m increase in GCI - due, of course, to the endogeneity of the GEX variable - so that the average change in GDPR is positive.

In all three cases the current balance is always in deficit, a result that is mainly caused by the high propensity to import. In the money-financed case the deficit is the biggest due to the greater change in income, thus causing imports to rise faster than in the other two cases, and to a greater reduction in exports as a result of greater increases in RPD than in the other two cases. This particular result is of paramount importance and highlights the potential of fiscal policy as a macroeconomic policy instrument in an open economy like that of the United Kingdom. In such an economy the impact of fiscal policy, and of monetary policy for that matter, is weakened because of the unpleasant side-effects due to the high propensity to import (Arestis and Karakitsos, 1980).

On the 'crowding-out' issue our results suggest that some crowding out of private expenditure by fiscal actions does come about but not in as a short period, as the results of the studies by Andersen and Jordan (1968), as well as those of Keran (1969, 1970) would suggest. The latter three studies, using data for a number of countries, clearly show that, with the exception of a money-financed increase in government expenditure, complete 'crowding out' always occurs, and, indeed, it materialises within a very short time period - a year. By contrast, our results[7] tend to support the conclusions reached in those studies (Laury, Lewis and Ormerod, 1978; Taylor, 1979; Lewis and Ormerod, 1979; Arestis and Karakitsos, 1980) which employ large models - the National Institute model, the Treasury model, the London Business School model - to demonstrate that although some 'crowding out' is prevalent in the United Kingdom, this result should not be interpreted to suggest that 'government spending does not matter'. It seems that government spending does matter but that its impact is considerable over a certain period only. Moreover, if government spending were to accelerate rapidly rather than be held to a once-for-all increase, the impact on gross national product would be considerable over the period of acceleration and also over some period beyond. It would therefore appear that these estimates of the fiscal multiplier are not as damaging to the Keynesian position as they would initially appear (Klein, 1973).

Tables 9.10 and 9.11 report the results of two exercises which assume exogenous changes in the current balance. In Table 9.10 the results of the exogenous change in world demand clearly show the expansionary impact on the level of economic activity, and the improvement in the current balance of the balance of payments. In the case of import controls - this way of imposing 'import controls' is also employed by Fetherston and Godley (1978) - the same pattern of results ensues, but there are, however, some important differences. Imports fall as well as exports - as a result of rising prices - but since the fall in imports is much greater than that of exports the current balance is substantially improved throughout the period (Table 9.

Next, we examine the case of incomes policy - Table 9.12. The main impact in this case is the fall in the inflation rate - the average fall over the period being -1.377. On the external front there does not seem to be much improvement in the current balance; if anything, there is an average deficit over the period of -0.511. It is thus natural to wonder what happens in the case where we combine an incomes policy with 'import controls'. The results of this experiment are reported in Table 9.13. Perhaps not surprisingly, this particular combination provides quite acceptable results. GDPR and its constituent components expand significantly over the whole period - although investment is on the low side and in some periods it actually falls due to the upward tendency of interest rates. Unemployment falls significantly, as does the inflation rate, while the current balance shows definite and substantial improvement over the entire period.

This particular combination of policies, along with fiscal/monetary ones to regulate aggregate demand, would therefore seem to be a satisfactory set of policy prescriptions for the UK authorities to adopt. But there are a number of problems associated with these types of policies. In the case of incomes policy there is no guarantee that trade unions would accept it for a long period of time, as experience with such policies has shown. Successful implementation of an incomes policy would require prior agreement with and acceptance by the trade unions, and these aspects of this policy present awkward problems for modelling purposes.

It has been argued by some economists (see, for example, Scott, Corden and Little, 1980) that import controls would only make matters worse. There is, to begin with, the question of retaliation by other countries to the United Kingdom imposing controls on her imports, and this would result in a lower volume of foreign trade. Furthermore, import prices will rise above the level that would result if the exchange rate, for example, were allowed to fall to cure a deficit in the balance of payments; this would come about because the burden of adjustment would fall on one category of imports, namely manufacturers. In addition, it is argued that with less foreign trade consumers would increase their demand for substitutes of imports which were either more expensive or of lower quality than the importables. Producers would be forced to buy substitutes for imported raw materials which were either more expensive or of lower quality than the imported ones. These latter two effects would inevitably, so the argument goes, reduce consumers' real income. Producers would also lose some economies of scale, since with less foreign trade they would have to rely on the smaller domestic market.

It must be stressed, however, that in addition to the difficulties of properly taking into account these criticisms when modelling the economy, there are good reasons to believe that most of these criticisms are ill-founded. Godley (1979), for example, has argued that retaliation and reduction in the volume of international trade should not necessarily occur following import controls; this argument rests on the assumption that if the composition of imports changed in favour of raw materials and away from manufactures, then since the exports of those countries that are rich in terms of raw materials would increase they would thus be able to increase their imports of manufactures from countries which lose trade due to the United Kingdom's import controls. Furthermore, prices would not rise above the level that would arise if devaluation were implemented instead, because in the case of import controls in the form of tariffs the latter is given back to economic agents in the form of tax reliefs so that, initially at least, there would be a tendency for prices to come down, not to increase as would be the case with devaluation.

If, then, foreign trade would not be lower with import controls, and prices would not be higher, the argument that consumers' real income would be reduced and that producers would lose some economies of scale is, to say the least, very weak indeed.

POLICY OPTIMISATION: THE OPTIMAL CONTROL APPROACH

In the simulation approach to policy questions, discussed above, given one's estimated model, values of endogenous variables are determined for alternative assumptions about the policy variables. In this way the simulation approach indicates to policy-makers the implications of alternative policies out of which they can pick a desired alternative. This approach, however, does not require the policy-makers to state their preferences in the form of set targets. The essential feature of the alternative approach, which we consider in this section, is that it specifies an objective function, in terms of instruments and targets, and derives solutions for the policy instruments and the corresponding targets, by utilising optimisation techniques; this is basically the optimal control approach to policy optimisation.

This framework can be elaborated as follows. It is assumed that the policy-makers state their preferences in the form of desired paths for certain strategic variables, the so-called *target* variables, such as the balance of payments, inflation, unemployment, etc. (for example, they might wish to steer the economy to a situation where there is zero inflation, 2 per cent unemployment, and a balanced balance of payments). These, then, would be the desired paths for the target variables. There is, however, a constraint to the policy-makers' attempt to reach the set desired paths for the target variables; this constraint is the postulated, and estimated, model which purports to show how the economy works. This could very well imply that the desired paths set by the policy-makers may not be feasible. In this case the policy-makers are supposed to rank their targets according to which one of them they wish to see satisfied most, if not fully. This, of course, means that there are penalty costs or weights attached to deviations of the optimal from the desired paths of the target variables; and by differentiating the penalty costs attached to different targets the ranking is achieved.

The policy-makers are assumed to attempt to achieve the desired paths of their target variables by manipulating those variables which are, in fact, under their control, such as the discount rate, tax rates, etc. - these are called the *instruments* or *controls*. The crucial problem for the policy-makers, then, is to establish the paths of their instruments over time so that their targets will assume the desired paths as closely as possible. The required paths for the instruments, however, may in some cases be too costly for the policy-makers to implement. For example, the required discount rate may have to assume too high a value, and this could create chaotic conditions in the financial markets; to the extent that the policy-makers wish orderly conditions to prevail in the financial markets, high interest rates are bound to be undesirable. For this reason it is assumed that the policy-makers have desired paths for the instruments, too; and just as in the case of targets, penalty costs are attached in those situations where there are deviations of the optimal from the desired paths of the instruments.

Formally speaking, this approach can be cast as a constrained optimisation problem, where the objective function is minimised subject to the econometric-model equations, the constraint.

The objective function is assumed to be quadratic[8] and is written in the following fashion:

$$J(Y,U) = \tfrac{1}{2}\,[(Y - Y^d)'\,Q_y\,(Y - Y^d) + (U - U^d)'\,Q_u\,(U - U^d)] \quad (9.10)$$

where Y and U are vectors of the target variables and instruments respectively, and the superscript d on Y and U denotes desired values; Q_y and Q_u are the penalty-costs matrices, with Q_y being symmetric and positive semi-definite, while Q_u is symmetric positive definite. Symmetric positive semi-definiteness and symmetric positive definiteness can be defined as follows. Let X denote a column vector of nth order - X' its transpose - and Q an nth order symmetric matrix. Then $X'QX$ is a quadratic form in the elements of X. If

$$X'QX > 0 \text{ for all } X \neq 0$$

then the quadratic form is positive definite and the matrix Q is said to be symmetric positive definite. If

$$X'QX \geq 0 \text{ for all } X$$

then the quadratic form is semi-definite and the matrix Q is symmetric positive semi-definite. Clearly, if Q is positive definite, it must be non-singular, for if it were singular then

$$X'QX = 0 \text{ for } X \neq 0$$

which is contrary to the definition of positive definiteness. In terms of economics the significance of these definitions is that Q_y could allow zero penalty costs on all targets, while Q_u does impose penalty costs on the instruments.

We, then, wish to minimise 9.10 by choosing the values of the instrument vector U, given the constraints of the model, written as

$$F\,(Y,U) = 0 \quad (9.11)$$

When the optimisation problem is posed this way,[9] it essentially becomes a problem of designing optimal policies in a deterministic world. These policies can, then, be judged according to whether the optimal paths of the target variables appoximate the desired paths. The difficulty with this approach is the formulation of the objective function; as in the case of an econometric model which is an approximation of how the economy works, similarly the objective function is an approximation of the preferences of the policy-makers. This is so, of course, because its specification requires knowledge of the policy-makers' desired values for both the target variables and the instruments, as well as their priorities concerning the achievement of their targets. All this information is not always readily available to the researcher.

It would be fruitful at this stage to highlight a fundamental difference between simulation and optimisation. Simulation can in fact be thought of as a special case of optimisation. In the case of simulation, values for the policy instruments are assumed and corresponding values for the endogenous variables are derived using the econometric model. In this sense there exists an objective function which reflects the preferences of the policy-makers in terms of the policy variables only. In the optimisation case the values Y may take are clearly influenced not just by the desired values of the policy variables but by the preferences of the policy-makers reflected in J(Y,U) (for more details on this point, see Rustem, 1979).

In order to illustrate the above we utilise the simple example of the section on 'The Meaning of Simulation' with the assumptions made there. This model consists of the following three equations:

$$Y_t = C_t + I_t + G_t \tag{9.12}$$

$$C_t = 1.0 + 0.75Y_{t-1} \tag{9.13}$$

$$I_t = 0.5 + 0.15\ (Y_{t-1} - Y_{t-2}) \tag{9.14}$$

Let it be assumed that we wish to optimise over two periods with respect to the endogenous variable Y_t - the same procedure can be applied for C_t and I_t (this is left to the reader as an exercise) - using G_t as our instrument. We begin by solving equations 9.12-9.14 for Y_t:

$$Y_t = 0.9\ Y_{t-1} - 0.15\ Y_{t-2} + 1.5 + G_t \tag{9.15}$$

Given, then, that $Y_{t-1} = 25$ and $Y_{t-2} = 20$, and also that we are interested in a two-period solution, we have:

$$Y_1 = 0.90(25) - 0.15(20) + 1.5 + G_1$$

$$Y_2 = 0.9\ Y_1 - 0.15(25) + 1.5 + G_2$$

or

$$- 0.9Y_1 + Y_2 = G_2 - 2.25$$

or in matrix form:

$$AY = G \tag{9.16}$$

where

$$Y = \begin{bmatrix} Y_1 \\ Y_2 \end{bmatrix}, \quad A = \begin{bmatrix} 1 & 0 \\ -0.9 & 1 \end{bmatrix}$$

and

$$G = \begin{bmatrix} G_1 + 21 \\ G_2 - 2.25 \end{bmatrix}$$

from which we can get

$$Y = A^{-1} G$$

or

$$Y = \begin{bmatrix} 1 & 0 \\ 0.9 & 1 \end{bmatrix} \begin{bmatrix} G_1 + 21 \\ G_2 - 2.25 \end{bmatrix}$$

and finally

$$Y = \begin{bmatrix} G_1 + 21 \\ 0.9G_1 + G_2 + 16.65 \end{bmatrix} \tag{9.17}$$

which is the expression for the target variable Y_t with respect to the instrument G_t over the two-period optimisation horizon.

The objective function is

$$J = \tfrac{1}{2} [(Y - Y^d)' Q_y (Y - Y^d) + (U - U^d)' Q_u (U - U^d)] \tag{9.18}$$

where

$$Y^d = \begin{bmatrix} 33 \\ 37.13 \end{bmatrix}$$

with the elements of this vector being the desired values for Y_1 = 10 per cent above its simulated value, and Y_2 = 10 per cent above its simulated value. Furthermore,

$$Q_y = \begin{bmatrix} 0.5 & 0 \\ 0 & 0.5 \end{bmatrix}$$

with the elements of the matrix being the weights on Y_1 and Y_2, assumed to be the same for both periods. Also,

$$Q_u = \begin{bmatrix} 0.2 & 0 \\ 0 & 0.2 \end{bmatrix}$$

with the elements being the weights on G_1 and G_2, again assumed to be the same for both periods. Finally,

$$U = \begin{bmatrix} G_1 \\ G_2 \end{bmatrix} \quad \text{and} \quad U^d = \begin{bmatrix} 10 \\ 10 \end{bmatrix}$$

where in the last vector the elements stand for the desired values on G_1 and G_2, assumed to be the same for each period.

We now wish to minimise 9.18; we thus have

$$\frac{\partial J}{\partial U} = \left(\frac{\partial Y}{\partial U}\right)' Q_y (Y - Y^d) + Q_u (U - U^d) = 0$$

where

$$\frac{\partial Y}{\partial U} = \begin{bmatrix} \dfrac{\partial Y_1}{\partial G_1} & \dfrac{\partial Y_1}{\partial G_2} \\ \dfrac{\partial Y_2}{\partial G_1} & \dfrac{\partial Y_2}{\partial G_2} \end{bmatrix}$$

which can be derived from 9.17 to give

$$\begin{bmatrix} 1 & 0.9 \\ 0 & 1 \end{bmatrix} \begin{bmatrix} 0.5G_1 - 6 \\ 0.45G_1 + 0.5G_2 - 10.24 \end{bmatrix} + \begin{bmatrix} 0.2G_1 - 2 \\ 0.2G_2 - 2 \end{bmatrix} = \begin{bmatrix} 0 \\ 0 \end{bmatrix}$$

or

$$\begin{bmatrix} 0.91G_1 + 0.45G_2 - 15.22 \\ \\ 0.45G_1 + 0.5G_2 - 10.24 \end{bmatrix} + \begin{bmatrix} 0.2G_1 - 2 \\ \\ 0.2G_2 - 2 \end{bmatrix} = \begin{bmatrix} 0 \\ \\ 0 \end{bmatrix}$$

or

$$1.11G_1 + 0.45G_2 - 17.22 = 0$$

$$0.45G_1 + 0.7G_2 - 12.24 = 0$$

from which

$$G_1^0 = 11.39 \quad \text{and} \quad G_2^0 = 10.16$$

being the optimal values for the instrument G_t for periods 1 and 2 respectively. Substituting these values in equation 9.15 we obtain

$$Y_1 + 0Y_2 = 32.39$$

$$-0.9Y_1 + Y_2 = 7.91$$

from which the optimal values for the target Y_t are derived for periods 1 and 2. These are

$$Y_1^0 = 32.39 \quad \text{and} \quad Y_2^0 = 37.06$$

OPTIMAL CONTROL IN THE ANNUAL MODEL

The above approach is now applied in the case of our annual model and for the period 1965-78. The crucial problem that one is immediately faced with is the specification of a satisfactory objective function. In order to do this we follow the approach developed by Westcott *et al.* (1981); the objective function thus obtained appears in Table 9.14. It is obvious from this table that our targets are CB, RPD and UNER. The instruments used to achieve these targets are WR, and exogenous components of QR, and GEX. The WR variable is exogenised and its optimal path determined; this path would then indicate to the policy-makers the way an incomes policy could be implemented in terms of the values that WR should take. The GEX instrument is the fiscal policy variable which can be used to regulate aggregate demand, and the R instrument is the imports control policy variable. In this way the exercise in this section can be thought of as an extension of the simulation exercise undertaken above. What we look for here is to find the optimal paths of both the instruments and targets, and to determine the extent to which the optimal values of the latter differ from their desired values.

The priorities of the policy-makers would, of course, determine the optimal paths of the instruments and the targets. The

Table 9.14 Objective function for annual model

	TARGETS			INSTRUMENTS		
	CB	RPD	UNER	WR	QR*	GEX†
R_i	0.070	1	0.256	1.00	1.344	0.067
x_i	0.10	10	3.30	9.64	1.00	0.00
x_i^d	0.00	0	2.00	30.00	0.95	1.5
$P_i = \frac{P_p}{R_i}$	142.86	10	39.00	10.00	7.443	150
$q_i = \frac{P_i}{(x_i - x_i^d)}$	1428.6	1	30.00	0.491	148.86	100

*The instrument in this case is the constant of the QR equation; this is achieved by multiplying the constant by a new variable which takes the value of 1.0 when simulating the model, and appropriate values when optimising the model.
†The instrument in this case is the same as in the simulations.

specification of the objective function reflects these priorities. The R_i row indicates changes in policy which the policy-makers rate of equal priority, taking a 1 per cent reduction in inflation as the standard. For example, a 0.4 per cent reduction in unemployment has a priority equal to a 1 per cent reduction in the inflation rate. The x_i row indicates the level of the variable upon which the R_is are made; the values along this line in Table 9.14 are the average simulated values, in the case of the targets, and the average of actual values, in the case of instruments. The x_i^d row represents the desired values for both targets and instruments, while row $P_i = 10/R_i$ - where 10 is the value of RPD used as the standard - indicates the priorities of the policy-makers at level x_i. Finally, row q_i provides the weights corresponding to the priorities determined in line P_i. The way the weights are calculated is as follows: given the equal priorities (R_i) for all three instruments, and all three targets, their x_is and x_i^ds and also the weight on RPD, assumed to be 1.0, we then, first of all, write the objective function as

$$J = \tfrac{1}{2}\,[q_1(CB - CB^d)^2 + q_2(RPD - RPD^d)^2 + q_3(UNER - UNER^d)^2$$
$$+ q_4(WR - WR^d)^2 + q_5(QR - QR^d)^2 + q_6(GEX - GEX^d)^2]$$

and for minimisation purposes we require

$$dJ = q_1(CB - CB^d)\ d(CB) + q_2(RPD - RPD^d)$$

$$+ q_3(UNER - UNER^d)\ d(UNER) + q_4(WR - WR^d)\ d(WR)$$

$$+ q_5(QR - QR^d)\ d(QR) + q_6(GEX - GEX^d)\ d(GEX) = 0$$

From this, now, we can get expressions which represent trade-offs between the different instruments and targets, and RPD, which is assumed to be the standard. For example,

$$\frac{d(CB)}{d(RPD)} = \frac{q_2(RPD - RPD^d)}{q_1(CB - CB^d)} = \frac{R_{CB}}{R_{RPD}}$$

gives us the trade-off between CB and RPD; from the values assumed in Table 9.14 it is obvious, then, that the last expression can be rewritten, with the appropriate substitutions, as

$$\frac{d(CB)}{d(RPD)} = \frac{10}{q_1(0.10)} = \frac{0.07}{1}$$

or

$$q_1 = \frac{10}{(0.10)(0.07)}$$

$$q_1 = 1428.6$$

which is the weight on CB. Working in this manner the weights for the rest of the instruments, as well as those for the targets, can be determined.

We next undertake two experiments: the first utilises the objective function of Table 9.14 for optimisation purposes - we label this experiment as OPT1; the second experiment makes use of the same objective function, but changes the weight on RPD, in fact it doubles it to 2.0, implying that more emphasis is now given to inflation - this experiment is labelled as OPT2. The results of these experiments appear in Tables 9.15, 9.16 and 9.17. In Table 9.15 the optimal values of OPT1 appear; in Table 9.16 we present the difference between OPT1 and the simulated values (SIM) - the latter reflect the actual history of the variables reported - and in Table 9.17 the differences between OPT2 and OPT1 are provided. In all cases we report the optimal values for the instruments and targets, as well as for the variable GDPR, so that the reader can get some idea of how real domestic product behaves throughout the optimisation period.

The story that emerges from Tables 9.15 and 9.16 is that, provided that the objective function postulated in Table 9.14 adheres to the policy-makers' targets and instruments over the period of optimisation, and provided that the policy-makers had correctly anticipated the paths of the exogenous variables, the optimal values for the targets and instruments over the period considered imply on

Table 9.15 Optimal values of OPT1

Year	CB	RPD	UNER	WR	QR*	GEX*	GDPR
1965	-0.088	7.338	0.838	12.380	8.840	14.558	41.297
1966	-0.074	5.451	0.449	9.401	8.891	16.292	41.319
1967	-0.071	3.597	1.470	4.992	9.113	18.132	40.937
1968	-0.039	2.717	1.919	3.906	10.425	20.206	44.554
1969	-0.060	3.161	1.510	4.146	11.365	21.121	45.439
1970	0.008	6.440	2.247	5.493	11.853	23.555	43.162
1971	-0.012	9.166	3.614	9.291	12.265	25.794	43.218
1972	0.146	7.978	3.355	8.118	13.736	30.661	48.483
1973	-0.083	5.774	2.441	9.460	13.662	31.192	48.065
1974	-0.123	15.378	3.123	13.990	12.153	37.912	47.271
1975	0.493	23.016	3.303	18.173	12.103	52.713	51.791
1976	0.132	12.191	3.210	16.382	12.652	54.091	50.126
1977	-0.259	11.866	3.464	8.873	13.724	61.460	53.956
1978	0.615	12.210	3.084	15.805	14.573	70.474	54.806
Mean	0.054	9.020	2.431	10.029	11.811	34.154	46.745

*These are the optimal values for the variables QR and GEX respectively; they are not the optimal values for the instruments utilised to influence these variables (as in Table 9.14). The same applies to Tables 9.16 and 9.17.

Table 9.16 Difference between optimal values (OPT1) and simulated values (SIM)

Year	CB	RPD	UNER	WR	QR	GEX	GDPR
1965	0.317	3.076	-0.637	8.080	-0.162	1.025	3.094
1966	0.279	1.828	-1.706	4.801	-0.288	1.559	3.542
1967	0.473	0.416	-1.468	1.092	-0.612	1.660	1.404
1968	0.320	-1.026	-0.665	-2.694	-0.374	2.134	1.641
1969	0.077	-0.439	-0.471	-1.154	0.023	2.120	1.545
1970	-0.474	-1.678	-0.182	-4.407	0.405	2.050	0.033
1971	-0.523	-1.374	0.340	-3.609	0.458	1.717	-0.840
1972	-1.637	-2.163	-0.333	-5.682	1.318	3.812	3.588
1973	-0.614	-1.614	-1.348	-4.240	0.307	1.401	1.592
1974	1.498	-2.212	-0.977	-5.810	-1.054	-0.003	1.550
1975	-0.243	-4.312	-1.460	-11.327	-0.543	1.441	5.168
1976	1.099	-1.111	-2.052	-2.918	-0.571	-1.495	3.487
1977	1.064	0.865	-1.617	2.273	-0.357	-0.246	3.217
1978	-1.359	0.687	-1.254	1.805	0.056	0.414	3.048
Mean	0.020	-0.647	-0.988	-1.699	-0.100	1.256	2.291

Table 9.17 Difference between OPT2 and OPT1

Year	CB	RPD	UNER	WR	QR	GEX	GDPR
1965	-0.022	0.415	0.018	1.090	0.058	0.064	-0.089
1966	-0.025	0.753	0.033	1.979	0.081	0.210	-0.022
1967	-0.014	0.691	0.081	1.814	0.051	0.227	-0.345
1968	-0.025	0.159	0.210	0.417	0.028	0.266	-0.530
1969	0.000	0.408	0.152	1.072	0.074	0.544	0.048
1970	0.004	-0.656	0.041	-1.723	-0.046	0.247	-0.305
1971	0.047	-0.861	0.078	-2.262	-0.079	0.280	-0.172
1972	-0.023	-0.811	-0.093	-2.130	0.000	0.402	0.596
1973	-0.014	-0.534	-0.303	-1.403	-0.013	0.265	0.487
1974	-0.104	-2.219	-0.195	-5.829	-0.209	-0.535	0.038
1975	-0.476	-4.670	-0.260	-12.265	-0.365	-2.174	1.222
1976	0.424	-1.680	-0.966	-4.413	-0.317	-2.123	3.201
1977	1.215	-0.623	-1.450	-1.636	-0.634	-4.405	2.562
1978	0.536	-1.433	-1.274	-3.763	-0.857	-5.157	2.470
Mean	0.109	-0.790	-0.281	-2.075	-0.159	-0.849	0.654

average a surplus in the balance of payments and lower unemployment, as well as lower inflation. In terms of the instruments utilised, imports would have had to be lower on average, government expenditure higher, and also an incomes policy should have been adopted which would have provided for lower wage increases than the ones that actually occurred; and real output (GDPR) would have been higher on average.

In terms of Table 9.17 let us suppose that the policy-makers would like to examine the consequences of putting twice as much emphasis as before on reducing inflation - q_2 is therefore doubled. The consequences of this change in policy are, on average, lower inflation, lower unemployment, and an improvement in the balance of payments, as well as a higher GDPR. The resulting lower inflation, because of the higher priority given now to reducing it, helps boost consumption, which increases output and decreases unemployment with government expenditure being lower as a consequence. The increased output would tend to increase imports, which are, nevertheless, contained by the tendency of imports to fall due to the lower inflation rate. On average, however, imports actually decrease, which means that the price effect is stronger than the income effect in this particular instance. This also explains the initial increase in imports, which is the result of the inflation rate being higher originally in the case of OPT2 than in OPT1. Note, however, that all these effects are rather small. The conclusion that one can draw from this latter result is that a change in priorities does have an effect on policies, but the change in priorities would have to be large for significant effects to materialise. Optimal policies are thus sensitive, but not over-sensitive, to changes in the priorities of policy-makers.

At a more general level, the analysis and exercises of this section indicate the independence of the objectives of economic policy; and they also help to clarify the importance and usefulness of the techniques of optimal control for the design and analysis of policy-making. At the same time, however, they clearly pinpoint the difficulties and the problems one is faced with when attempting to apply these techniques to everyday problems of policy.

Finally, we should stress that there are a number of problems we have not raised in this section; in particular we have not considered the implications of removing the following three assumptions:

(a) perfect foresight of exogenous variables;
(b) exact behavioural equations; and
(c) constant coefficients.

To do so would take us to the realm of 'stochastic optimal control', as opposed to the 'deterministic optimal control', which has been expounded in this section. This exercise would be beyond the scope of this book.[10]

Appendix: OLS—Estimates of Full Annual Model

(1) $$(APC)_t = \underset{(3.81)}{0.44654} - \underset{(3.18)}{0.00414}\,(RL_t - RPD_t) - \underset{(3.73)}{0.00466}\,(RPD)_t$$

$$+ \underset{(3.11)}{0.22311}\left(\frac{LA}{YD}\right)_t + \underset{(3.86)}{0.34405}\left(\frac{TYDR}{YDR}\right)_t - \underset{(2.26)}{0.00084}\,(RPD)_{t-2}$$

$$R^2 = 0.932$$

$$\rho = \underset{(6.05)}{0.81869},\ S = 0.006,\ S/ME = 0.007,\ \chi_1^2(5) = 8.88,$$

$$\chi_3^2(1) = 1.55,\ F(1,13) = 0.53$$

(2) $$(CON)_t = (APC)_t \times (YD)_t$$

(3) $$(CONR)_t = \frac{(CON)_t}{(PCD)_t}$$

(4) $$(PCD)_t = \underset{(70.86)}{0.93788}\,(PD)_t$$

$$R^2 = 0.997$$

$$\rho = \underset{(6.14)}{0.81517}$$

(5) $$(LA)_t = \underset{(1.95)}{6.48887} + \underset{(15.64)}{1.15330}\left[\frac{(M3)_t + (M3)_{t-1}}{2}\right]$$

$$+ \underset{(1.77)}{0.34546}\left[\frac{\Delta(GS)_t + \Delta(GS)_{t-1}}{2}\right]$$

$$R^2 = 0.993$$

$$\rho = \underset{(6.30)}{0.85355}$$

(6) $$(TYDR)_t = [(YDR)_t + (YDR)_{t-1} + (YDR)_{t-2} + (YDR)_{t-3} + (YDR)_{t-4}]/5$$

(7) $$(YDR)_t = \frac{(YD)_t}{(PCD)_t}$$

(8) $$(IP)_t = -\underset{(3.52)}{2.45838} + \underset{(2.23)}{0.01671}\,(CU)_t + \underset{(12.30)}{0.42127}\,(IF)_t$$

$$+ \underset{(4.34)}{1.51754}\,(CC)_t + \underset{(2.83)}{0.09602}\,[(GDPR)_{t-1} - (GDPR)_{t-2}]$$

$$- \underset{(3.46)}{0.02894}\left[(RL)_{t-2} - \left(\frac{(RPD)_{t-1} + (RPD)_{t-2} + (RPD)_{t-3}}{3}\right)\right]$$

$$+ \underset{(3.48)}{0.42623}\,(IP)_{t-1}$$

$$R^2 = 0.994$$

$$\rho = -\underset{(2.10)}{0.60971},\ S = 0.101,\ S/ME = 0.021,\ \chi_1^2(5) = 7.04,$$

$$\chi_3^2(1) = 12.49,\ F(1,12) = 7.30$$

(9) $$(CU)_t = \underset{(5.53)}{64.10057} + \underset{(6.35)}{84.57442}\left[\frac{(IPR)_{t-1} - (IPR)_{t-2}}{(IPR)_{t-2}}\right]$$

$$+ \underset{(2.43)}{0.29894}\,(CU)_{t-1}$$

$$R^2 = 0.491$$

$$\rho = -\underset{(2.87)}{0.58592},\ S = 2.361,\ S/ME = 0.025,\ \chi_1^2(1) = 0.09,$$

$$\chi_3^2(1) = 0.17,\ F(1,16) = 0.13$$

(10) $$(IPR)_t = \underset{(8.00)}{2.88357}\,[(GDPR)_t - (GDPR)_{t-1}] + \underset{(183.57)}{0.98957}\,(IPR)_{t-1}$$

$$R^2 = 0.987$$

$$D\text{-}W = 2.08,\ S = 1.568,\ S/ME = 0.017,\ \chi_1^2(1) = 1.85,$$

$$\chi_3^2(1) = 0.10,\ F(1,18) = 0.10$$

(11) $$(STB)_t = \underset{(7.12)}{0.08396}\,[(IPR)_t - (IPR)_{t-1}] + \underset{(3.66)}{0.06018}\,[(IPR)_{t-1} - (IPR)_{t-2}] + \underset{(3.24)}{0.07094}\,(GSA1) - \underset{(2.19)}{0.03899}\left[(RL)_{t-1} - \left(\frac{(RPD)_t + (RPD)_{t-1} + (RPD)_{t-2}}{3}\right)\right]$$

$R^2 = 0.853$

D-W = 2.29, S = 0.171, S/ME = 0.456, $\chi_1^2(3) = 1.21$,

$\chi_3^2(1) = 1.68$, F(1,16) = 0.81

(12) $$(XR)_t = \underset{(6.80)}{5.95105} + \underset{(34.18)}{0.03703}\,(WD)_t + \underset{(1.77)}{0.00870}\,(WPA)_t + \underset{(3.44)}{0.02444}\,(WPA)_{t-1} - \underset{(2.50)}{2.79870}\,(PXFD)_{t-1} - \underset{(2.99)}{4.68520}\,(PXFD)_{t-2}$$

$R^2 = 0.999$

D-W = 2.35, S = 0.142, S/ME = 0.013, $\chi_1^2(3) = 2.12$,

$\chi_3^2(1) = 0.72$, F(1,14) = 0.24

(13) $$(PXFD)_t = \underset{(24.94)}{0.56188} + \underset{(6.59)}{0.73584}\,(PD)_t - \underset{(3.20)}{0.68306}\,(PD)_{t-1} + \underset{(2.49)}{0.37743}\,(PD)_{t-2}$$

$R^2 = 0.989$

D-W = 1.75, S = 0.030, S/ME = 0.028, $\chi_1^2(1) = 0.04$,

$\chi_3^2(1) = 1.59$, F(1,16) - 0.61

(14) $$(PXD)_t = \left(\frac{PXFD}{ER}\right)_t$$

(15) $$(QR)_t = -\underset{(1.46)}{2.80944} + \underset{(1.91)}{0.17133}\,(GDPR)_t + \underset{(2.98)}{4.45197}\,(PD)_{t-1} - \underset{(3.20)}{3.18068}\,(PQD)_{t-1} + \underset{(3.18)}{0.50211}\,(QR)_{t-1}$$

$R^2 = 0.993$

$\rho = \underset{(2.15)}{0.55286}$, S = 0.254, S/ME = 0.024, $\chi_1^2(3) = 5.99$,

$\chi_3^2(1) = 3.42$, F(1,14) = 1.61

(16) $$(GEX)_t = (GCI)_t + (GT)_t + (NLG)_t$$

$$(17)\quad (RGCIM)_t = -\underset{(2.81)}{0.24988} + \underset{(2.10)}{0.00412}\,[(UNER)_t - (UNER)_{t-1}]$$

$$- \underset{(3.07)}{0.00202}\,(GDPR)_t + \underset{(2.76)}{0.00709}\,(DV)_t + \underset{(3.27)}{0.00951}\,(DEM)_t$$

$$+ \underset{(6.40)}{0.20777}\left(\frac{GCID}{PMD}\right)_t$$

$$R^2 = 0.967$$

$$D\text{-}W = 1.46,\ S = 0.004,\ S/ME = 0.020,\ \chi_1^2(4) = 7.69,$$

$$\chi_3^2(1) = 7.63,\ F(1,14) = 3.51$$

$$(18)\quad (GCI)_t = (RGCIM)_t \times (GDPM)_t$$

$$(19)\quad (RGTM)_t = \underset{(3.19)}{0.00571}\,(UNER)_t + \underset{(1.96)}{0.00062}\,(RPD)_t + \underset{(3.45)}{0.00168}\,(GDPR)_t$$

$$+ \underset{(2.95)}{0.01047}\,(DV)_t + \underset{(3.87)}{0.00169}\,(DEMO)_t$$

$$R^2 = 0.947$$

$$D\text{-}W = 1.32,\ S = 0.007,\ S/ME = 0.042,\ \chi_1^2(5) = 4.56,$$

$$\chi_3^2(1) = 1.05,\ F(1,15) = 0.67$$

$$(20)\quad (GT)_t = (RGTM)_t \times (GDPM)_t$$

$$(21)\quad (GDPM)_t = (GDPN)_t + (ITAX)_t - (SUB)_t$$

$$(22)\quad (GDPN)_t = (GDPR)_t \times (PD)_t$$

$$(23)\quad (TAX)_t = (ITAX)_t + (DTAXP)_t + (ODTAX)_t$$

$$(24)\quad (ITAX)_t = -\underset{(8.30)}{0.53438} + \underset{(8.27)}{0.06483}\,(TDE)_{t-1} + \underset{(3.71)}{0.31060}\,(DV)_t$$

$$+ \underset{(15.11)}{0.77316}\,(ITAX)_{t-1}$$

$$R^2 = 0.999$$

$$\rho = -\underset{(2.01)}{0.47085},\ S = 0.218,\ S/ME = 0.026,\ \chi_1^2(2) = 5.51$$

$$\chi_3^2(1) = 0.02,\ F(1,15) = 0.01$$

$$(25)\quad (TDE)_t = (GDPM)_t - [(XR)_t \times (PXD)_t] + [(QR)_t \times (PQD)_t]$$

$$- (ITAX)_t + (SUB)_t$$

(26) $$(DTAXP)_t = \underset{(8.54)}{0.31990}\,[(CPY)_t - (CPY)_{t-1}] + \underset{(5.20)}{0.06781}\,(RPD)_t + \underset{(2.62)}{0.02959}\,[(RPD)_{t-1} - (RPD)_{t-2}] + \underset{(75.14)}{0.95919}\,(DTAXP)_{t-1}$$

$R^2 = 0.999$

D-W = 1.89, S = 0.208, S/ME = 0.030, $\chi_1^2(3) = 7.51$, $\chi_3^2(1) = 0.0001$, F(1,16) = 0.0001

(27) $$(CPY)_t = (TAXR)_t \times (PY)_t$$

(28) $$(PY)_t = (EY)_t + (NIBG)_t$$

(29) $$(EY)_t = -\underset{(1.74)}{16.08544} + \underset{(18.44)}{1.26971}\,(GDPN)_t - \underset{(5.27)}{0.43196}\,(GDPN)_{t-1} + \underset{(1.77)}{0.72956}\,(EMPL)_t$$

$R^2 = 0.999$

D-W = 2.17, S = 0.696, S/ME = 0.015, $\chi_1^2(2) = 3.48$, $\chi_3^2(1) = 1.75$, F(1,16) = 0.91

(30) $$(YD)_t = (PY)_t - (DTAXP)_t - (NIC)_t - (NTA)_t$$

(31) $$(GDPR)_t = (CONR)_t + (IP)_t + (STB)_t + (IPC)_t + \left(\frac{GCI}{GCID}\right)_t + (XR)_t - (QR)_t - \left(\frac{ITAX}{PITD}\right)_t + \left(\frac{SUB}{PSUBD}\right)_t$$

(32) $$(PD)_t = (PD)_{t-1} + [(PD)_{t-1} \times (RPD)_t \times 0.01000]$$

(33) $$(RPD)_t = \underset{(3.84)}{1.85988} + \underset{(9.22)}{0.33152}\,(RPQD)_{t-1} + \underset{(7.21)}{0.37083}\,(WR)_t - \underset{(1.53)}{0.19332}\,(GOM)_t - \underset{(4.09)}{3.49920}\,(DVO)_t + \underset{(3.91)}{2.19890}\,(DVO1)_t$$

$R^2 = 0.989$

D-W = 1.97, S = 0.786, S/ME = 0.107, $\chi_1^2(5) = 9.54$, $\chi_3^2(1) = 5.01$, F(1,14) = 4.46

$$(34)\quad (WR)_t = -\underset{(14.81)}{72.48433} + \underset{(16.75)}{0.58496}\,(RPD)_t - \underset{(11.77)}{2.66323}\,(UNER)_t$$

$$+ \underset{(17.66)}{0.50632}\,[(RPD)_{t-1} - (RPD)_{t-2}]$$

$$+ \underset{(15.06)}{199.63243}\,(NA)_t + \underset{(6.02)}{42.41130}\,(GN)_t$$

$$- \underset{(4.02)}{1.16942}\,(DV1)_t - \underset{(7.09)}{2.16608}\,(DV2)_t + \underset{(6.48)}{3.41683}\,(DV3)_t$$

$R^2 = 0.997$

D-W = 2.15, S = 0.494, S/ME = 0.055, $\chi_1^2(7) = 11.87$,

$\chi_3^2(1) = 8.56$, $F(1,11) = 5.17$

$$(35)\quad (EMPL)_t = (LS)_t - (UNE)_t$$

$$(36)\quad (UNE)_t = [(UNER)_t \times (LS)_t]/100$$

$$(37)\quad (UNER)_t = \underset{(5.21)}{5.50970} - \underset{(2.84)}{0.04328}\,[(CU)_t - (CU)_{t-1}] - \underset{(5.24)}{0.08325}\,(IPR)_t$$

$$+ \underset{(10.08)}{0.96367}\,(UNER)_{t-1} - \underset{(4.41)}{0.43508}\,(UNER)_{t-2}$$

$$+ \underset{(6.00)}{0.25131}\,(TREND)_t$$

$R^2 = 0.983$

D-W = 1.86, S = 0.200, S/ME = 0.071, $\chi_1^2(2) = 2.08$,

$\chi_3^2(1) = 8.99$, $F(1,14) = 3.87$

$$(38)\quad \ln\left(\frac{M3}{PD}\right)^d = -\underset{(2.40)}{0.92025} - \underset{(2.29)}{0.21774}\,\ln(RS)_t + \underset{(2.97)}{0.46141}\,\ln(GDPR)_t$$

$$+ \underset{(4.14)}{0.87816}\,\ln\left(\frac{M3}{PD}\right)_{t-1} + \underset{(3.26)}{0.18427}\,\ln\left(\frac{(ROB)_t}{(ROB)_{t-1}}\right)$$

$R^2 = 0.940$

D-W = 1.86, S = 0.048, S/ME = 0.017, $\chi_1^2(3) = 4.37$,

$\chi_3^2(1) = 0.98$, $F(1,15) = 0.73$

$$(39)\quad \ln(M3)_t^s = \underset{(1.81)}{0.58469} + \underset{(1.35)}{0.05479}\,\ln\left(\frac{(RS)_t}{(RS)_{t-1}}\right) + \underset{(3.10)}{0.48157}\,\ln(BA)_t$$

$$- \underset{(2.04)}{0.14719}\,\ln(BR)_t + \underset{(4.36)}{0.66933}\,\ln(M3)_{t-1}$$

$$R^2 = 0.994$$

$$\rho = \underset{(3.16)}{0.79231}, \quad S = 0.039, \quad S/ME = 0.013, \quad \chi_1^2(3) = 4.86$$

$$\chi_3^2(1) = 0.44, \quad F(1,14) = 0.21$$

(40) $$\ln(M3)_t^d = \ln(M3)_t^s = \ln(M3)_t$$

(41) $$\ln(RL)_t = -\underset{(2.00)}{1.05645} + \underset{(5.94)}{0.35194} \ln(RS)_t + \underset{(2.05)}{0.41309} \ln(GDPR)_t$$

$$+ \underset{(2.07)}{0.85706} \ln\left(\frac{(PD)_t}{(PD)_{t-1}}\right) + \underset{(4.01)}{0.42517} \ln(RL)_{t-1}$$

$$R^2 = 0.988$$

$$D\text{-}W = 2.00, \quad S = 0.046, \quad S/ME = 0.022, \quad \chi_1^2(3) = 2.33,$$

$$\chi_3^2(1) = 0.22, \quad F(1,15) = 0.17$$

(42) $$(BA)_t = \Delta(BA)_t + (BA)_{t-1}$$

(43) $$\Delta(BA)_t = (PSBR)_t + \Delta(FR)_t - \Delta(GS)_t$$

(44) $$(PSBR)_t = (GEX)_t - (TAX)_t + (OGREV)_t$$

(45) $$\Delta(FR)_t = (CB)_t + (DKM)_t$$

(46) $$(CB)_t = [(PXD)_t \times (XR)_t] - [(PQD)_t \times (QR)_t] + (OCB)_t$$

End-notes

CHAPTER 1

1. The expression 'best, linear and unbiased estimator' (BLUE) will often be used in the book. Here we provide a brief interpretation. For a more rigorous explanation of this and other econometric concepts we may freely use, see Johnston (1972). The ordinary least squares (OLS) estimator for the regression

$$\hat{Z}_t = \hat{a} + \hat{\beta}X_t$$

is

(i) *best*, that is, it has the minimum possible variance within the class of linear unbiased (see below) estimators

$$(\text{var}\ (\hat{\beta}) < \text{var}\ (\tilde{\beta})\ \text{where}\ \tilde{\beta} = \text{any other estimator of}\ \beta)$$

when the error term in the stochastic equation

$$Z_t = a + \beta X_t + u_t$$

obeys the classical assumption $E(uu') = \sigma^2 I$, which implies absence of autocorrelation and heteroscedasticity; sometimes $\hat{\beta}$ is called an *efficient* estimator.

(ii) *linear* in relation to Z_t since

$$\hat{\beta} = \Sigma W_t Z_t$$

where $W_t = \dfrac{x_t}{\Sigma x_t^2}$ for $x_t = X_t - \bar{X}$

(iii) *unbiased*, that is, $E(\hat{\beta}) = \beta$ when $E(u_t) = 0$ and $E(u_t X_t) = 0$ for all t, the latter assumption implying independence between u and the regressor. For $E(\beta) \neq \beta$ the estimator is biased. These small-sample properties can easily be generalised in the case of multiple regression.

2. An estimator is said to be more efficient than some other estimator if it always has a smaller variance. An estimator that is more efficient than any other is called 'absolutely efficient', or simply 'efficient'.
3. Very frequently estimators are biased; we therefore look for a second-best property; we say that an estimator $\hat{\beta}$ is *consistent* if

   $$\text{plim}\hat{\beta} = \beta$$

   that is, the probability limit of β is the true value of the coefficient, or

   $$\lim_{n \to \infty} \Pr \{|\hat{\beta} - \beta|<\varepsilon\} = 1$$

   for $\varepsilon > 0$, where ε is any arbitrary small number, which means that as the number of observations (n) tends to infinity both the bias and the variance tend to zero. The property described by the expressions is called an *asymptotic property*, in that it holds at the *limit* of a process of adding successively more observations. The same conceptual framework can be used to talk about asymptotic unbiasedness, asymptotic variance, asymptotic efficiency and asymptotic distribution.
4. For a discussion of the importance and problems of measurement of human capital, see Chang, Hilton and Yaseen (1979).
5. Model 1.64 is said to be *recursive* if (i) the B matrix is triangular, that is, elements either above or below the main diagonal are all zero, (ii) the variance-covariance matrix of errors is diagonal, that is, errors across equations are independent, and (iii) the errors must be free from serial correlation and correlation with past values of the errors in other equations. When these conditions are satisfied, OLS estimates of 1.64 are consistent and asymptotically efficient. An interesting feature of recursiveness is that it assumes an unidirectional state of dependence or causality. The coefficient matrix for endogenous variables can be arranged in triangular form with each variable influencing variables which lie below it but not influenced by any of them. There is no feedback and thus no simultaneity problem.

CHAPTER 2

1. There are of course important differences between consumers' expenditure and consumption. These differences are brought together later on in this chapter.
2. Adam Smith, *The Wealth of Nations*, quoted by Dobb (1975, p. 59).
3. We note that in recent years there have been attempts to look yet again at the relationship between aggregate disposable income and aggregate consumers' expenditure, perhaps because existing models

failed to predict the peculiarly high levels of the personal saving ratio since 1972.

4. For the constituents of the category 'other goods' see *Economic Trends - Annual Supplement*, London, HMSO, 1977, p. 158.
5. For a discussion of the shortcomings of the 'use' definition of consumption and problems of measurement, see Mayer (1972, pp. 12-16).
6. It rose from an average of 8 per cent in the late 1960s to a peak of just over 15 per cent in the second half of 1975; for an example of annual forecasts which illustrates the problem see Deaton (1975). The main forecasting models of the UK economy are reported and discussed in Renton (1975); a subsequent volume on economic modelling in the United Kingdom is Ormerod (1979a).
7. Two alternative specifications have also been estimated: first, the exponential form of 2.8, i.e.

$$C/Y = mi^{d1} W^{d2} (\bar{Y}/Y)^{d3} u$$

and, second, a relationship obtained on the basis of permanent income being measured as a weighted average of present and past levels of income, approximately expressed as

$$C/Y = c_0 + c_1 i + c_2 w + c_3 (C_{-1}/Y) + u_t$$

On the basis of their empirical performance the above have been found inferior to the linear form and they are not therefore reported in this study (for more details on these, see Arestis and Hadjimatheou, 1982).

8. There are two time-series estimates of the personal sector's wealth: (i) the estimates of the Department of Applied Economics at Cambridge, covering the period 1957-66, and (ii) the evidence submitted to the Royal Commission on the Distribution of Income and Wealth by the Central Statistical Office. The estimates for the overlap year of 1966 are significantly different, reflecting the different basis of estimation adopted (for further details see *Economic Trends*, January 1978,pp. 97-107). Furthermore, the balance-sheets of the personal sector (*Economic Trends*, January 1978) suggest that the device by which time series of wealth are constructed on the basis of savings taken as the only addition to wealth - a procedure that has been used in a number of UK studies, e.g. Stone (1964) - leads to completely inadequate and erroneous approximations.
9. Liquid assets have been used extensively in empirical studies of the consumption function. For a detailed summary see Ferber (1973. Recent UK studies which use liquid assets in consumption functions are Townend (1976), Davidson *et al.* (1978), Bean

(1978), Hadjimatheou (1979), Cuthbertson (1980), and Arestis and Hadjimatheou (1982).

10. A further substitution effect can arise due to the movement of mortgage and hire-purchase repayments with interest rates. As these repayments are partly contractual, an increase in interest rates could lower consumers' expenditure.
11. For a more detailed discussion on this point see Tobin and Dolde (1971, pp. 102-11) and Boskin (1978). Another effect on consumption of interest-rate changes is 'a consequence of the fact that the real rate of interest helps to determine the services yielded by the stock of consumer durables' (Poole, 1972, p. 211).

CHAPTER 3

1. Keynes refers to the expectation of future yields from capital assets as one of three fundamental psychological factors which play an important role in his general theory. More recently the crucial role of expectations in this context has been emphasised by Eisner (1974).
2. Also commenting on the nature of uncertainty Shackle (1970, p. 76) explains: 'The very concept of *novelty* implies essential and deep-rooted uncertainty, for the novel is the hitherto unknown, even the unimagined. If there can be new knowledge, there must have been either wrong knowledge or a gap in knowledge. In either case an awareness of the possibility that accepted knowledge is wrong or is insufficient is precisely what we mean by uncertainty.'
3. The rate of investment plays an important role in the determination of the rate of steady-state growth in post-Keynesian economics (Robinson, 1956). Furthermore, the introduction of new technology is usually assumed to be dependent on the speed of new capital formation.
4. For comparative evidence see Denison (1968) and Bacon and Eltis (1978).
5. A more detailed account of changes in the composition of GDFCF in the United Kingdom since the beginning of the present century is given by Lund (1971).
6. It can also be shown that the level of stockbuilding conforms fully to this pattern of change. In other words it is the volatility in stockbuilding, rather than changes in GDP, that dominate and generate fluctuations in the ratio of stockbuilding to GDP.
7. The constant elasticity of substitution production function

$$Y = \gamma\{\delta K^{-\rho} + (1 - \delta)L^{-\rho}\}^{-v/\rho}$$

was popularised by Arrow, Chenery, Minhas and Solow (1961). It follows from the assumption of profit-maximising entrepreneurs facing competitive markets and the observation that $Y/L = \alpha W^{\lambda}$, i.e. that output per head (Y/L) is a changing proportion of the wage rate (W). It is a generalisation of the Cobb-Douglas production function which is obtained as a special case for $\lambda = 1$. For $v = 1$ we have the case of constant returns to scale; γ is a scale parameter changing with neutral technical progress; δ indicates the degree to which technology is capital-intensive and ρ is the substitution parameter equal to $(1 - \sigma)/\sigma$, with σ being the elasticity of substitution. (For a derivation and further discussion see Heathfield, 1971; see also Wallis, 1973.)

8. For a description of this process see Matthews (1959, pp. 89-91).

CHAPTER 4

1. For a discussion of alternative measures of import penetration see Wells and Imber (1977).
2. Deppler and Ripley (1978) show, however, that when a time trend is used as an additional regressor in estimated import functions the UK income elasticity is lower than those obtained for West Germany, France and Japan. But there are substantial differences in time trends. The United Kingdom has a significantly positive time trend for imports and a zero trend for exports, in contrast to Japan and West Germany, for which no significant import trend was found.
3. The rationale for including a time trend in import functions is frequently based on the need to provide for the effect on non-price competitiveness, that is, a largely non-measurable variable encompassing the act of selling and various aspects of the product including design, ease of maintenance, quality, reliability, delivery time and after-sales service. This applies for both imports and exports.
4. Winters (1976) also fails to obtain a significant coefficient on a 'pressure on capacity' variable. Furthermore, in common with Enoch (1978) and this study, he fails to find a significant coefficient for a time trend.
5. The particular way in which the world prices variable (WP) appears in the equation merely signifies the optimum lag structure selected on the basis of experimentation with alternative lag structures. This result confirms the presence of substantially long price lags in the export function obtained by Enoch (1978).
6. For money income elasticities of demand for UK exports at a highly disaggregated level see Thirlwall (1980).

CHAPTER 5

1. This term is used when reference is made to the Bank of England and the Treasury (with the responsible minister being the Chancellor of the Exchequer).
2. Credit, here, is used as a general term meaning funds loaned to borrowers - not just credit extended by commercial banks, which gives rise to demand deposits, but credit extended by the widest variety of sources.
3. For a detailed discussion and analysis of these proposals see Gowland (1978).

4. Assets qualified to be included in the reserve asset ratio were as follows: balances with the Bank of England (other than special deposits), British government and Northern Ireland government Treasury Bills, company tax reserve certificates, money at call with the London money market, British government stocks with one year or less to final maturity, local authority bills eligible for rediscount at the Bank of England, and (up to a maximum of 2 per cent of eligible liabilities) commercial bills eligible for rediscount at the Bank of England.
5. OGREV stands for 'other government revenue', which includes national insurance contributions, trading surpluses, rent, interest and dividends, transfers, etc.
6. The inter-bank rate is utilised as a proxy for the 'own' rate, for which, however, data exist only since 1964; for the period before 1964 we employed Bank Rate data.

CHAPTER 6

1. The present presentation of government receipts and expenditure was adopted in 1977 and is described in *Economic Trends* (March 1977).
2. An account of some empirical evidence is provided in a later section of this chapter; for a full review of the empirical evidence, see Hadjimatheou (1976).
3. For a review of the 'public choice' literature, see Mueller (1976); see also Tullock (1965).
4. A full account of the relative price effect is provided by Rees and Thompson (1972), and by the HM Treasury (1972) study.

CHAPTER 7

1. The derivation of this relationship from a single 'typical' labour market to a non-linear, aggregate, negative relationship entails a number of problems. See Peston (1971) for an admirable summary of these problems, and also Trevithick and Mulvey (1978, pp. 42-3). On the non-linearity assumption, see the studies by Phelps *et al.* (1970), Mortensen (1970), Grossman (1974), Barro and Grossman (1976, ch. 5), and a summary in Santomero and Seater (1978, p. 503). Finally, see Corry and Laidler (1967), who argue that if quits rise as excess demand increases it might be possible for the negative relationships to disappear. Vanderkamp (1968), however, has shown that the empirical evidence does not support this contention.
2. The definition of this notion can be found in Friedman (1968, p. 8):

> At any moment of time, there is some level of unemployment which has the property that it is consistent with equilibrium in the structure of *real* wage rates ... The 'natural rate of unemployment', in other words, is the level that would be ground out by the Walrasian system of general equilibrium equations, provided there is imbedded in them the actual structural characteristics of the labor and commodity markets,

including market imperfections, stochastic variability in demands and supplies, the cost of gathering information about job vacancies and labor availabilities, the costs of mobility, and so on.

The natural rate of unemployment, therefore, is a real phenomenon; in addition, Tobin (1972) has argued that the natural rate also depends upon the regional dispersion of unemployment.

3. The term 'rational expectations' was first introduced to the literature by Muth (1961), who argued 'that expectations, since they are informed predictions of future events, are essentially the same as the predictions of the relevant economic theory' (p. 316). Its use, however, to challenge macroeconomic policy of the Keynesian kind is a more recent development; see, for example, the Sargent and Wallace (1976) contribution.
4. See McNees (1978) for a similar and other criticisms of Sargent's (1973) study.

CHAPTER 8

1. Summaries of these 'big' models are provided in Renton (1975) and Ormerod (1979a).
2. For an elaboration of all these, and other, points of the post-Keynesian paradigm see, for example, Eichner (1979).

CHAPTER 9

1. One should note that the coefficients of Y_t, Y_{t-1} and Y_{t-2} are the same as those of C_t, C_{t-1} and C_{t-2} in equation 9.5 as well as with the coefficients of I_t, I_{t-1} and I_{t-2} in equation 9.6. This is to be expected; see Klein (1974, p. 234), as well as Orcutt (1948).
2. Baumol (1970) provides an introduction to difference equations and to their solution.
3. In those cases where a high-order difference equation is involved, which might not be easily solved, its convergence can be determined by the Schur theorem, which does not require the actual solution of the difference equation. See Chiang (1967, pp. 551-2) for details.
4. An imaginary component arises when we have

$$\frac{(b \quad + i \ ) \pm (- [b \quad + i \ ) \quad - 4i \ ])^{\frac{1}{2}}}{2} =$$

$$\frac{(b \quad + i \ ) \pm (b \quad + i \ ) \quad - 4i \ )^{\frac{1}{2}} \ . \ \ i}{2}$$

where $i = (-1)^{\frac{1}{2}}$.

5. For a similar discussion on the types of direct impacts as well as the feedback responses, see the study by Meyer (1975, p. 74); see also the studies by Friedman (1978), Arestis (1979), and Arestis and Karakitsos (1980).

6. Additional negative feedback responses could arise as a result of a wealth-induced rise in interest rates; this can come about when the demand for money is significantly influenced by some wealth variable (Floyd and Hynes, 1978; Butkiewicz, 1979). In the case of our study no such impact exists - our demand for money does not contain a wealth variable, and there are good reasons for this. First of all, a satisfactory wealth series does not exist in the case of the United Kingdom. But even if it existed and was included in this equation, the wealth elasticity of the demand for money should be expected to be low (Goodhart, 1975, pp. 48-9). Furthermore, Modigliani and Ando (1976, pp. 27-9) have argued that on both theoretical and empirical grounds a wealth effect should not enter the demand for money relationship.
7. Studies using US data provide similar findings: 'in fact most of the models here show such multipliers reaching a peak in two or three years and then declining thereafter in fluctuating paths. At the end of five to ten years, some of the models show that continued sustained fiscal stimulus has ever-increasing perverse impacts' (Fromm and Klein, 1973, p. 393).
8. Livesey (1973) and Theil (1964) provide arguments to support the usefulness and validity of working with a quadratic objective function; see also Chow (1975).
9. This approach to policy optimisation has been developed by Rustem and Zarrop (1979).
10. For non-linear models, such as the model developed in this book, these problems are basically intractable; see, however, Karakitsos, Rustem and Zarrop (1980) for an interesting approach.

Bibliography

Akerlof, G. A. (1979) 'The Case against Conservative Macroeconomics: An Inaugural Lecture' *Economica* (August) pp. 219-37.

Almon, S. (1965) 'The Distributed Lag Between Appropriations and Expenditures', *Econometrica* (January) pp. 178-96.

Andersen, L. C. and A. E. Burger (1969) 'Asset Management and Commercial Bank Portfolio Behaviour', *Journal of Finance* (May) pp. 207-22.

Andersen, L. C. and J. L. Jordan (1968) 'Monetary and Fiscal Actions: A Test of their Relative Importance in Economic Stabilization', *Federal Reserve Bank of St Louis Review* (November) pp. 11-24.

*Ando, A. and F. Modligliani (1963) 'The "Life-Cycle" Hypothesis of Saving: Aggregate Implications and Tests', *American Economic Review* (March) pp. 55-84.

Archibald, G. C. (1969) 'The Phillips Curve and Distribution of Unemployment', *American Economic Review* (May) pp. 124-34.

Arestis, P. (1979) 'The "Crowding Out" of Private Expenditure by Fiscal Actions: An Empirical Investigation', *Public Finance*, no. 1, pp. 36-50.

Arestis, P. and G. Hadjimatheou (1982) 'The Determinants of the Average Propensity to Consume in the UK', *Applied Economics* (March) pp. 111-23.

Arestis, P. and E. Karakitsos (1980) 'Fiscal Actions, Optimal Control and Crowding-out Within the NIESR Model', *Greek Economic Review* (December) pp. 220-40.

Arrow, K. J., H. B. Chenery, B. S. Minhas and R. B. Solow (1961) 'Capital-Labour Substitution and Economic Efficiency', *Review of Economics and Statistics* (August) pp. 225-50.

Artis, M. J. (1981) 'Is there a Wage Equation?', in A. S. Courakis (ed.), *Inflation, Depression and Economic Policy in the West* (Mansell: London) pp. 65-80.

Artis, M. J. and M. K. Lewis (1974) 'The Demand for Money: Stable or Unstable?', *The Banker* (March) pp. 239-47.

Artis, M. J. and M. K. Lewis (1976) 'The Demand for Money in the United Kingdom: 1963-1973', *Manchester School* (June) pp. 147-81.

*Ash, J. C. K. and D. J. Smyth (1973) *Forecasting the UK Economy* (Saxon House: Farnborough).

Bacon, R. and W. Eltis (1978) *Britain's Economic Problem: Too Few Producers* (Macmillan: London).

Ball, R. J., T. Burns and P. J. Warburton (1979) 'The London Business School Model of the UK Economy: An Exercise in International Monetarism', in P. Ormerod (ed.), *Economic Modelling* (Heinemann: London) pp. 86-114.

Ball, R. J., J. R. Eaton and M. D. Steuer (1966) 'The Relationship between United Kingdom Export Performance in Manufactures and the Internal Pressure of Demand', *Economic Journal* (September) pp. 501-18.

Bank of England Quarterly Bulletin (1971a) 'Key Issues in Monetary and Credit Policy', speech by Sir Leslie O'Brien, Governor of the Bank of England, to the International Banking Conference in Munich (June) pp. 195-8.

Bank of England Quarterly Bulletin (1971b) 'Competition and Credit Control' (June) pp. 189-94.

Bank of England Quarterly Bulletin (1971c) 'Competition and Credit Control: The Discount Market' (September) pp. 314-16.

Bank of England Quarterly Bulletin (1971d) 'Reserve Ratios: Further Definitions' (December) pp. 482-9.

Bank of England Quarterly Bulletin (1974) 'Credit Control: A Supplementary Scheme' (March) pp. 37-40.

Bank of England Quarterly Bulletin (1978) 'Economic Commentary' (March) pp. 3-21.

Baran, P. A. (1968) 'The Concept of the Economic Surplus', in D. Horowitz (ed.), *Marx and Modern Economics* (MacGibbon & Kee: London) pp. 326-50.

Baran, P. A. and P. M. Sweezy (1966) *Monopoly Capital* (Penguin: Harmondsworth).

Barker, T. S. (1970) 'Aggregation Error and Estimates of the UK Import Demand Function', in K. Hilton and D. F. Heathfield (eds), *The Econometric Study of the United Kingdom* (Macmillan: London) pp. 115-43.

*Barker, T. S. (ed.) (1976) *Economic Structure and Policy* (Chapman & Hall: London).

Barker, T. S. (1977) 'International Trade and Economic Growth: An Alternative to the Neoclassical Approach', *Cambridge Journal of Economics* (June) pp. 153-77.

Barker, T. S. (1979) 'Identification of Activity Effects, Trends and Cycles in Import Demand', *Bulletin of the Oxford Institute of Economics and Statistics* (February) pp. 63-8.

Barro, R. J. and H. I. Grossman (1976) *Money, Employment and Inflation* (Cambridge University Press: New York and Cambridge).

Baumol, W. J. (1967) 'The Macroeconomics of Unbalanced Growth', *American Economic Review* (June) pp. 415-26.

*Baumol, W. J. (1970) *Economic Dynamics* (Macmillan: New York).

Baumol, W. J. and W. E. Oates (1975) *The Theory of Environmental Policy* (Prentice-Hall: Englewood Cliffs, N.J.).

Bean, C. R. (1978) 'The Determination of Consumers' Expenditure in the UK', unpublished paper, HM Treasury, AP(77), 35.

Bean, C. R. (1979) 'An Econometric Model of Manufacturing Investment in the UK', paper presented to the SSRC Economic Modelling Group, London School of Economics (March 1979).

Beckerman, W. (1966) 'The Determinants of Economic Growth', in P.D. Henderson (ed.), *Economic Growth in Britain* (Weidenfeld & Nicolson: London) pp. 55-83.

Beenstock, M. and P. Warburton (1980) 'UK Imports and the International Trading Order', London Business School Economic Forecasting Unit, Discussion Paper No. 83 (July).

*Bischoff, C. W. (1971) 'Business Investment in the 1970s: A Comparison of Models', *Brookings Papers on Economic Activity*, no. 1, pp. 13-58.

Blaug, M. (1973) *Economic Theory in Retrospect* (Heinemann: London).

Bleany, M. (1976) *Underconsumption Theories: A History and Critical Analysis* (International Publishers: New York).

Boatwright, B. and J. Eaton (1972) 'Investment Functions for Manufacturing Investment in the UK', *Economica* (November) pp. 403-19.

Boskin, M. J. (1978) 'Taxation, Saving and the Rate of Interest', *Journal of Political Economy* (April) pp. S3-S27.

*Boughton, J. M. (1979) 'Demand for Money in Major OECD Countries', *OECD Economic Outlook*, Occasional Studies (January).

Brainard, W. C. and J. Tobin (1968) 'Pitfalls in Financial Model Building', *American Economic Review* (May) pp. 99-122.

Brown, C. J. F. and T. D. Sheriff (1979) 'De-industrialisation: A Background Paper' in F. Blackaby (ed.), *De-industrialisation* (Heinemann: London) pp. 233-62.

Buchanan, J. M., J. Burton and R. E. Wagner (1978) *The Consequences of Mr Keynes* (Institute of Economic Affairs: London).

*Budd, A. (1979) 'The Present State of the Art', in P. Ormerod (ed.), *Economic Modelling* (Heinemann: London) pp. 1-22.

*Buiter, W. H. (1980) 'The Macroeconomics of Dr Pangloss: A Critical Survey of the New Classical Macroeconomics', *Economic Journal* (March) pp. 34-50.

Burman, J. P. (1970) 'Capacity Utilisation and the Determination of Fixed Investment', in K. Hilton and D. F. Heathfield (eds), *The Econometric Study of the United Kingdom* (Macmillan: London) pp. 185-202.

Butkiewicz, J. L. (1979) 'Outside Wealth, the Demand for Money and the Crowding Out Effect', *Journal of Monetary Economics* (April) pp. 249-58.

Cagan, P. H. (1956) 'The Monetary Dynamics of Hyperinflation', in M. Friedman (ed.), *Studies in the Quantity Theory of Money* (University of Chicago Press: Chicago) pp. 25-117.

Chang, E. R., K. Hilton and H. A. Yaseen (1979) 'The Stock of Human Capital in the UK 1975: A Preliminary Estimate', in K. D. Patterson and K. Schott (eds), *The Measurement of Capital* (Macmillan: London) pp. 198-211.

Chiang, A. C. (1967) *Fundamental Methods of Mathematical Economics* (McGraw-Hill: New York).

*Chow, G. C. (1975) *Analysis and Control of Dynamic Economic Systems* (Wiley: New York).

*Christ, C. (1968) 'A Simple Macroeconomic Model with a Government Budget Restraint', *Journal of Political Economy* (January) pp. 53-67.

Chrystal, K. A. and J. Alt (1979a) 'Some Problems in Formulating and Testing a Politico-Economic Model of the UK', University of Essex Discussion Paper.

Chrystal, K. A. and J. Alt (1979b) 'Public Sector Behaviour: The State of the Political Business Cycle', paper presented to the Association of University Teachers in Economics Conference at Exeter University (March).

Chrystal, K. A. and J. Alt (1979c) 'A Model of the Non-industrial Public Sector in Britain', University of Essex Discussion Paper 129 (July).

*Clark, P. K. (1979) 'Investment in the 1970s: Theory, Performance and Prediction', *Brookings Papers on Economic Activity*, no. 1, pp. 73-124.

Clower, R. W. (1965) 'The Keynesian Counter-revolution: A Theoretical Appraisal', in F. Hahn and E. Brechling (eds), *The Theory of Interest Rates* (Macmillan: London) pp. 103-25.

Coghlan, R. T. (1978) 'A Transactions Demand for Money', *Bank of England Quarterly Bulletin* (March) pp. 48-60.

*Coghlan, R. T. (1980) *The Theory of Money and Finance* (Macmillan: London).

Coghlan, R. T. and P. M. Jackson (1979) 'The UK Personal Savings Ratio: Past, Present and Future', *Scottish Journal of Political Economy* (November) pp. 307-24.

Corry, B. and D. E. W. Laidler (1967) 'The Phillips Relation: A Theoretical Explanation', *Economica* (May) pp. 189-97.

Courakis, A. S. (1978) 'Serial Correlation and a Bank of England Study of the Demand for Money: An Exercise in Measurement without Theory', *Economic Journal* (September) pp. 537-48.

*Cripps, F. and M. Fetherston (1979) 'Cambridge Economic Policy Group Methodology', in P. Ormerod (ed.), *Economic Modelling* (Heinemann: London) pp. 40-52.

Crockett, A. D. (1970) 'Timing Relationships between Movements of Monetary and National Income Variables', *Bank of England Quarterly Bulletin* (December) pp. 459-68.

Cross, R. B. and D. E. W. Laidler (1975) 'Inflation, Excess Demand and Expectations in Fixed Exchange Rate Open Economies: Some Preliminary Empirical Results', in J. M. Parkin and G. Zis (eds), *Inflation in the World Economy* (Manchester University Press: Manchester) pp. 221-55.

Crouch, R. L. (1967) 'A Model of the UK Monetary Sector', *Econometrica* (July-October) pp. 398-418.

Crouch, R. L. (1968) 'Money Supply Theory and the UK's Monetary Contraction, 1954-56', *Bulletin of the Oxford University Institute of Economics and Statistics*, vol. 130, pp. 143-52.

Cuthbertson, K. (1980) 'The Determination of Expenditure on Consumer Durables', *National Institute Economic Review* (September) pp. 62-72.

Daly, V. and G. Hadjimatheou (1981) 'Stochastic Implications of the Life Cycle-Permanent Income Hypothesis: Evidence for the UK Economy', *Journal of Political Economy* (June) pp. 596-9.

*Davidson, J., D. Hendry, F. Srba and S. Yeo (1978) 'Econometric Modelling of the Aggregate Time-series Relationship between Consumers' Expenditure and Income in the United Kingdom', *Economic Journal* (December) pp. 661-92.

*Deaton, A. (1975) *Models and Projections of Demand in Post-War Britain* (Chapman & Hall: London).

*Deaton, A. (1977) 'Involuntary Saving through Unanticipated Inflation', *American Economic Review* (December) pp. 899-910.

Denison, E. F. (1968) 'Economic Growth', in R. E. Caves (ed.), *Britain's Economic Prospects* (Allen & Unwin: London) pp. 231-78.

Deppler, M. C. and D. M. Ripley (1978) 'The World Trade Model: Merchandise Trade', *International Monetary Fund Staff Papers* (March) pp. 147-206.

Dicks-Mireaux, L. A. (1961) 'The Interrelationship between Cost and Price Changes 1946-1959: A Study of Inflation in Post-War Britain', *Oxford Economic Papers* (October) pp. 267-92.

Dobb, M. (1975) *Theories of Value and Distribution since Adam Smith* (Cambridge University Press: Cambridge).

Dornbusch, R. (1976) 'The Theory of Flexible Exchange Rate Regimes and Macroeconomic Policy', *Scandinavian Journal of Economics* (May) pp. 255-75.

*Duesenberry, J. (1949) *Income, Saving and the Theory of Consumer Behavior* (Harvard University Press: Cambridge, Mass.).

Duesenberry, J. (1958) *Business Cycles and Economic Growth* (McGraw-Hill: New York).

Duffy, M. and A. Renton (1970) 'A Model of UK Exports of Manufactures to Industrial Countries', *Applied Economics* (September) pp. 153-77.

*Eichner, A. S. (ed.) (1979) *A Guide to Post-Keynesian Economics* (Macmillan: London).

Eisner, R. (1974) 'Comment', *Journal of Economic Literature* (March) pp. 49-50.

Enoch, C. A. (1978) 'Measures of Competitiveness in International Trade', *Bank of England Quarterly Bulletin* (June) pp. 181-95.

*Evans, M. K. (1969) *Macroeconomic Activity* (Harper & Row: New York).

Fair, R. C. and D. M. Jaffee (1972) 'Methods of Estimation for Markets in Disequilibrium', *Econometrica* (May) pp. 497-514.

Feige, E. L. (1967) 'Expectations and Adjustments in the Monetary Sector', *American Economic Review* (May) pp. 462-73.

Feldstein, M. and J. Flemming (1971) 'Tax Policy, Corporate Saving and Investment Behaviour in Britain', *Review of Economic Studies* (October) pp. 415-34.

Ferber, R. (1973) 'Consumer Economics: A Survey', *Journal of Economic Literature* (December) pp. 1303-42.

Fetherston, M. J. and K.J. Coutts (1979) 'Technical Manual on the CEPG Model of the UK', mimeo, Department of Applied Economics, University of Cambridge.

Fetherston, M. J. and W. A. H. Godley (1978) '"New Cambridge" Macroeconomics and Global Monetarism: Some Issues in the Conduct of UK Economic Policy', in K. Brunner and A. H. Meltzer (eds), *Public Policies in Open Economies*, Carnegie-Rochester Conference Series No. 9 (North-Holland: Amsterdam) pp. 33-65.

Fisher, D. (1968) 'The Demand for Money in Britain: Quarterly Results, 1951-67', *Manchester School* (December) pp. 329-44.

Fisher, I. (1930) *Theory of Interest* (Macmillan: London).

Floyd, J. E. and J. A. Hynes (1978) 'Deficit Finance and "First-Round" Crowding Out: A Clarification', *Canadian Journal of Economics* (February) pp. 97-105.

*Foot, M. D. K. W., C. A. E. Goodhart and A. C. Hotson (1979) 'Monetary Base Control', *Bank of England Quarterly Bulletin* (June) pp. 149-59.

*Frey, B. S. (1978) *Modern Political Economy* (Martin Robertson: London).

Frey, B. S. and F. Schneider (1978) 'A Politico-Economic Model of the United Kingdom', *Economic Journal* (June) pp. 243-53.

*Friedman, B. M. (1978) 'Crowding Out or Crowding In? Economic Consequences of Financing Government Deficits', *Brookings Papers on Economic Activity*, no. 3, pp. 593-654.

Friedman, B. M. (1979) 'Optimal Expectations and the Extreme Information Assumptions of "Rational Expectations" Macro-models', *Journal of Monetary Economics* (January) pp. 23-41.

Friedman, M. (ed.) (1956) *Studies in the Quantity Theory of Money* (University of Chicago Press: Chicago).

*Friedman, M. (1957) *A Theory of the Consumption Function* (Princeton University Press: Princeton, N.J.).

Friedman, M. (1968) 'The Role of Monetary Policy', *American Economic Review* (April) pp. 1-17.

Friedman, M. (1972) 'Comment on the Critics', *Journal of Political Economy* (September-October) pp. 906-50.

Friedman, M. (1975) *Unemployment Versus Inflation? An Evaluation of the Phillips Curve*, IEA Occasional Paper No. 44 (Institute of Economic Affairs: London).

Friedman, M. (1977) 'Inflation and Unemployment', *Journal of Political Economy* (June) pp. 451-72.

Friedman, M. and D. Meiselman (1963) 'The Relative Stability of Monetary Velocity and the Investment Multiplier in the USA, 1897-1958', in *Stabilization Policies*, Commission on Money and Credit, Research Study No. 2 (Prentice-Hall: Englewood Cliffs, N.J.) pp. 165-269.

Fromm, G. and L. R. Klein (1973) 'A Comparison of Eleven Econometric Models of the US', *American Economic Review* (May) pp. 385-93.

Garganas, N. C. (1975) 'An Analysis of Consumer Credit and its Effects on Purchases of Consumer Durables', in G. A. Renton (ed.), *Modelling the Economy* (Heinemann: London) pp. 610-53 (with discussion).

Gershuny, J. (1979) *After Industrial Society* (Macmillan: London).

Godley, W. A. H. (1979) 'Britain's Chronic Recession - Can Anything Be Done?, in W. Beckerman (ed.), *Slow Growth in Britain: Causes and Consequences* (Clarendon Press: Oxford) pp. 226-33.

Godley, W. A. H. and T. F. Cripps (1980) 'Academic Criticism of the CEPG Analysis', *Economic Policy Review* (Department of Applied Economics, University of Cambridge) pp. 35-42.

Goodhart, C. A. E. (1973a) 'Monetary Policy in the United Kingdom', in K. Holbik (ed.), *Monetary Policy in Twelve Industrial Countries* (Federal Reserve Bank of Boston) pp. 465-524.

Goodhart, C. A. E. (1973b) 'Analysis of the Determinants of the Stock of Money', in M. Parkin and A. R. Nobay (eds), *Essays in Modern Economics* (Longman: London) pp. 243-61.

Goodhart, C. A. E. (1975) *Money, Information and Uncertainty* (Macmillan: London).

*Goodhart, C. A. E. (1981) 'Problems of Monetary Management: The UK Experience', in A. S. Courakis (ed.), *Inflation, Depression and Economic Policy in the West* (Mansell: London) pp. 111-43.

Goodhart, C. A. E. and A. D. Crockett (1970) 'The Importance of Money', *Bank of England Quarterly Bulletin* (June) pp. 159-98.

*Gough, I. (1979) *The Political Economy of the Welfare State* (Macmillan: London).

Gowland, D. (1978) *Monetary Policy and Credit Control* (Croom Helm: London).

Granger, C. W. J. and P. Newbold (1977) *Forecasting Economic Time Series* (Academic Press: London).

Griliches, Z. (1967) 'Distributed Lags, A Survey', *Econometrica* (January) pp. 16-49.

Grossman, H. I. (1974) 'The Cyclical Pattern of Unemployment and Wage Inflation', *Economica* (November) pp. 403-13.

Gurley, J. G. (1960) *Liquidity and Financial Institutions in the Postwar Economy*, Study Paper No. 14, Joint Economic Committee, 86th Congress, 2nd Session (Washington, D.C.).

Gurley, J. G. and E. S. Shaw (1960) *Money in a Theory of Finance* (Brookings Institution: Washington, D.C.).

Gustafsson, B. (ed.) (1979) *Post-industrial Society* (Croom Helm: London).

Hacche, G. (1974) 'The Demand for Money in the United Kingdom: Experience since 1971', *Bank of England Quarterly Bulletin* (September) pp. 284-305.

Hadjimatheou, G. (1976) *The Housing and Mortgage Markets: The UK Experience* (Saxon House: Farnborough).

Hadjimatheou, G. (1976) 'Economic Theory and Expanding State Activity', *Thames Papers in Political Economy* (Autumn).

Hadjimatheou, G. (1979) 'An Explanation of the Decline in the Average Propensity to Consume in the UK', *British Review of Economic Issues* (November) pp. 1-13.

Hall, R. (1978) 'Stochastic Implications of the Life Cycle-Permanent Income Hypothesis, Theory and Evidence', *Journal of Political Economy* (December) pp. 971-87.

Hamburger, M. J. (1967) 'Interest Rates and the Demand for Consumer Durable Goods', *American Economic Review* (December) pp. 1131-53.

Hamburger, M. J. (1977) 'The Demand for Money in an Open Economy: Germany and the United Kingdom', *Journal of Monetary Economics* (January) pp. 25-40.

Harvey, A. C. (1981) *The Econometric Analysis of Time Series* (Philip Allan: Oxford).

Heathfield, D. F. (1971) *Production Functions* (Macmillan: London).

*Hendry, D. F. (1979) 'Predictive Failure and Econometric Modelling in Macroeconomics: The Transactions Demand for Money', in P. Ormerod (ed.), *Economic Modelling* (Heinemann: London) pp. 217-42.

*Hendry, D. F. (1980) 'Econometrics - Alchemy or Science? An Inaugural Lecture', *Economica* (November) pp. 387-406.

*Hendry, D. F. and G. E. Mizon (1978) 'Serial Correlation as a Convenient Simplification, not a Nuisance: A Comment on a Study of the Demand for Money by the Bank of England', *Economic Journal* (September) pp. 549-63.

*Hendry, D. F. and T. von Ungern-Sternberg (1980) 'Liquidity and Inflation Effects on Consumers' Expenditure', in A.S. Deaton (ed.), *Essays in the Theory and Measurement of Consumers' Behaviour* (Cambridge University Press: Cambridge).

Hicks, J. R. (1937) 'Mr Keynes and the Classics: A Suggested Interpretation', *Econometrica* (April) pp. 147-59.

Hicks, J. R. (1939) *Value and Capital* (Oxford University Press: Oxford).

Hicks, J. R. (1950) *A Contribution to the Theory of the Business Cycle* (Oxford University Press: Oxford).

Hicks, J. R. (1975) 'What is Wrong with Monetarism?', *Lloyds Bank Review* (October) pp. 1-13.

Hicks, J. R. (1979) *Causality in Economics* (Blackwell: Oxford).

Hines, A. G. (1964) 'Trade Unions and Wage Inflation in the United Kingdom, 1893-1961', *Review of Economic Studies* (October) pp. 221-52.

Hines, A. G. and G. Catephores (1970) 'Investment in UK Manufacturing Industry, 1956-67' in K. Hilton and D. F. Heathfield (eds), *The Econometric Study of the United Kingdom* (Macmillan: London) pp. 203-24.

HM Treasury (1972) *Public Expenditure White Paper: Handbook on Methodology* (HMSO: London).

*HM Treasury (1979) 'Some Problems in the Development of the Treasury Model', in P. Ormerod (ed.), *Economic Modelling* (Heinemann: London) pp. 53-85.

Holmes, J. (1971) 'A Condition for Independence of Permanent and Transitory Components of a Series', *Journal of the American Statistical Association* (March) pp. 13-15.

Houthakker, H. S. and S. P. Magee (1969) 'Income and Price Elasticities in World Trade', *Review of Economics and Statistics* (May) pp. 111-25.

Howard, D. H. (1978) 'Personal Saving Behaviour and the Rate of Inflation', *Review of Economics and Statistics* (November) pp. 547-54.

Hughes, J. J. and A. P. Thirlwall (1977) 'Trends and Cycles in Import Penetration in the UK', *Bulletin of the Oxford Institute of Economics and Statistics* (November) pp. 301-17.

Hughes, J. J. and A. P. Thirlwall (1979) 'Trends and Cycles in Import Penetration in the UK: Reply', *Bulletin of the Oxford Institute of Economics and Statistics* (February) pp. 78-80.

*Humphrey, D. H. (1976) 'Disaggregated Import Functions for the UK, West Germany and France', *Bulletin of the Oxford Institute of Economics and Statistics* (November) pp. 281-98.

Hutton, J. and P. Minford (1975) *A Model of UK Manufactured Exports and Export Prices*, Government Economic Service Occasional Paper No. 11.

*Johnston, J. (1972) *Econometric Methods* (McGraw-Hill: New York).

Johnston, J. and M. Timbrell (1973) 'Empirical Tests of a Bargaining Theory of Wage Rate Determination', *Manchester School* (June) pp. 141-67.

*Jorgenson, D. W. (1963) 'Capital Theory and Investment Behaviour', *American Economic Review* (May) pp. 247-59.

Kahn, M. S. and K. Z. Ross (1975) 'Cyclical and Secular Income Elasticities of the Demand for Imports', *Review of Economics and Statistics* (August) pp. 357-61.

Kaldor, N. (1966) *Causes of the Slow Rate of Economic Growth of the United Kingdom* (Cambridge University Press: Cambridge).

Kalecki, M. (1971) 'Determinants of Investment', in M. Kalecki, *Selected Essays on the Dynamics of the Capitalist Economy 1933-70* (Cambridge University Press: Cambridge) pp. 110-23.

Karakitsos, E., B. Rustem and M. B. Zarrop (1980) 'Robust Economic Policy under Uncertainty', paper presented to the 4th World Congress of the Econometric Society (Aix-en-Provence).

Kavanagh, N. J. and A. A. Walters (1966) 'The Demand for Money in the UK 1877-1961: Preliminary Findings', *Bulletin of the Oxford University Institute of Economics and Statistics* (May) pp. 93-116.

Kelley, A. C. (1976) 'Demographic Change and the Size of the Government Sector', *Southern Economic Journal* (October) pp. 1056-66.

Keran, M. W. (1969) 'Monetary and Fiscal Influences on Economic Activity - The Historical Evidence', *Federal Reserve Bank of St Louis Monthly Review* (February) pp. 5-24.

Keran, M. W. (1970) 'Monetary and Fiscal Influences on Economic Activity: The Foreign Experience', *Federal Reserve Bank of St Louis Monthly Review* (February) pp. 16-28.

*Keynes, J. M. (1964) *The General Theory of Employment, Interest and Money* (Macmillan: London).

Keynes, J. M. with H. D. Henderson (1931) 'Can Lloyd George Do It?', in J.M. Keynes, *Essays in Persuasion* (MacMillan: London) pp. 118-34.

Klein, L. R. (1973) 'Commentary on "The State of the Monetarist Debate"', *Federal Reserve Bank of St Louis Monthly Review* (September) pp. 9-14.

*Klein, L. R. (1974) *A Textbook of Econometrics*, 2nd edn (Prentice-Hall: Englewood Cliffs, N.J.).

Klein, L. R. (1978) 'The Supply Side', *American Economic Review* (March) pp. 1-7.

Krause, L. B. (1968) 'British Trade Performance', in R. E. Caves (ed.), *Britain's Economic Prospects* (Allen & Unwin: London) pp. 198-228.

Kregel, J. A. (1979) 'Income Distribution', in A. S. Eichner (ed.), *A Guide to Post-Keynesian Economics* (Macmillan: London) pp. 46-60.

Laidler, D. E. W. (1971) 'The Influence of Money on Economic Activity: A Survey of Some Current Problems', in G. Clayton (ed.), *Monetary Theory and Monetary Policy in the 1970s* (Oxford University Press: Oxford) pp. 73-135.

Laidler, D. E. W. and J. M. Parkin (1970) 'The Demand for Money in the UK, 1955-67: Preliminary Estimates', *Manchester School* (September) pp. 187-208.

Laidler, D. E. W. and J. M. Parkin (1972) 'The Demand for Money in the United Kingdom, 1955-67: Preliminary Estimates', in H. G. Johnson (ed.), *Readings in British Monetary Economics* (Clarendon Press: Oxford) pp. 181-200.

*Laidler, D. E. W. and J. M. Parkin (1975) 'Inflation - A Survey', *Economic Journal* (December) pp. 741-809.

Latane, H. A. (1954) 'Cash Balances and the Interest Rate - A Pragmatic Approach', *Review of Economics and Statistics* (November) pp. 456-60.

*Latter, A. R. (1979) 'Some Issues in Economic Modelling at the Bank of England', in P. Ormerod (ed.), *Economic Modelling* (Heinemann: London) pp. 25-39.

Laury, J. S. E., G. R. Lewis and P. Ormerod (1978) 'Properties of Macroeconomic Models of the UK Economy: A Comparative Study', *National Institute Economic Review* (February) pp. 52-72.

Leijonhufvud, A. (1968) *On Keynesian Economics and the Economics of Keynes* (Oxford University Press: Oxford).

Leontief, W. (1971) 'Theoretical Assumptions and Nonobservable Facts', *American Economic Review* (March) pp. 1-7.

*Lewis, G. R. and P. Ormerod (1979) 'Policy Simulations and Model Characteristics', in S. T. Cook and P. M. Jackson (eds), *Current Issues in Fiscal Policy* (Martin Robertson: London) pp. 156-82.

Lipsey, R. G. (1960) 'The Relationship Between Unemployment and the Rate of Change of Money Wage Rates in the United Kingdom, 1862-1957: A Further Analysis', *Economica* (February) pp. 1-31.

*Lipsey, R. G. (1978) 'The Place of the Phillips Curve in Macroeconomic Models', in A. R. Bergstrom, A. J. L. Catt, M. H. Peston and B. D. J. Silverstone (eds), *Stability and Inflation* (Wiley: New York) pp. 49-75.

Lipsey, R. G. and M. Parkin (1972) 'Incomes Policy: A Reappraisal', in M. Parkin and M. T. Sumner (eds), *Incomes Policy and Inflation* (Manchester University Press: Manchester) pp. 85-111.

Livesey, D. A. (1973) *Can Macroeconometric Planning Problems Ever Be Treated as a Quadratic Regulator Problem?*, Institution of Electrical Engineers Conference Publication, no. 101, pp. 1-14.

London Business School (1980) 'Quarterly Econometric Model of the United Kingdom Economy', mimeo, London Business School.

*Lovell, M. (1964) 'Determinants of Inventory Investment', in E. F. Denison and L. R. Klein (eds), *Models of Income Determination* (Princeton University Press: Princeton, N.J.) pp. 177-231.

Lucas, R. E. (1976) 'Econometric Policy Evaluation: A Critique', in K. Brunner and A. H. Meltzer (eds), *The Phillips Curve and Labour Markets* (North-Holland: Amsterdam) pp. 19-46.

Lund, P. J. (1971) *Investment - The Study of an Economic Aggregate* (North-Holland: Amsterdam).

McNees, S. K. (1978) 'An Empirical Assessment of "New Theories" of Inflation and Unemployment', in *After the Phillips Curve: Persistence of High Inflation and High Unemployment*, Conference Series No. 19 (Federal Reserve Bank of Boston) pp. 29-46.

*McNees, S. K. (1979) 'The Accuracy of Macroeconometric Models and Forecasts of the US Economy', in P. Ormerod (ed.), *Economic Modelling* (Heinemann: London) pp. 245-64.

Marx, K. (1976) *Capital*, Vol. 1 (Penguin; Harmondsworth).

Matthews, R. C. O. (1959) *The Trade Cycle* (Cambridge University Press: Cambridge).

Matthews, R. C. O. (1968) 'Why has Britain had Full Employment since the War?', *Economic Journal* (September) pp. 555-69.

Matthews, R. C. O. (1971) 'The Role of Demand Management', in A. Cairncross (ed.), *Britain's Economic Prospects Reconsidered* (Allen & Unwin: London) pp. 13-35.

*Mayer, R. (1972) *Permanent Income, Wealth and Consumption* (University of California Press: California).

*Mayer, T. (1980) 'Economics as a Hard Science: Realistic Goal or Wishful Thinking?', *Economic Inquiry* (April) pp. 165-78.

Meltzer, L. A. (1941) 'The Nature and Stability of Inventory Cycles', *Review of Economic Statistics* (August) pp. 113-29.

Meyer, L. H. (1975) 'The Balance Sheet Identity, the Government Financing Constraint, and the Crowding-Out Effect', *Journal of Monetary Economics* (January) pp. 65-78.

Meyer-zu-Schlochtern, F. and A. Yajima (1970) *OECD Trade Model: 1970 Version*, OECD Occasional Studies (December).

Mica, P. (1978) *Capacity Utilization in UK Manufacturing Industry* (NEDO: London).

Midland Bank Review (1977) 'The Paradox of Personal Saving' (March) pp. 12-18.

Midland Bank Review (1980) 'Can Mrs Thatcher do it?', paper prepared by the Clare Group (Autumn) pp. 9-19.

Modligliani, F. and A. Ando (1976) 'Impacts of Fiscal Actions on Aggregate Income and the Monetarist Controversy: Theory and Evidence', in J. L. Stein (ed.), *Monetarism* (North-Holland: Amsterdam) pp. 17-42.

Moore, B. and J. Rhodes (1976) 'The Relative Decline of the UK Manufacturing Sector', *Economic Policy Review*, Department of Applied Economics, University of Cambridge (March) pp. 36-41.

Morgan, A. D. (1975) 'Tariff Reductions and UK Imports of Manufactures: 1955-71', *National Institute Economic Review* (May) pp. 38-54.

Mortensen, D. T. (1970) 'A Theory of Wage and Employment Dynamics', in E. S. Phelps *et al.*, *Microeconomic Foundations of Employment and Inflation Theory* (Norton: New York) pp. 167-201.

Mueller, D. C. (1976) 'Public Choice: A Survey', *Journal of Economic Literature* (June) pp. 395-433.

Muth, J. F. (1961) 'Rational Expectations and the Theory of Price Movements', *Econometrica* (July) pp. 315-35.

Nadiri, I. and S. Rosen (1969) 'Interrelated Factor Demand Functions', *American Economic Review* (September) pp. 457-71.

National Institute of Economic and Social Research (1979) *Listing of the Interim NIESR Model*, Discussion Paper No. 28, NIESR.

Neild, R. R. (1963) *Pricing and Employment in the Trade Cycle* (Cambridge University Press: Cambridge).

Nordhaus, W. D. (1972) 'The World-wide Wage Explosion', *Brookings Papers on Economic Activity*, no. 2, pp. 431-63.

Nordhaus, W. D. (1975) 'The Political Business Cycle', *Review of Economic Studies* (April) pp. 169-90.

Norton, W. E. (1969) 'Debt Management and Monetary Policy in the UK', *Economic Journal* (September) pp. 475-94.

O'Connor, J. (1973) *The Fiscal Crisis of the State* (St. Martin's Press: New York).

Odling-Smee, J. C. (1967) 'The Rise in the UK Personal Saving Ratio', *Oxford Bulletin of Economics and Statistics* (August) pp. 281-7.

Odling-Smee, J. C. (1973) 'Personal Saving Revisited: More Statistics, Fewer Facts', *Oxford Bulletin of Economics and Statistics* (February) pp. 21-9.

Orcutt, G. H. (1948) 'A Study of the Autoregressive Nature of the Time Series used for Tinbergen's Model of the Economic System of the United States, 1919-1932', *Journal of the Royal Statistical Society*, vol.X, series B, pp. 1-53.

*Ormerod, P. (ed.) (1979a) *Economic Modelling* (Heinemann: London).

*Ormerod, P. (1979b) 'The National Institute Model of the UK Economy: Some Current Problems', in P. Ormerod (ed.), *Economic Modelling* (Heinemann: London) pp. 115-41.

Ormerod, P. (1980) 'Manufactured Export Prices in the United Kingdom and the "Law of One Price"', *Manchester School* (September) pp. 265-83.

Paish, F. W. (1970) *How the Economy Works and Other Essays* (Macmillan: London).

Panić, M. (1975) 'Why the UK's Propensity to Import is High', *Lloyds Bank Review* (January) pp. 1-10.

Parkin, M. (1973) 'Reserve Assets and the Supply of Money', *Manchester School* (March) pp. 88-105.

*Parkin, J. M. and M. T. Sumner (eds) (1972) *Incomes Policy and Inflation* (Manchester University Press: Manchester).

Parkin, J. M., M. T. Sumner and R. Ward (1976) 'The Effects of Excess Demand, Generalised Expectations and Wage-Price Controls on Wage Inflation in the UK, 1951-1971', in K. Brunner and A. H. Meltzer (eds), *The Economics of Price and Wage Controls*, Carnegie-Rochester Conference Series No. 7 (North-Holland: Amsterdam) pp. 193-221.

Peacock, A. T. and M. Ricketts (1978) 'The Growth of the Public Sector and Inflation', in F. Hirsch and J. H. Goldthorpe (eds), *The Political Economy of Inflation* (Martin Robertson: London) pp. 117-36.

Peacock, A. T. and J. Wiseman (1961) *The Growth of Public Expenditure in the United Kingdom* (Oxford University Press: Oxford).

Peacock, A. T. and J. Wiseman (1979) 'Approaches to the Analysis of Government Expenditure Growth', *Public Finance Quarterly* (January) pp. 3-23.

Pearce, I. F. (1976) 'Introduction', in I. F. Pearce *et al.*, *A Model of Output, Employment, Wages and Prices in the UK* (Cambridge University Press: Cambridge) pp. 1-20.

Pesaran, M. and A. Deaton (1978) 'Testing Non-Nested Non-Linear Regression Models', *Econometrica* (May) pp. 677-94.

Pesek, B. and T. Saving (1967) *Money, Wealth and Economic Activity* (Macmillan: New York).

Peston, M. (1971) 'The Micro-Economics of the Phillips Curve', in H. G. Johnson and A. R. Nobay (eds), *The Current Inflation* (Macmillan: London) pp. 125-42.

Phelps, E. S. (1968) 'Money-Wage Dynamics and Labour Market Equilibrium', *Journal of Political Economy* (July-August) pp. 678-711.

Phelps, E. S., *et al.* (1970) *Microeconomic Foundations of Employment and Inflation Theory* (Norton: New York).

Phillips, A. W. (1958) 'The Relation Between Unemployment and the Rate of Change of Money Wage Rates in the United Kingdom, 1861-1957', *Economica* (November) pp. 283-99.

*Pindyck, R. S. and D. L. Rubinfeld (1976) *Econometric Models and Economic Forecasts* (McGraw-Hill: New York).

Poole, W. (1972) 'The Role of Interest Rates and Inflation in the Consumption Function', *Brookings Papers on Economic Activity*, no. 1, pp. 211-20 (with discussion).

Prais, S. J. and H. S. Houthakker (1971) *The Analysis of Family Budgets* (Cambridge University Press: Cambridge).

Price, L. D. D. (1972) 'The Demand for Money in the United Kingdom: A Further Investigation', *Bank of England Quarterly Bulletin* (March) pp. 43-55.

Prothero, D. L. and K. F. Wallis (1976) 'Modelling Macro-Economic Time Series', *Journal of the Royal Statistical Society*, vol. 139, pp. 468-500 (with discussion).

Radcliffe Committee (1959) *Report of the Committee on the Working of the Monetary System*, Cmnd 827 (HMSO: London).

*Rao, P. and R. L. Miller (1971) *Applied Econometrics* (Wadsworth: California).

Rees, P. M. and F. P. Thompson (1972) 'The Relative Price Effect in Public Expenditure: Its Nature and Method of Calculation', *Statistical News* (HMSO: London, August).

Rees, R. D. and P. R. G. Layard (1971) *The Determinants of UK Imports*, Government Economic Service Occasional Paper No. 3.

Renton, G. A. (1975) *Modelling the Economy* (Heinemann: London).

Robinson, J. (1954) 'The Production Function and the Theory of Capital', *Review of Economic Studies*, vol. 21, pp. 81-106.

Robinson, J. (1956) *The Accumulation of Capital* (Macmillan: London).

Rustem, B. (1979) 'Policy Optimisation Algorithms for Non-Linear Econometric Models', Programme of Research into Optimal Policy Evaluation (PROPE) Imperial College Discussion Paper No. 33.

Rustem, B. and M. B. Zarrop (1979) 'Newton-type Methods for the Optimisation and Control of the Non-linear Econometric Models', *Journal of Economic Dynamics and Control* (August) pp. 283-300.

*Santomero, A. M. and J. J. Seater (1978) 'The Inflation-Unemployment Trade-off: A Critique of the Literature', *Journal of Economic Literature* (June) pp. 439-544.

Sargent, T. J. (1973) 'Rational Expectations, the Real Rate of Interest, and the Natural Rate of Unemployment', *Brookings Papers on Economic Activity*, no. 2, pp. 429-72.

*Sargent, T. J. and N. Wallace (1976) 'Rational Expectations and the Theory of Economic Policy', *Journal of Monetary Economics* (April) pp. 169-83.

Saunders, P. G. and A. R. Nobay (1972) 'Price Expectations, the Phillips Curve and Incomes Policy', in J. M. Parkin and M. T. Sumner (eds), *Incomes Policy and Inflation* (Manchester University Press: Manchester) pp. 237-49.

Savage, D. (1979) 'Monetary Targets and the Control of the Money Supply', *National Institute Economic Review* (August) pp. 44-52.

Savage, D. (1980) 'Some Issues of Monetary Policy', *National Institute Economic Review* (January) pp. 78-85.

Sayers, R. S. (1960) 'Monetary Thought and Monetary Policy in England', *Economic Journal* (December) pp. 710-24.

Scott, M.FG., W. M. Corden and I. M. D. Little (1980) *The Case Against General Import Restrictions*, Trade Policy Research Centre, Thames Essay No. 24.

Shackle, G. L. S. (1970) *Expectations, Enterprise and Profit* (Allen & Unwin: London).

Shackle, G. L. S. (1971) 'Discussion Paper' in G. Clayton, J. C. Gilbert and R. Sedgwick (eds), *Monetary Theory and Monetary Policy in the 1970s*, Proceedings of the 1970 Sheffield Money Seminar (Oxford University Press: Oxford) pp. 32-4.

Shanks, M. (1977) *Planning and Politics* (Allen & Unwin: London).

Sheppard, D. K. (1971) *The Growth and Role of UK Financial Institutions 1880-1962* (Methuen: London).

Siegel, J. J. (1979) 'Inflation Induced Distortions in Government and Private Saving Statistics', *Review of Economics and Statistics* (February) pp. 83-90.

Solow, R. M. (1969) *Price Expectations and the Behaviour of the Price Level* (Manchester University Press: Manchester).

Stewart, J. (1976) *Understanding Econometrics* (Hutchinson: London).

Stewart, M. (1977) *The Jekyll and Hyde Years - Politics and Economic Policy since 1964* (Dent: London).

Stone, R. (1964) 'Private Saving in Britain, Past, Present and Future', *Manchester School* (May) pp. 79-112.

Taplin, G. R. (1973) 'A Model of World Trade', in J. R. Ball (ed.), *The International Linkage of National Economic Models* (North-Holland: Amsterdam).

Taubman, P. (1968) 'Personal Saving: A Time Series Analysis of Three Measures of the Same Conceptual Series', *Review of Economics and Statistics* (February) pp. 125-7.

Taylor, C. T. (1979) '"Crowding-Out": Its Meaning and Significance', in S. T. Cook and P. M. Jackson (eds), *Current Issues in Fiscal Policy* (Martin Robertson: London) pp. 86-107.

Taylor, C. T. and A. R. Threadgold (1979) *'Real' National Savings and its Composition*, Bank of England Discussion Paper No. 6.

Taylor, L. D. (1971) 'Saving out of Different Types of Income', *Brookings Papers on Economic Activity*, no. 2, pp. 383-415 (with discussion).

Theil, H. (1964) *Optimal Decision Rules for Government and Industry* (North-Holland: Amsterdam).

Thirlwall, A. P. (1978) 'The UK's Economic Problem: A Balance of Payments Constraint?', *National Westminster Bank Review* (February) pp. 24-32.

*Thirlwall, A. P. (1980) *Balance-of-Payments Theory and the United Kingdom Experience* (Macmillan: London).

Tobin, J. (1963) 'Commercial Banks as Creators of Money', in D. Carson (ed.), *Banking and Monetary Studies* (Homewood: New York) pp. 408-19.

Tobin, J. (1967) 'Unemployment and Inflation: the Cruel Dilemma', in A. Phillips and O. E. Williamson (eds), *Prices: Issues in Theory, Practice and Public Policy* (University of Pennsylvania Press: Pennsylvania) pp. 101-7.

Tobin, J. (1969) 'A General Equilibrium Approach to Monetary Theory', *Journal of Money, Credit and Banking* (February) pp. 15-29.

Tobin, J. (1972) 'Inflation and Unemployment', *American Economic Review* (March) pp. 1-18.

Tobin, J. and W. C. Dolde (1971) 'Wealth, Liquidity and Consumption', in *Consumer Spending and Monetary Policy: The Linkages*, Federal Reserve Bank of Boston Monetary Conference Series No. 5. pp. 99-146.

Townend, J. C. (1976) 'The Personal Saving Ratio', *Bank of England Quarterly Bulletin* (March) pp. 53-61.

Treasury (1979) *Macroeconomic Model: Technical Manual* (HMSO: London).

Trevithick, J. A. and C. Mulvey (1978) *The Economics of Inflation* (Martin Robertson: London).

*Trivedi, P. K. (1976) 'Import Equations - A Preliminary Study', in I. F. Pearce *et al.* (eds), *A Model of Output, Employment, Wages and Prices in the UK* (Cambridge University Press: Cambridge) pp. 142-56.

Tsurumi, H. (1971) 'A Note on Gamma Distributed Lags', *International Economic Review*, vol. 12, pp. 317-24.

Tufte, E. R. (1978) *Political Control of the Economy* (Princeton University Press: Princeton, N.J.).

Tullock, G. (1965) *The Politics of Bureaucracy* (Public Affairs Press: Washington).

Turnovsky, S. J. (1972) 'The Expectations Hypothesis and the Aggregate Wage Equation: Some Empirical Evidence for Canada', *Economica* (February) pp. 1-17.

Vanderkamp, J. (1968) 'The Phillips Relation: A Theoretical Explanation - A Comment', *Economica* (May) pp. 179-84.

Wagner, A. (1890) *Finanzwissenschaft*, 3rd edn (Leipzig).

Wallis, K. F. (1973) *Topics in Applied Econometrics* (Gray-Mills: London).

Wallis, K. F. (1974) 'Seasonal Adjustment and Relations between Variables', *Journal of the American Statistical Association*, vol. 69, pp. 18-31.

Walters, A. (1978) *Economists and the British Economy*, IEA Occasional Paper No. 54 (Institute of Economic Affairs: London).

Weber, E. W. (1970) 'The Effect of Interest Rates on Consumption', *American Economic Review* (September) pp. 591-600.

Weber, E. W. (1971) 'Interest Rates and the Short-run Consumption Function', *American Economic Review* (June) pp. 421-25.

Weber, E. W. (1975) 'Interest Rates, Inflation and Consumer Expenditures', *American Economic Review* (December) pp. 843-58.

Wells, J. D. and J. C. Imber (1977) 'The Home and Export Performance of United Kingdom Industries', *Economic Trends* (August) pp. 78-89.

Wescott, J. H., E. Karakitsos, B. Rustem and R. Becker (1981) 'Memorandum of Evidence on Monetary Policy', House of Commons, Treasury and Civil Service Committee (HMSO: London).

Whitley, J. D. (1979) 'Imports of Finished Manufactures: The Effects of Prices, Demand and Capacity', *Manchester School* (December) pp. 325-48.

Whitley, J. D. and R. A. Wilson (1979) 'Trends and Cycles in Import Penetration in the UK: Comment', *Bulletin of the Oxford Institute of Economics and Statistics* (February) pp. 69-77.

Winters, L. A. (1976) 'Exports', in T. S. Barker (ed.), *Economic Structure and Policy* (Chapman & Hall: London) pp. 131-61.

Index